Collins

NICHOLSON

WATERWAYS GUIDE 4

Four Counties & the Welsh Canals

CONTENTS

T0340427

Published by Nicholson
An imprint of HarperCollins Publishers
Westerhill Road, Bishopbriggs, Glasgow G64 2QT
www.harpercollins.co.uk

HarperCollins Publishers
Macken House, 39/40 Mayor Street Upper, Dublin 1, Ireland

Waterways Guides published by Nicholson since 1969
This edition first published by Nicholson and Ordnance Survey 1997
New editions published by Nicholson 2000, 2003, 2006, 2009, 2012, 2015, 2019, 2023

This product uses map data licensed from Ordnance Survey © Crown copyright and database rights (2022) Ordnance Survey (100018598)

The representation in this publication of a road, track or path is no evidence of the existence of a right of way.

Researched and written by Jonathan Mosse, David Lobban and Judith Pile.

The publishers gratefully acknowledge the assistance given by Canal & River Trust and their staff in the preparation of this guide. Grateful thanks are also due to the Environment Agency, members of the Inland Waterways Association, British Canoeing, and CAMRA representatives and branch members.

All photographs © Jonathan Mosse except:
pp22–41 travellight/Shutterstock, p42 FreespiritEnvironment/Alamy Stock Photo, pp171–181 Marbury/Shutterstock.

Every care has been taken in the preparation of this guide. However, the Publisher accepts no responsibility whatsoever for any loss, damage, injury or inconvenience sustained or caused as a result of using this guide.

HarperCollins does not warrant that any website mentioned in this title will be provided uninterrupted, that any website will be error free, that defects will be corrected, or that the website or the server that makes it available are free of viruses or bugs. For full terms and conditions please refer to the site terms provided on the website.

A catalogue record for this book is available from the British Library

Printed in Malaysia

ISBN 978-0-00-854668-7

10 9 8 7 6 5 4 3 2

This book contains FSC™ certified paper and other controlled sources to ensure responsible forest management.

For more information visit: www.harpercollins.co.uk/green

Wending their quiet way through town and country, the inland navigations of Britain offer boaters, walkers and cyclists a unique insight into a fascinating, but once almost lost, world. When built this was the province of the boatmen and their families, who lived a mainly itinerant lifestyle: often colourful, to our eyes picturesque but, for them, remarkably harsh. Transporting the nation's goods during the late 1700s and early 1800s, negotiating locks, traversing aqueducts and passing through long narrow tunnels, canals were the arteries of trade during the initial part of the industrial revolution.

Then the railways came: the waterways were eclipsed in a remarkably short time by a faster and more flexible transport system, and a steady decline began. In a desperate fight for survival canal tolls were cut, crews toiled for longer hours and worked the boats with their whole family living aboard. Canal companies merged, totally uneconomic waterways were abandoned, some were modernised but it was all to no avail. Large scale commercial carrying on inland waterways had reached the finale of its short life.

At the end of World War II a few enthusiasts roamed this hidden world and harboured a vision of what it could become: a living transport museum which stretched the length and breadth of the country; a place where people could spend their leisure time and, on just a few of the wider waterways, a still modestly viable transport system.

The restoration struggle began and, from modest beginnings, Britain's inland waterways are now seen as an irreplaceable part of the fabric of the nation. Long-abandoned waterways, once seen as an eyesore and a danger, are recognised for the valuable contribution they make to our quality of life, and restoration schemes are integrating them back into the network. Let us hope that the country's network of inland waterways continues to be cherished and well-used, maintained and developed as we move through the 21st century.

If you would like to comment on any aspect of the guides, please write to Nicholson Waterways Guides, Collins, Westerhill Road, Bishopbriggs, Glasgow G64 2QT or email nicholson@harpercollins.co.uk.

Also available:

Collins NICHOLSON

Waterways guides and map

The Waterways of Britain

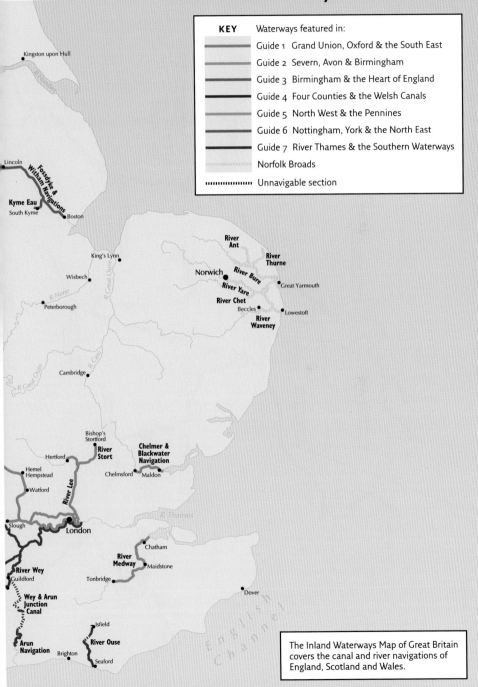

KEY

Waterways featured in:

Guide 1   Grand Union, Oxford & the South East
Guide 2   Severn, Avon & Birmingham
Guide 3   Birmingham & the Heart of England
Guide 4   Four Counties & the Welsh Canals
Guide 5   North West & the Pennines
Guide 6   Nottingham, York & the North East
Guide 7   River Thames & the Southern Waterways

Norfolk Broads

.... Unnavigable section

Kingston upon Hull

R Humber

Lincoln
Fossdyke & Witham Navigations
Kyme Eau
South Kyme
Boston

King's Lynn
Wisbech
Peterborough
R Nene
R Great Ouse

River Ant
Norwich
River Bure
River Thurne
River Yare
River Chet
Great Yarmouth
Beccles
Lowestoft
River Waveney

R Cam
Cambridge
R Great Ouse

Bishop's Stortford
River Stort
Chelmer & Blackwater Navigation
Hertford
Chelmsford
Maldon
Hemel Hempstead
Watford
River Lee
Slough
London

Chatham
River Medway
Maidstone
River Wey
Guildford
Tonbridge
Dover
Wey & Arun Junction Canal
Isfield
Arun Navigation
Brighton
River Ouse
Seaford

R Thames

English Channel

The Inland Waterways Map of Great Britain covers the canal and river navigations of England, Scotland and Wales.

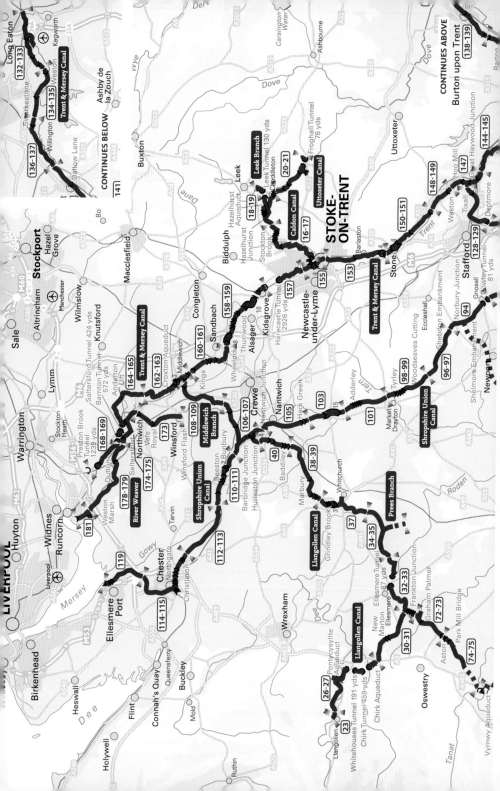

GENERAL INFORMATION FOR WATERWAYS USERS

INTRODUCTION

Boaters, walkers, fishermen, cyclists and gongoozlers (on-lookers) all share in the enjoyment of our quite amazing waterway heritage. Canal & River Trust (CRT) and the Environment Agency, along with other navigation authorities, are empowered to develop, maintain and control this resource. A series of guides, codes, and regulations have come into existence over the years, evolving to match a burgeoning – and occasionally conflicting – demand. Set out in this section are key points as they relate to everyone wishing to enjoy the waterways.

The *Boater's Handbook* is available from all navigation authorities. It contains a complete range of safety information, boat-handling know-how, warning symbols and illustrations, and can be downloaded from www.canalrivertrust.org. uk/enjoy-the-waterways/boating/a-guide-to-boating/boaters-handbook. It is complimented by this excellent video: www.youtube.com/watch?v=IXn47JYXs44.

CONSIDERATE BOATING

Considerate Boating gives advice and guidance to all waterway users on how to enjoy the inland waterways safely and can be downloaded from www.canalrivertrust.org.uk/boating/navigating-the-waterways/considerate-boating. It is also well worth visiting www.considerateboater.com. These publications are also available from the Customer Services Team which is staffed *Mon-Fri 08.00-21.00; Sat and B Hols 08.00-19.00 & Sun 09.00-19.00.* The helpful staff will answer general enquiries and provide information about boat licensing, mooring, boating holidays and general activities on the waterways. They can be contacted on 0303 040 4040; customer. services@canalrivertrust.org.uk; Canal & River Trust, Head Office, First Floor North, Station House, 500 Elder Gate, Milton Keynes MK9 1BB. Visit www.canalrivertrust.org.uk for up to date information on almost every aspect of the inland waterways from news and events to moorings.

Emergency Helpline Available from Canal & River Trust outside normal office hours on weekdays and throughout weekends. If lives or property are at risk or there is danger of serious environmental contamination then immediately contact 0800 47 999 47; www.canalrivertrust.org.uk/contact-us/contacting-us-in-an-emergency.

ENVIRONMENT AGENCY

The Environment Agency (EA) manages around 600 miles of the country's rivers, including the Thames and the River Medway. For general enquiries or to obtain a copy of the *Boater's Handbook*, contact EA Customer Services on 03708 506 506; enquiries@environment-agency. gov.uk. To find out about their work nationally (or to download a copy of the *Handbook)* and for lots of other useful information, visit www.gov. uk/government/organisations/environment-agency. The website www.visitthames.co.uk provides lots on information on boating, walking, fishing and events on the river.

Incident Hotline The EA maintain an Incident Hotline. To report damage or danger to the natural environment, damage to structures or water escaping, telephone 0800 80 70 60.

LICENSING – BOATS

The majority of the navigations covered in this book are controlled by CRT and the EA and are managed on a day-to-day basis by Regional Waterway Offices (details of these are in the introductions to each waterway). All craft using the inland waterways must be licensed and charges are based on the dimensions of the craft. In a few cases, these include reciprocal agreements with other waterway authorities (as indicated in the text). CRT and the EA offer an optional Gold Licence which covers unlimited navigation on the waterways of both authorities. Permits for permanent mooring on CRT waterways are issued by CRT.

Contact Canal & River Trust Boat Licensing Team on 0303 040 4040; www.canalrivertrust. org.uk/boating/licensing; Canal & River Trust Licensing Team, PO Box 162, Leeds LS9 1AX.

For the Thames and River Medway contact the EA. River Thames: 0118 953 5650; www.gov.uk/government/organisations/environment-agency; Environment Agency, PO Box 214, Reading RG1 8HQ. River Medway: 01732 223222 or visit the website.

BOAT SAFETY SCHEME

CRT and the EA operate the Boat Safety Scheme aimed at maintaining boat safety standards and featuring four-yearly testing, primarily intended to identify third party risks. A Boat Safety Scheme Certificate (for new boats, a Declaration of Conformity) is necessary to obtain a craft licence from all navigation authorities. CRT also requires proof of insurance for Third Party Liability for a minimum of £2,000,000 for powered boats. Contact details are: 0333 202 1000; www.boatsafetyscheme.org; Boat Safety Scheme, First Floor North, Station House, 500 Elder Gate, Milton Keynes MK9 1BB. The website offers useful advice on preventing fires and avoiding carbon monoxide poisoning.

TRAINING

The Royal Yachting Association (RYA) runs one and two day courses leading to the Inland Waters Helmsman's Certificate, specifically designed for novices and experienced boaters wishing to cruise the inland waterways. For details of RYA schools, telephone 023 8060 4100 or visit www.rya.org.uk. Contact your local boat clubs, too. The National Community Boats Association (NCBA) run courses on boat-handling and safety on the water. Telephone 07899 822113 or visit www.national-cba.co.uk.

CANOES, KAYAKS AND PADDLEBOARDS

(see also pages 100 and 170)
All portable, unpowered craft such as canoes, kayaks, dinghies, rowing boats, paddleboards and even light inflatable craft require a license to access the majority of British waterways. A British Canoeing "waterway licence" provides the best value for money at less than 50% of the cost of individual licenses from the Canal and River Trust, the Environment Agency and the Broads Authority and gives access to over 5000 miles of inland waterways. A wide range of information is also available from British Canoeing (www.britishcanoeing.org.uk) and www.gopaddling.info is a useful source of launch points. More detailed, canal specific information is available from the Canal and River Trust at www.canalrivertrust.org.uk/enjoy-the-waterways/canoeing-and-kayaking-near-me, while paddling in tunnels is covered at www.canalrivertrust.org.uk/enjoy-the-waterways/canoeing-and-kayaking-near-me/paddling-through-tunnels.

TOWPATHS

Few, if any, artificial cuts or canals in this country are without an intact towpath accessible to the walker at least and the Thames is the only river in the country with a designated National Trail along its path from source to sea (for more information visit www.nationaltrail.co.uk). However, on some other river navigations, towpaths have on occasion fallen into disuse or, sometimes, been lost to erosion. The indication of a towpath in this guide does not necessarily imply a public right of way. Cyclists are asked to abide by the Towpath Code

available at www.canalrivertrust.org.uk/enjoy-the-waterways/cycling, while an excellent selection of rides are detailed at www.canalrivertrust.org.uk/enjoy-the-waterways/cycling/canal-cycling-routes. Horse riding and motorcycling are forbidden on all towpaths.

INDIVIDUAL WATERWAY GUIDES

No national guide can cover the minutiae of detail concerning every waterway, and some CRT Waterway Managers produce guides to specific navigations under their charge. Copies of individual guides (where available) can be downloaded from www.canalrivertrust.org.uk/enjoy-the-waterways/boating/planning-your-boat-trip. Please note that times – such as operating times of bridges and locks – do change year by year and from winter to summer. For free copies of a range of helpful leaflets for all users of the River Thames – visit www.visitthames.co.uk/about-the-river/publications.

STOPPAGES

CRT and the EA both publish winter stoppage programmes which are sent out to all licence holders, boatyards and hire companies. Inevitably, emergencies occur necessitating the unexpected closure of a waterway, perhaps during the peak season. You can check for stoppages on individual waterways between specific dates on www.canalrivertrust.org.uk/notices/winter, lockside noticeboards or by telephoning 0303 040 4040; for stoppages and river conditions on the Thames, visit www.gov.uk/river-thames-conditions-closures-restrictions-and-lock-closures or telephone 0845 988 1188.

NAVIGATION AUTHORITIES AND WATERWAYS SOCIETIES

Most inland navigations are managed by CRT or the EA, but there are several other navigation authorities. For details of these, contact the Association of Inland Navigation Authorities on 0844 335 1650 or visit www.aina.org.uk. The boater, conditioned perhaps by the uniformity of our national road network, should be sensitive to the need to observe different codes and operating practices.

The Canal & River Trust is a charity set up to care for England and Wales' legacy of 200-year-old waterways, holding them in trust for the nation forever, and is linked with an ombudsman. CRT has a comprehensive complaints procedure and a free explanatory leaflet is available from Customer Services. Problems and complaints should be addressed to the local Waterway Manager in the first instance. For more information, visit their website.

The EA is the national body, sponsored by the Department for Environment, Food and Rural Affairs, to manage the quality of air, land and water in England and Wales. For more information, visit its website.

The Inland Waterways Association (IWA) campaigns for the use, maintenance and restoration of Britain's inland waterways, through branches all over the country. For more information, contact them on 01494 783453; iwa@waterways.org.uk; www.waterways.org.uk; The Inland Waterways Association, Island House, Moor Road, Chesham HP5 1WA. Their website has a huge amount of information of interest to boaters, including comprehensive details of the many and varied waterways societies.

STARTING OUT

Extensive information and advice on booking a boating holiday is available from the Inland Waterways Association, www.visitthames.co.uk and www.canalrivertrust.org.uk/boating/boat-trips-and-holidays. Please book a waterway holiday from a licensed operator – this way you can be sure that you have proper insurance cover, service and support during your holiday. It is illegal for private boat owners to hire out their craft. If you are hiring a holiday craft for the first time, the boatyard will brief you thoroughly. Take notes, follow their instructions and do ask if there is anything you do not understand. CRT have produced a 40 min DVD which is essential viewing for newcomers to canal or river boating. Available to view free at www.canalrivertrust.org.uk/boatersdvd or obtainable (charge) from the CRT Customer Service Centre 0303 040 4040; www.canalrivertrust.org.uk/shop.

PLACES TO VISIT ALONG THE WAY

This guide contains a wealth of information, not just about the canals and rivers and navigating on them, but also on the visitor attractions and places to eat and drink close to the waterways. Opening and closing times, and other details often change; establishments close and new ones open. If you are making special plans to eat in a particular pub, or visit a certain museum it is always advisable to check in advance.

MORE INFORMATION

An internet search will reveal many websites on the inland waterways. Those listed below are just a small sample:

National Community Boats Association is a national charity and training provider, supporting community boat projects and encouraging more people to access the inland waterways. Telephone 0845 0510649; www.national-cba.co.uk.
National Association of Boat Owners is dedicated to promoting the interests of private boaters on Britain's canals and rivers. Visit www.nabo.org.uk.
www.canalplan.org.uk is an online journey-planner and gazetteer for the inland waterways.
www.canals.com is a valuable source of information for cruising the canals, with loads of links to canal and waterways related websites.
www.ukcanals.net lists services and useful information for all waterways users.

GENERAL CRUISING NOTES

Most canals and rivers are saucer shaped, being deepest at the middle. Few canals have more than 3-4ft of water and many have much less. Keep to the centre of the channel except on bends, where the deepest water is on the outside of the bend. When you meet another boat, keep to the right, slow down and aim to miss the approaching craft by a couple of yards. If you meet a loaded commercial boat keep right out of the way and be prepared to follow his instructions. Do not assume that you should pass on the right. If you meet a boat being towed from the bank, pass it on the outside. When overtaking, keep the other boat on your right side.

Some CRT and EA facilities are operated by pre-paid cards, obtainable from CRT and EA regional and local waterways offices, lock keepers and boatyards. Weekend visitors should purchase cards in advance. A handcuff/anti-vandal key is commonly used on locks where vandalism is a problem. A watermate/sanitary key opens sanitary stations, waterpoints and some bridges and locks. Both keys and pre-paid cards can be obtained via CRT Customer Service Centre.

Safety

Boating is a safe pastime. However, it makes sense to take simple safety precautions, particularly if you have children aboard.
- Never drink and drive a boat – it may travel slowly, but it weighs many tons.
- Be careful with naked flames and never leave the boat with the hob or oven lit.

Familiarise yourself and your crew with the location and operation of the fire extinguishers.

- Never block ventilation grills. Boats are enclosed spaces and levels of carbon monoxide can build up from faulty appliances or just from using the cooker.
- Be careful along the bank and around locks. Slipping from the bank might only give you a cold-water soaking, but falling from the side of, or into a lock is more dangerous. Beware of slippery or rough ground.
- Remember that fingers and toes are precious! If a major collision is imminent, never try to fend off with your hands or feet; and always keep hands and arms inside the boat.
- Weil's disease is a particularly dangerous infection present in water which can attack the central nervous system and major organs. It is caused by bacteria entering the bloodstream through cuts and broken skin, and the eyes, nose and mouth. The flu-like symptoms occur two–four weeks after exposure. Always wash your hands thoroughly after contact with the water. Visit www.leptospirosis.org for details.

Speed
There is a general speed limit of 4 mph on most CRT canals and 5 mph on the Thames. There is no need to go any faster – the faster you go, the bigger a wave the boat creates: if your wash is breaking against the bank, causing large waves or throwing moored boats around, slow down. Slow down also when passing engineering works and anglers; when there is a lot of floating rubbish on the water (try to drift over obvious obstructions in neutral); when approaching blind corners, narrow bridges and junctions.

Mooring
Generally you may moor where you wish on CRT property, as long as you are *not causing an obstruction*. Do not moor in a winding hole or junction, the approaches to a lock or tunnel, or at a water point or sanitary station. On the Thames, generally you have a right to anchor for 24 hours in one place provided no obstruction is caused, however you will need explicit permission from the land owner to moor. There are official mooring sites along the length of the river; those provided by the EA are free, the others you will need to pay for. Your boat should carry metal mooring stakes, and these should be driven firmly into the ground with a mallet if there are no mooring rings. Do not stretch mooring lines across the towpath and take account of anyone who may walk past. Always consider the security of your boat when there is no one aboard. On tideways and commercial waterways it is advisable to moor only at recognised sites, and allow for any rise or fall of the tide.

Bridges
On narrow canals slow down well in advance and aim to miss one side (usually the towpath side) by about 9 inches. *Keep everyone inboard when passing under bridges and ensure there is nothing on the roof of the boat that will hit the bridge.* If a boat is coming the other way, the craft nearest to the bridge has priority. Take special care with moveable structures – the crew member operating the bridge should be strong and heavy enough to hold it steady as the boat passes through.

Going aground
You can sometimes go aground if the water level on a canal has dropped or you are on a particularly shallow stretch. If it does happen, try reversing *gently*, or pushing off with the boat hook. Another method is to get your crew to rock the boat from side to side using the boat hook, or move all crew to the end opposite to that which is aground. Or, have all crew leave the boat, except the helmsman, and it will often float off quite easily.

Tunnels
Again, ensure that everyone is inboard. Make sure the tunnel is clear before you enter, and use your headlight. Check the instruction boards by the entrance and be aware that you may be sharing the tunnel with canoeists and paddleboarders. Consult www.canalrivertrust.org.uk/enjoy-the-waterways/canoeing-and-kayaking-near-me/paddling-through-tunnels for further deails.

Fuel
Diesel can be purchased from most boatyards and some CRT depots. To comply with HMRC regulations you must declare an appropriate split between propulsion and heating so that the correct level of VAT can be applied. However, few boatyards stock petrol. Where a garage is listed under a town or village's facilities, petrol (and DERV) are available.

Water
It is advisable to top up daily.

Pump out

Self-operated pump out facilities are available at a number of locations on the waterways network. These facilities are provided by CRT and can be operated via a 25-unit prepayment card. Details of how to buy a pump out card either online, by phone or in person are available from www.canalrivertrust.org.uk. The cards provide for one pump out or 25 units of electricity. Cards can be obtained from CRT Waterway Offices, some Marinas and boatyards, shops and cafés.

Boatyards

Hire fleets are usually turned around at a weekend, making this a bad time to call in for services.

VHF Radio

The IWA recommends that all pleasure craft navigating the larger waterways used by freight carrying vessels, or any tidal navigation, should carry marine-band VHF radio and have a qualified radio operator on board.

PLANNING A CRUISE

Don't try to go too far too fast. Go slowly, don't be too ambitious, and enjoy the experience. Mileages indicated on the maps are for guidance only. A *rough* calculation of time taken to cover the ground is the lock-miles system:

Add the number of *miles* to the number of *locks* on your proposed journey, and divide the resulting figure by three. This will give you an approximate guide to the number of *hours* your travel will take.

TIDAL WATERWAYS

The typical steel narrow boat found on the inland waterways is totally unsuitable for cruising on exposed tidal water. However, passage is possible in most estuaries if careful consideration is given to the key factors of weather conditions, tides, crew experience, the condition of the boat and its equipment and, perhaps of overriding importance, the need to take expert advice. In many cases it will be prudent to employ the skilled services of a local pilot. Within the text, where inland navigations connect with a tidal waterway, details are given of sources of advice and pilotage. It is also essential to inform your insurance company of your intention to navigate on tidal waterways as they may very well have special requirements or wish to levy an additional premium. This guide is to the inland waterways of Britain and therefore recognizes that tideways – and especially estuaries – require a different approach and many additional skills. We do not hesitate to draw the boater's attention to the appropriate source material.

LOCKS AND THEIR USE

A lock is a simple and ingenious device for transporting your craft from one water level to another. When both sets of gates are closed it may be filled or emptied using gates, or ground paddles, at the top or bottom of the lock. These are operated with a windlass. On the Thames, the locks are manned all year round, with longer hours from April to October. You may operate the locks yourself at any time.

If a lock is empty, or 'set' for you, the crew open the gates and you drive the boat in. If the lock is full of water, the crew should check first to see if any boat is waiting or coming in the other direction. If a boat is in sight, you must let them through first: do not empty or 'turn' the lock against them. This is not only discourteous, and against the rules, but wastes precious water.

In the diagrams the *plan* shows how the gates point uphill, the water pressure forcing them together. Water is flooding into the lock through the underground culverts that are operated by the ground paddles: when the lock is 'full', the top gates (on the left of the drawing) can be opened. One may imagine a boat entering, the crew closing the gates and paddles after it.

In the *elevation*, the bottom paddles have been raised (opened) so that the lock empties. A boat will, of course, float down with the water. When the lock is 'empty' the bottom gates can be opened and the descending boat can leave.

Remember that when going *up* a lock, a boat should be tied up to prevent it being thrown about by the the rush of incoming water; but when going *down* a lock, a boat should never be tied up or it will be left high and dry.

At the lock interface between a canal and a river, signs are appearing to indicate the river height. They show four possible states. Red – danger. Yellow and falling. Yellow and rising. Green – no danger. The alternative to the signs is the coloured strip on the lock wall around water level. The signs give you extra information in the yellow band – as to whether the level is going up or down – and tell you about locations remote from where you are now.

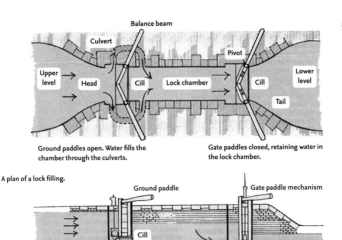

Ground paddles open. Water fills the chamber through the culverts.

Gate paddles closed, retaining water in the lock chamber.

A plan of a lock filling.

Ground paddles closed preventing water from the upper level filling the chamber.

Gate paddles open. Water flows from the chamber to the lower level.

An elevation of a lock emptying.

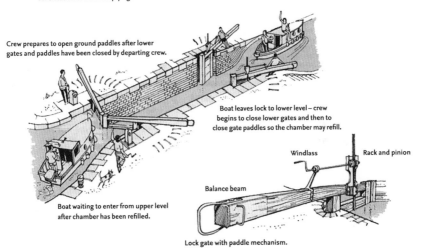

Crew prepares to open ground paddles after lower gates and paddles have been closed by departing crew.

Boat leaves lock to lower level – crew begins to close lower gates and then to close gate paddles so the chamber may refill.

Boat waiting to enter from upper level after chamber has been refilled.

Lock gate with paddle mechanism.

- Make safety your prime concern. *Keep a close eye on young children.*
- Always take your time, and do not leap about.
- Never open the paddles at one end without ensuring those at the other end are closed.
- Keep to the landward side of the balance beam when opening and closing gates. Whilst it may be necessary to put your back behind the balance beam to gain a better purchase when starting to close a gate, always move to the correct position as soon as possible.

- Never leave your windlass slotted onto the paddle spindle – it will be dangerous should anything slip.
- Keep your boat away from the top and bottom gates to prevent it getting caught on the gate or the lock cill.
- Never drop the paddles – always wind them down.
- Be wary of fierce *top gate* paddles, especially in wide locks. Operate them slowly, and close them if there is *any* adverse effect.
- Always follow the navigation authority's instructions, where given on notices or by their staff.

13

Consall Forge

CALDON CANAL

MAXIMUM DIMENSIONS	MILEAGE
to Consall Forge	*STOKE TOP LOCK*
Length: 72'	(Trent & Mersey Canal) *to:*
Beam: 7'	Hanley: 2 miles
Headroom: 6' 8"	Foxley: 4½ miles
through Froghall Tunnel	Stockton Brook Summit: 7 miles
Length: 65'	Hazelhurst Junction (Leek Branch): 9½ miles
Beam: 7'	*LEEK TERMINUS:* 12¼ miles
Headroom: 5' 6"	Cheddleton Flint Mill: 11½ miles
(see also Navigational Notes on page 21)	*FROGHALL TERMINUS:* 17 miles

MANAGER

0303 040 4040
enquiries.westmidlands@canalrivertrust.org.uk

Locks: 17

Canoeing and Paddleboarding: Category 1.
However, see Navigational Notes on page 20.

The Caldon Canal – or, more correctly, the Caldon Branch of the Trent & Mersey Canal – was designed as an outlet on to the canal system for the Caldon limestone quarries near Froghall. It was opened as a single branch to Froghall in 1779, tramways being constructed to bring the vast quantities of limestone down from Cauldon Low quarries a couple of miles to the east. Froghall soon became a very busy terminus. Eighteen years later the Caldon's owners, the Trent & Mersey Canal Company, decided to build a secondary branch from the Caldon Canal to Leek, the main purpose of the extension being to use the line as a feeder from their new reservoir at Rudyard. The fact that the feeders from Rudyard had to enter the summit level of the canal, and the later advent of the railway, brought about significant changes in the layout of the canal between Endon and Hazelhurst, and resulted in the fascinating cross-over junction that exists at Denford today. In 1811 yet another branch was completed from Froghall down the Churnet Valley for 13 miles to Uttoxeter. This branch had a short life, and in 1845 a railway line was built, much of the track using the canal bed. However the first lock and the basin at Froghall have now, remarkably, been restored.
The limestone from Froghall remained the chief commodity carried on the Caldon Canal for years. With its 17 locks and roundabout route the Caldon must have been an obvious target for railway competitors. However, the canal, with the rest of the Trent & Mersey, was owned by the North Staffordshire Railway from the 1840s onward, so presumably the NSR saw no point in competing against itself. But at the beginning of the 20th C a new railway line was eventually opened and inevitably canal traffic slumped badly. The canal then gradually deteriorated until it became more or less unnavigable in the early 1960s.
The Caldon Canal Society led the struggle to re-open the route; public interest grew and local authorities recognised the great recreational potential of this beautiful waterway for the thousands of people living in the nearby Potteries. Much was achieved in the way of essential works by the British Waterways Board (now Canal & River Trust) and volunteer efforts. The canal was finally fully reopened to navigation in 1974, representing a splendid addition to the cruising network, and a much-needed linear park for the potteries. Indeed, once beyond Engine Lock, this waterway offers some of the finest cruising to be found anywhere in the country.
Incidentally, the difference in spelling of the quarry name 'Cauldon' and the title of the canal itself, dates back to a simple spelling mistake in the original Act which was never corrected!

Hanley

The Caldon Branch of the Trent & Mersey Canal leaves the main line at Stoke Top Lock, and soon passes a statue of James Brindley, builder of the Trent & Mersey. The first two locks up are combined in a staircase – the only one in north Staffordshire. Planet Lock is soon reached with *shops, a chemist and pubs* close by. A short distance west of Milton Bridge 18 there is a small memorial garden commemorating the life of Susie Cooper, one of the most influential and important pottery designers of 20thC. This is on the site of the family grocery store where she worked as a schoolgirl. There is also a useful *parade of shops, including a chemist, stores, off licence, fish & chips and takeaways,* ¼ mile east of Bridge 18. Engine Lock follows, so called because a huge beam engine used to be housed nearby to pump water from mine workings. By bridge 21 the unnavigable feeder from Knypersley Reservoir joins the waterway. Five locks at Stockton Brook raise the canal up to the summit level 484ft above sea level.

● **Hanley**
Staffs. All services. Hanley is one of the six towns that were amalgamated in 1910 to form the present Stoke-on-Trent.
The Potteries Walk north from bridge 8 along Lichfield Street. Ahead is The Potteries Shopping Centre: to the left, off Potteries Way, you will find:
The Potteries Museum & Art Gallery Bethesda Street, Hanley ST1 3DW (01782 232323; www.stokemuseums.org.uk). Where the history of the area is brought to life. There is also a fine ceramics collection. Wi-Fi. *Open all year Wed-Sat 10.00-17.00 & Sun 11.00-16.00.* Free.
Emma Bridgewater Factory Shop Lichfield Street, Hanley ST1 3EJ (01782 201328; www.emmabridgewaterfactory.co.uk). Just north of bridge 8. Earthenware, textiles and gifts. *Open Mon-Sat 10.00-17.00; Sun & B Hols 10.00-16.00.*
Etruria Industrial Museum Vale Road, Stoke-on-Trent ST1 4RB (07900 267711; www.etruriamuseum.org.uk). At the junction with the Trent & Mersey.

This is a Victorian steam-powered potter's miller's works, built in 1857 and which ground bone, flint and stone for the pottery industry, until closure in 1972. It has now been restored as part of an industrial complex incorporating a blacksmith's shop with working steam-powered machinery. Originally the raw materials and ground products were transported by canal, and present-day canal travellers will find plenty of moorings available. *Open Fri 11.00–15.30.* Tearoom and shop. Charge.

Tourist Information Centre The Potteries Museum & Art Gallery, Bethesda Street, Stoke on Trent, Staffordshire, ST1 3DW (01782 236000; www.visitstoke.co.uk). The visitor map of the Potteries, available here, gives full details of factory visits. *Open daily 10.00–17.00.*

● **Milton**
Staffs. PO, tel, stores, fish & chips, chemist, off-licence, takeaways. A little village on the side of a hill, forming an agreeable background to the canal.

● **Knypersley Reservoir**
3½ miles north of Milton. This feeds water to the Trent & Mersey summit level via the Caldon Canal. Surrounded by woodland, the reservoir is a delightful setting for picnicking and rambling.

● **Stockton Brook**
Staffs. PO, tel, stores, garage. A pleasant and useful place. The five locks have a charming position, with views back down the headwaters of the River Trent. There is a splendid Victorian waterworks at the bottom of the flight, and *pubs and shops* near the middle.

WALKING AND CYCLING
The towpath is generally in good condition throughout and has benefitted from a recent upgrade.

NAVIGATIONAL NOTES
1 Bridges 8, 9 and 11 are very low.
2 Your Watermate key will be required for Ivy House Lift Bridge, 11 and Norton Green Lift Bridge, 21.
3 You will need a windlass to operate Bridge 23
4 Overnight mooring between Locks 1–2 and the winding hole at Milton.

Boatyards

Ⓑ **CRT Etruria Yard** at junction with Trent & Mersey Canal (0303 040 4040). 🚽🚿 Pump out, toilet, showers (including facilities for disabled people), 48-hour moorings outside the museum.

Pubs and Restaurants

🍺 **1 The Terrace Inn** 185 Leek Road, Shelton, Stoke-on-Trent ST4 2BW (07989 848021; www.dorbiere.co.uk/the-terrace). Close to the University, this open-plan student pub serves real ales and food *daily 12.00–20.00.* Garden, traditional pub games and sports TV. *Open 11.00–21.00 (Sun 12.00).*

🍺 **2 The Millrace** 21 Maunders Road, Milton ST2 7DU (01782 926757). By Bridge 18. A handsome and friendly pub with coal fires and a traditional bar area. Real ales and sandwiches *always available.* Children welcome. Quiz *Sun.* Traditional pub games and sports TV. *Open daily 16.00–00.00 (Sat-Sun 13.00).* Shops nearby.

🍺 **3 The Foxley** Foxley Lane, Milton ST2 7EH (01782 535684). Traditional two-room pub beside the navigation, dispensing real ale and food *Tue-Sun 12.00–20.00.* Dog- and child-friendly, canalside garden. Live music *Sat.* Traditional pub games and sports TV. *Open Mon 15.00–22.30; Tue-Sat 12.00–23.00 (Fri-Sat 00.00) & Sun 12.00–23.00.*

🍺 **4 The Foaming Quart** 5 Frobisher Street, Norton Green ST6 8PD (01782 911171). Attractive two-roomed pub serving real ale. Dogs welcome *(not weekends).* Traditional pub games and sports TV. *Open daily 12.00–00.00.*

🍺✕ **5 The Rose & Crown** Stanley Road, Stockton Brook ST9 9LL (01782 503893; www.roseandcrownstanley.com). Comfortable village hostelry serving real ales and food *L and E Tue-Thu (not Tue L) and Fri-Sun 12.00-20.30 (Sun 17.00).* Family-friendly. Quiz *Mon.* Traditional pub games and real fires. *Open Tue-Thu L and E and Fri-Sun 12.00–00.00.*

🍺 **6 The Sportsman** 1074 Leek New Road, Stockton Brook ST9 9NT (01782 505307). Close to Railway Lock. Cosy traditional pub, where skittles are played. Real ale and sandwiches available. Dog- and family-friendly. Quiz *Wed.* Traditional pub games and sports TV. *Open 12.00–00.00 (Sun 23.00).*

✕🍷 **7 Greenway Hall Golf Club** Stanley Road, Stockton Brook ST9 9LJ (01782 503158; www.greenwayhallgolfclub.co.uk). Open to non-residents, serving breakfast, light meals and an à la carte menu, *08.00–21.00 (Sat-Sun) 07.00.*

🍺✕ **8 The Hollybush** 1 Stanley Road, Stockton Brook ST9 9NL (01782 502116; www.egorestaurants.co.uk/stockton-brook-menu). Plush, modern pub-cum-restaurant, close to the canal, serving real ale and a wide selection of food *daily 11.00–22.00.* Family-friendly. *Open daily 11.00–22.30.*

See also **Pubs and Restaurants** for the Trent & Mersey Canal on page 154.

Hazelhurst Locks

The canal passes to the east of Endon, negotiates the bend after Doles Bridge and approaches Hazelhurst, where it divides. There are *shops* 250yds north west of Bridge 28 and here Endon Stores sells CRT swipe cards, needed for the facilities at Park Lane Bridge 31 (there are *showers, toilets and a pump out* here). At the junction the main line falls through three locks before turning east and then south to accompany the River Churnet, while the Leek Branch bears right along the hillside, then crosses the main line on a large aqueduct. The railway and Endon Brook are also traversed by aqueducts and eventually the Leek Branch reaches the north side of this narrow valley. A lagoon provides the opportunity to wind just before the 130yd Leek Tunnel. Beyond the tunnel, only a short stretch of canal remains, ending on a fine stone aqueduct over the River Churnet. Boats over 45ft in length should wind at Bridge 9. The last half-mile beyond the Churnet Aqueduct and straight along to Leek Basin has been filled in. However, it is little more than half a mile's walk to reach the *supermarket and garage*, which lies close to the former terminus (*see* Walking and Cycling below). The town centre is another ½ mile further on. The main line to Froghall drops through three attractive and isolated locks and passes under the Leek Branch beside the site of the original, connecting staircase locks. The canal and the River Churnet now run side by side for the next 7 miles. Cheddleton Flint Mill makes a fascinating stop.

- ● **Stanley**
  Staffs. PO box, tel. A stiff climb southwards from bridge 28 leads to this brown-stone hill village. There are fine views across the valley to Endon.
- ● **Endon**
  Staffs. Tel, stores, chemist, off-licence, laundrette, garage. The real village is up the hill just north of the main road and is attractive, especially during its traditional well-dressing ceremony. Endon Basin built in 1907, and once a canal/railway interchange basin, is now used as the Stoke-on-Trent Boat Club's base. The *24hr* laundrette is in the garage beside the Black Horse pub.
- ● **Leek**
  Staffs. All services (except station). A silk town, which also gained a reputation for its dyeing and embroidery: the Leek School of Embroidery was founded here in the 1870s by Lady Wardle, and it was about this time that William Morris, founder of the Arts & Crafts Movement, worked here. James Brindley, the canal engineer, started in business as a millwright in Leek. The parish church of St Edward (ST13 6AB) is 14th-C, but was restored in 1856, and the chancel rebuilt in 1867.
  Brindley's Mill 214 Mill Street, Leek ST13 8FA (01538 395530; (www.brindleysmill.co.uk).

Situated on the A523 Leek – Macclesfield road, approximately ½ mile west of the town centre. It is a working corn mill built in 1752 by James Brindley, the canal engineer, when he worked as a millwright in Leek. Milling display, Brindley's notebook and theodolite. *Opening times vary so please visit website for details.*

Tourist Information Centre Nicholson Institute, Stockwell Street, Leek ST13 6DW (01538 395530; www.staffsmoorlands.gov.uk/article/2229/Tourist-information-centre). *Open Mon-Sat 10.00-16.00.*

Deep Hayes Country Park Park Lane, near Cheddleton, Leek ST9 9QQ (www.woodlandtrust.org.uk/visiting-woods/woods/deep-hayes-country-park). South east of Denford. This was once an industrial area, where coal and clay were extracted, iron was smelted and bricks were made. The pools were built in 1848 by the Potteries Waterworks Company to compensate for water taken from the River Churnet. Now it is a delightful mixture of woods and meadows. The Visitor Centre is *open Sat, Sun & B Hols 14.00-16.00 in summer and Sat & Sun 14.00-16.00 in winter.*

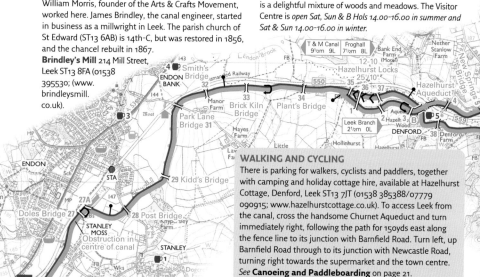

WALKING AND CYCLING

There is parking for walkers, cyclists and paddlers, together with camping and holiday cottage hire, available at Hazelhurst Cottage, Denford, Leek ST13 7JT (01538 385388/07779 090915; www.hazelhurstcottage.co.uk). To access Leek from the canal, cross the handsome Churnet Aqueduct and turn immediately right, following the path for 150yds east along the fence line to its junction with Barnfield Road. Turn left, up Barnfield Road through to its junction with Newcastle Road, turning right towards the supermarket and the town centre. See **Canoeing and Paddleboarding** on page 21.

● **Cheddleton**

Staffs. Stores, off-licence, fish & chips. A main road rumbles through the village, but away from this is the charming Flint Mill, by the canal. The village is grouped around the ancient stone church of St Edward the Confessor. Little of the original building remains, but some 14th-C work is worth a look. The stores are *open daily 07.00-22.00.*

Cheddleton Flint Mill Cheadle Road, Cheddleton ST13 7HL (0161 408 5083; www.cheddletonflintmill. com). Superbly restored mill where you can watch two water wheels driving the flint grinding pans, in a charming and picturesque setting. Machinery collection includes a 100hp Robey steam engine and a 1770 haystack boiler. For group visits please telephone in advance. *Open Mon & Wed 12.00-16.00 but telephone to check.* Donations.

Pubs and Restaurants

🍺✕ **1 The Travellers Rest** Tompkin Road, Stanley ST9 9LX (01782 502580; www.facebook.com/ thetravellersreststanley) An attractive hostelry, set in the middle of the village, ½ mile up the hill to the south east of Bridge 28. Real ale and food available *Mon-Fri L and E, Sat-Sun 12.00-21.00 (Sun 20.30).* Children welcome, garden. Holiday cottages to let. B&B. *Open Mon-Thu L and E & Fri-Sun 11.45-23.00.*

🍺✕ **2 The Rose & Crown** Stanley Road, Stanley Moor ST9 9LL (01782 503893; www.roseandcrownstanley. com). With its bar decorated with pictures of film stars, this pub serves real ale and food *Tue-Sun L and E (not Sun E).* Dog- and family-friendly. Traditional pub games and real fires. *Open Tue-Fri L and E & Sat-Sun 12.00-00.00 (Sun 23.00).*

🍺✕ **3 Toby Carvery** Leek Road, Endon ST9 9BE (01782 502115; www.tobycarvery.co.uk/restaurants/ midlands/endonstokeontrent#). Real ale, along with food *until 22.00.* Family-friendly, outside seating. Traditional pub games and sports TV. *Open daily 11.30-23.00.*

🍺 **4 The Black Horse** 381 Leek Road, Endon ST9 9BA (01782 502239; www.theblackhorseendon.co.uk). Smart, comfortable hostelry serving real ale and food *12.00-21.00. Weekend* live music, traditional pub games and sports TV. *Open daily 12.00-00.00.*

🍺✕ **5 The Hollybush Inn** Denford Road, Leek ST13 7JT (01538 371819; www.hollybushleek.co.uk). Popular, dog- and family-friendly, canalside pub (beside Bridge 38) dispensing real ales and homemade food *daily 12.00-20.30.* Beer garden and real fires. Live music *Thu. Open daily 11.00-23.00 (Sun 12.00).*

🍺 **6 The Wheel** Leek Road, Longsdon ST9 9QF (01538 385012; www.facebook.com/thewheel.longsdon). A country pub serving real ale. Home-made meals available *Mon-Sat L and E, Sun 12.00-21.00.* Children welcome *until 21.00.* Garden and children's play area. Traditional pub games and sports TV. *Open Mon-Sat L and E & Sun 12.00-23.00.*

BOAT TRIPS
Joshua Day Boat Hire (07716 738350; www. joshuadayboathire.co.uk) offer self-drive boat hire from Denford for up to 10 people.

🍺✕ **7 The Red Lion** 37 Cheadle Road, Cheddleton ST13 7HN (01538 369401; www. facebook.com/redlioncheddleton). Close to Bridge 42. Homely pub, with an open fire, serving real ales and appetising and inexpensive) food *Mon-Thu E; Fri 15.00-20.30 & Sat-Sun 12.00-20.30.* Dog- and child-friendly, garden. Traditional pub games. *Open Mon-Thu E; Fri 15.00-00.00 & Sat-Sun 12.00-00.00.*

✕♟ **8 The Flintlock at Cheddleton** 11 Cheadle Rd, Cheddleton, Leek ST13 7HN (01538 361380; www.facebook.com/flintlockcheddleton). An informal fine dining restaurant, with a large lounge area overlooking the canal. Excellent menu, majoring on traceable local produce, accompanied by friendly, attentive service. *Open Thu-Sat L; Sat E & Sun L.*

🍺 **9 The Black Lion** 12 Hollow Ln, Cheddleton, Leek, Staffordshire ST13 7HP (01538 360620; www.facebook.com/TheBlackLionCheddleton). Village local, accessed from Bridge 38, serving real ales and food *daily L.* Patio and beer garden, dog- and family-friendly. Traditional pub games, real fires and Sports TV. *Open daily 12.00-23.00 (Fri-Sat 00.00).*

🍺 **10 Cheddleton Old School Tea Rooms and Craft Centre** Hollow Lane, Cheddleton ST13 7HP (01538 528942; www.facebook.com/ theoldschooltearoomandcraftcentre). Just beyond the Black Lion, this friendly, welcoming establishment takes muddy boots in its stride. Appetising food – ranging from pastries to full meals – and a selection of crafts to browse. *Open Wed-Sun 10.00-15.00.*

Boatyards

Ⓑ**Countryside Cruising Holidays** Westwood House, Brookhouse Lane, Wetley Rocks, Stoke-on-Trent ST9 0BU (01782 551172/07855 714527; www.countrysidecruising. co.uk). Narrowboat hire.

WALKING AND CYCLING

There are fine walks from Froghall Wharf – you can purchase a leaflet from the Visitor Centre at the wharf for a nominal fee or download a free pdf at www.staffordshire.gov.uk. The Blue Walk visits the old tramways to the east, passing a pub; the Green Walk visits woods to the north, along with a limekiln and two pubs; and the Red Walk follows the line of the canal to Consall Forge, passing a Falcon & Otter Sanctuary on its return. Just follow the coloured waymarks. The Staffordshire Way, a 93-mile route stretching between Mow Cop Castle and Kinver Edge, follows the part of the towpath above Consall Forge.

Froghall

Passing Cheddleton, between the Boat Inn and Cheddleton Station, the canal continues its pretty journey. At Oakmeadowford Lock it enters the River Churnet, and the two waterways share the same course for about a mile to Consall Forge (*see* Navigational Note 1). Here you will find the Black Lion, a very fine old-fashioned *pub* alongside the canal and steam railway. For most of this section, the Churnet valley is enclosed by steep and thickly wooded hills, whose sides reach right down to the river and adjacent canal. It is a superlative landscape, seeming to be almost untouched and unspoilt by man's incursions. Yet it has been busy in the past, when boats and trains laden with limestone from Cauldon competing for trade. Now there is little to break the peace of this splendidly secluded place. The canal proceeds along the north east side of the steep valley, with the river now to the south, passing old limekilns on the way to Flint Mill Lock and what was the adjacent flint mill. Between the railway bridge and bridge 50B is Consall railway station – the waiting room stands alone, cantilevered out over the canal. Beyond the mill, the navigation creeps along the side of a wooded hill as the valley floor drops away. Derelict industrial works then indicate that Froghall has been reached. There are *moorings* west of the amazingly low tunnel for those whose boat is too large to pass through, and a *winding hole*. The delightful terminus is just beyond the tunnel: there is a full-length *winding hole*, a fine wharf house and stables, moored craft, lime kilns and a *picnic area*. Tea rooms at both Cheddleton and Kingsley & Froghall Stations are well worth visiting.

NAVIGATIONAL NOTES

1 The Canal and River Churnet share a common course between Oakmeadowford Lock and Consall Forge, and care should be exercised along here, especially paddlers after heavy rain. Check level gauge at the tail of the lock to determine whether it is safe to proceed. Paddlers are advised to inspect the state of the water before committing to proceed.

2 Froghall is a very low tunnel, 76 yards in length. Unpowered boats may use it but must display a bright white, forward facing light on each boat. If you do not have this, or would prefer not to paddle, you can portage on the right, via the flat towpath which crosses a main road.

3 Boats up to 65' which cannot pass through Froghall Tunnel can wind just before it. Maximum dimensions for the tunnel are 5' 0" from the waterline to the cabin-top and 5' 0" across top of cabin from edge to edge. The tunnel is also impassable to boats over 65'.

4 There is a profile Gauge at the tail of Flint Mill Lock and this is also the location of the last winding hole capable of turning a full-length boat.

Caldon Canal *Froghall*

5 The last mile or so of canal is very narrow – in places two narrowboats cannot pass. It can also be challenging for paddlers. However, for boats able to negotiate the tunnel, there are good moorings through Lock 1 on the Uttoxeter Canal.

Consall Forge Pottery Mill Cottages, Consall Forge, Wetley Rocks ST9 0AJ (01538 266625; www.4ateapot.co.uk). Hand-thrown craft pottery and ceramics, especially teapots. *Open daily 10.00–17.00 but telephone to confirm before visiting.*

Churnet Valley Railway Kingsley & Froghall Station, Froghall ST10 2HA (01538 360522; www.churnetvalleyrailway.co.uk). Near Bridge 44. Opened by the North Staffordshire Railway in 1849 between North Rode and Macclesfield, the last stretch of this line closed in 1988. Purchased by enthusiasts, a steam-operated passenger train first ran again in August 1996. This superb line, which retains a 1950s ambience is open from Leekbrook, through Ipstones, Cheddleton and Consall to Kingsley & Froghall, and there is a buffet service on every train.

● **Froghall**
Staffs. PO box, tel. Tucked away in the heart of unspoilt Staffordshire, Froghall has been an outpost of industry ever since the advent of the canal fostered the growth of the Cauldon lime quarries a few miles east. The limestone was carted down the hills by a plate tramway, built originally in 1758 and the first to use iron rails. This was re-aligned in 1785, and finally re-built in 1800. A cable railway replaced the whole lot in 1849. The limestone was transhipped into waiting canal boats at Froghall Basin, serviced by the locomotives *Frog*, *Toad* and *Bobs*. Production ceased in 1920, with much of the trade being lost to the railways. Just west of the final bridge by the basin was the junction with the old canal arm to Uttoxeter (explaining the distances on the milestones): this locked down to the Churnet valley. The branch was closed in 1847 and the railway now occupies most of the canal's course, although much of the canal bed can still be traced. Until recently Froghall's industry was comprised almost entirely of factories and dwellings associated with Thomas Boltons copper works, where the original transatlantic cables where manufactured. Sadly for its 110 strong workforce, the firm went into receivership in March 2014. You can arrange for *gas* to be delivered to your boat by Staffordshire Farm Supplies, *Mon-Sat:* contact 01538 266718; www.countrystorewebshop.co.uk).

CANOEING AND PADDLEBOARDING
A number 18 bus – operating *07.30-18.30 (Sun 09.30-17.30)* – connects Hanley (bus station) Endon, Denford Road, Longsdon and Leek (bus station) making a one-way paddle a practical possibility along this very attractive waterway. *See also* **Walking and Cycling** on page 18.

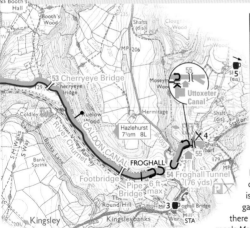

Pubs and Restaurants

● **1 The Boat Inn** Basford Bridge Lane, Cheddleton ST13 7EQ (01538 360521; www.facebook.com/theboatinncheddleton). Handsome stone-built pub, with long low-ceilinged bar decorated with plates and jugs. Real ale is served, bar meals are available *Mon-Sat L and E (not Mon E) & Sun 12.00-20.00.* Children welcome. Outside seating on the canalside patio. Camping and newspapers. *Open Mon-Sat 11.00-23.00 (Fri-Sat 00.00) & Sun 12.00-23.00.*

●✗ **2 The Black Lion** Consall Forge, Wetley Rocks ST9 0AJ (01782 550294; www.blacklionpub.co.uk). A splendid canalside pub of outstanding isolation, in a beautiful setting and with a fine garden. Although the interior is quite straightforward, there is an open fire and real ale to enjoy, along with meals *Mon-Thu L & Fri-Sun L and E.* Real cider. Child-and dog-friendly. Camping, traditional pub games and Wi-Fi. *Open Mon-Tue 11.00-17.30; Wed-Thu 11.00-20.00 (Thu 10.00) Fri-Sat 11.00-23.00 & Sun 12.00-22.30.*

●✗ **3 The Railway Inn** Froghall Road, Froghall ST10 2HA (01538 710700; www.facebook.com/therailwayinnfroghall). Beside Kingsley & Froghall Station, serving real ale and home-cooked meals *daily*. Garden, dog- and family-friendly. Wi-Fi. B&B. *Open Mon-Tue E & Wed-Sun 12.00-23.00.*

✗♀ **4 Hetty's Tea Shop** Foxt Road, Froghall ST10 2HL (01538 266288; www.hettysteashop.co.uk). Stylish tearoom serving breakfast *until 12.00*, light meals, sandwiches, panini, ciabatta, salads, teas, coffee, wine, beer and cake. *Open Thu-Sun 10.00-16.00.* Gift shop and upstairs accommodation for rent.

●✗ **5 The Fox & Goose** Foxt ST10 2HN (01538 266886). Village hostelry serving real ales and food *Wed-Fri E & Sat-Sun 12.00-21.00.* Child- and dog-friendly, garden. Quiz *Thu*. Traditional pub games. *Open Tue-Fri E & Sat-Sun 12.00-23.30.*

LLANGOLLEN CANAL

MAXIMUM DIMENSIONS

Length: 72'
Beam: 6' 10"
Headroom: 7'
Draught:
Hurleston to Pontcysyllte: 2' 3"
Pontcysyllte to Llangollen: 2'

MANAGER

0303 040 4040
enquiries.westmidlands@canalrivertrust.org.uk

MILEAGE

HURLESTON JUNCTION (Shropshire Union) *to:*
Frankton Junction: 29 miles
Pontcysyllte Aqueduct: 40 miles
LLANGOLLEN: 44½ miles
Llantysilio: 46 miles

Locks: 21

Canoeing and Paddleboarding: Category 1.
However, see Navigational Notes on page 35.

In 1791 a plan was published for a canal from the Mersey to the Severn, to pass through Chester, and the iron and coal fields around Ruabon, Ellesmere and Shrewsbury. There were to be branches to the limestone quarries at Llanymynech, and to the Chester Canal via Whitchurch. The new terminus on the Mersey was to be at the little fishing village of Netherpool, known after 1796 as Ellesmere Port. After extensive arguments about routes, the company received its Act in 1793. William Jessop was appointed engineer, and work began. By 1796 the Wirral line from Chester to Ellesmere Port was open, and was immediately successful, carrying goods and passengers (in express flyboats) to Liverpool. The same year, the Llanymynech Branch was completed. The company continued to expand and build inwards, but failed to make the vital connections with the Dee and the Severn; the line south to Shrewsbury never got further than Weston, and the line northwards to Chester stopped at Pontcysyllte. By 1806 the Ellesmere company had opened 68 miles of canal, which included lines from Hurleston on the Chester Canal to Plas Kynaston via Frankton, and from Chester to Ellesmere Port; there were branches to Llanymynech, Whitchurch, Prees and Ellesmere, and a navigable feeder to Llangollen; the two great aqueducts at Chirk and Pontcysyllte were complete. However, it was a totally self-contained system, its only outlet being via the old Chester Canal at Hurleston. Despite this, the Ellesmere Canal was profitable; it serviced a widespread local network, and gave an outlet to Liverpool (via the River Mersey) for the ironworks and the coalfields that were grouped at the centre of the system. This profitability was dependent upon good relations with the Chester Canal Company. An attempted take over in 1804 failed, but in 1813 the inevitable merger took place, and the Ellesmere & Chester Canal Company was formed. Today the Llangollen Canal is quite justly one of the most popular canals in the country, with fascinating architecture, spectacular aqueducts and splendid scenery. As a result it can become crowded during the summer months. Those who cruise out of the peak season, or avoid the mid-week rush to Llangollen, will have a more relaxing time. And of course you can always divert along the initial navigable section of the Montgomery Canal from Frankton Junction.

WALKING AND CYCLING

The towpath is just passable *for walkers* throughout its length. Cyclists will not find the towpath easy going, in spite of a few smooth stretches such as the resurfaced section from Llantysilio to Gledrid Bridge 19. Cycling across aqueducts and through tunnels **is not permitted**. Whilst there is very limited access for powered craft beyond the marina in Llangollen, the towpath is in excellent condition and makes a very enjoyable walk all the way to Horseshoe Falls.

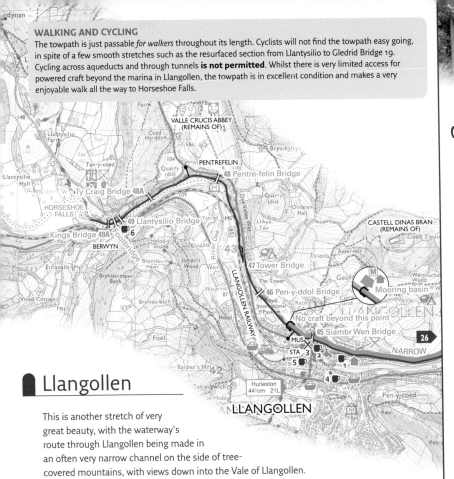

Llangollen

This is another stretch of very great beauty, with the waterway's route through Llangollen being made in an often very narrow channel on the side of tree-covered mountains, with views down into the Vale of Llangollen.

The canal passes high above the town, flowing through picturesque white bridges and passing the backs of charming and modestly eccentric houses. But it doesn't stop there: the excellent towpath continues beyond the mooring basin, alongside the small feeder channel which weaves its way up the valley, accompanied by the River Dee, past a country hotel and chain bridge over the river. The feeder terminates at the beautiful Horseshoe Falls with the diminutive Llantysilio Church just above it. The falls are formed by a long semi-circular weir across the Dee, built by Telford to provide constant water flow along the feeder channel and into the canal – 12 million gallons a day – ending up in Hurleston Reservoir at the eastern end of the canal. The Dee valley, with its many attractions including steam trains on the restored railway, make for a very pleasant circular walk of approximately four miles.

NAVIGATIONAL NOTES

1. There is **no** turning point west of the mooring marina at Llangollen, so boats longer than about 10ft (with a draught greater than 2' 3") must not venture up the feeder. However, this makes an excellent route for paddlers, there being little danger of meeting powered craft coming the other way (but *see* **Canoeing and Paddleboarding** on page 35).

2. There are ample moorings either side of Bridge 45, east on the canal towpath and west at the mooring basin. A combined ticket for either site must be obtained from the hut or shop on the west side of Bridge 45. The ticket is for either site but the combined maximum stay is only *48hrs in total.*'

23

● **Llangollen**

Denbighshire. PO, tel, stores, chemist, butcher, delicatessen, greengrocer, hardware, bank, baker, off-licence, fish & chips, garage. Founded in the 7th C by St Collen, the town has become established as one of North Wales' major tourist venues, especially during the month of July, when the International Musical Eisteddfod attracts performers and visitors from all around the world. Its superb setting in the upper Dee Valley has made it a great centre for outdoor pursuits, including pony trekking, climbing, walking and canoeing. For the less energetic there are canal trips, steam railway rides, the wonderful house of Plas Newydd, a Victorian School Museum and a Motor Museum. Visitors to the surrounding hills can explore Castell Dinas Bran, Valle Crucis Abbey and Elisegs Pillar, as well as enjoying superb walks. It was the construction of Telford's A5 road from London to Holyhead in 1815, which firmly placed Llangollen on the tourist map, but another 60 years were to pass before the streets of the town were to exchange their earthen surface for stone, quarried from Trevor Rocks. The town was a staging post on a drover's road, the routes used to move livestock to the distant markets of eastern England. In 1854 George Borrow recorded a meeting with a massive pig being driven along the road near Llangollen in his book *Wild Wales*. He noted that it weighed 'eighteen score of pounds' and 'walked with considerable difficulty'. At this time a pig would change hands at between 18 and 20 shillings - 'dire was the screaming of the porkers, yet the purchaser invariably seemed to know how to manage his bargain'. At the centre of the town is the parish church of St Collen, who was thought to be the first abbot of Valle Crucis Abbey. The 15th-C carved oak roof and stained glass window of St Collen are well worth seeing. The Ladies of Llangollen (*see* below) are buried in the churchyard.

International Musical Eisteddfod Eisteddfod Office, 1st Floor, Royal International Pavilion, Abbey Road, Llangollen LL20 8SW (01978 862001; www. international-eisteddfod.co.uk). For *one week every July* the town attracts singers, dancers and musicians from all over the world, who perform both in organised concerts, and impromptu street events. The gallery displays local and national touring exhibitions, and local craft work is displayed in the Craft Showcase, where items can be purchased. There are concerts, festivals and other events all year round at the Pavilion (01978 860111; www. llangollenpavilion.co.uk).

St Collen's Parish Church Regent St, Llangollen LL20 8HL (01978 861768; www.stcollenschurch.org. uk). This church was probably founded by St Collen, who was the first abbot of nearby Valle Crucis Abbey, and its establishment dates from the 7th century. The present building is of Norman origin, with many later additions and alterations. It has a beautifully carved oak roof, dating from the 15th C, and the stained glass window dedicated to St Collen is worth locating. In the churchyard is the tomb of the Ladies of Llangollen (*see* Plas Newydd across) and Mary Carryll, their maid.

Llangollen Railway The Station, Abbey Rd, Llangollen LL20 8SN (01978 860979; www.llangollen-railway.co.uk). The original Llangollen station was called Whitehurst Halt, and was situated close to Froncysyllte, from where the hotels in the town ran a taxi service to fetch the visitors. The building of the line was completed in 1862 after many delays, since the work, supervised by the chief engineer Henry Robertson, took much longer than anticipated. Vast numbers of navvies were employed, but in spite of their working on Sundays (to the disgust of the locals), the bad winter of 1860-1 brought their work to a halt. The first passenger train finally arrived on 2nd June 1862. The line was later extended to Corwen, when the present station was opened in 1865, and subsequently as far as Dolgellau. Soon trips to the coast at Barmouth were to become very popular amongst the locals. The line closed to passenger traffic in 1965, and to goods in 1968, and the station and tracks were left to fall into a ruinous state. Fortunately local enthusiasts came to its rescue, and they now operate steam and heritage diesel trains to Carrog (LL21 9BD) on over 8 miles of track in the direction of Corwen throughout most of the year. They also operate special dining trains (*Apr–Sept*) and driver experience.

Llangollen Motor Museum Pentrefelin Mill, Pentrefelin, Llangollen LL20 8EE (07780 306220; www.llangollenmotormuseum.co.uk) Near bridge 48. Housed in a building dating from the 1830s which was once a slate dressing works, this museum successfully recreates the atmosphere of a working 1950s garage, with tools and other motoring items lying around, and complete with living quarters. Cars, motorcycles, toys and memorabilia dating from the early part of the 20th C until the 1970s can be seen, and there is usually some restoration work under way. The Canal Exhibition explains, in pictures and words, how the canals were built and operated, their decline and their more recent revival. Working models of the Barton swing aqueduct, the Anderton boat lift, Worsley coal mine and how a lock is built and operated. *Opening hours vary so visit website for details.*

Plas Newydd Hill Street, Llangollen LL20 8AW (01978 862834; www.llangollen.org.uk/index.php/ things-to-do/attractions/item/61-plas-newydd-the-ladies-of-llangollen). On the southern outskirts of town. From 1779–1831 it was the home of the eccentric Lady Eleanor Butler and Miss Sarah Ponsonby, 'the two most celebrated virgins in Europe'. Their visitors, who included Browning, Tennyson, Walter Scott and Wordsworth, presented them with antique curios, which are now on display in the elaborately panelled rooms. Part of the 12-acre grounds is a public park. House *open daily Apr-Sep 10.00-16.00, last admission 15.30*. Charge. Entry to to the grounds is free, and these are *open all year round*.

Castell Dinas Bran 1/2 mile north of canal. The ruins of the castle built for Eliseg, Prince of Powys, can be seen from the waterway while approaching the town, and stand on a 1100ft mountain accessible to energetic walkers from various points along the canal, including bridge 45. A prince known as Bran is thought to have built the original fortification on this site, following a dispute with his brother Beli. Their mother was Corwena, who lived near what is now Corwen. The castle is thought to have had links with the legendary Holy Grail. The visible remains date from the late 13th C, and were built by the Princes of Powys.

Eliseg's Pillar ¼ mile north of the abbey. Erected in the 18th C to commemorate Eliseg, who built the fortress on the top of Dinas Bran.

Eglwyseg Rocks To the north east of the town, this is an impressive and brilliantly white escarpment of carboniferous limestone laid down some 400 million years ago, when this area was covered by the sea. It is now very popular with fossil hunters.

Tourist Information Centre Y Chapel, Castle Street, Llangollen LL20 8NU (01978 860828; www.llangollen.org.uk/index.php/where-to-stay/tourist-information-centre-2). Good choice of guide books and Wi-Fi. *Open Fri–Wed 09.30-17.00 (Sun 16.00).*

● **Llantysilio**
Denbighshire. Overlooking Horseshoe Falls. Parts of the interior of the church are taken from the nearby Valle Crucis Abbey.

Valle Crucis Abbey Llantysilio, Llangollen LL20 8DD (01978 860326/03000 252239; cadw.gov.wales/visit/places-to-visit/valle-crucis-abbey). 1½ miles north west of the town. Finely preserved ruins of the Cistercian abbey founded in 1201 by Madoc, Prince of Powys, and rebuilt in more lavish style after a fire in 1250. The abbey fell into neglect following the dissolution of the monasteries in 1539. Its finest feature is the vaulted chapter house and screened library cupboard. There is also the only surviving monastic fish pond to be seen in Wales. Occasional theatrical and musical events are held in the grounds. *Open May-Oct, Thu-Mon 10.00-17.00. Last admission 30 mins before closing.* Charge.

Pubs and Restaurants (pages 22–23)

There is a wide variety of friendly pubs and restaurants in Llangollen, including:

🍺✕ **1 The Ponsonby Arms** Mill Street, Llangollen LL20 8RY (01978 447985). On the A539 east of bridge 45. Serving an excellent selection of real ales and cider, together with food *daily in season.* Child- and dog-friendly, garden. Quiz *Tue.* Traditional pub games, newspapers, real fires, sports TV ad Wi-Fi. Camping nearby. *Open in season Tue to Sun 12.00-23.00 (Fri-Sun 00.00). Winter opens at 17.00 (Fri-Sun 15.00).*

🍺✕ **2 The Bridge End Hotel** Mill Street, Llangollen LL20 8RY (01978 861703; www.bridgeendhotel.co.uk). Below bridge 45. Large and comfortable pub serving real ale. Bar and restaurant meals *daily from 12.00 but L only Sun & Tue-Wed.* Dog- and child-friendly, garden. Sports TV and Wi-Fi. B&B. *Open 11.00-21.30 (Sat 22.00).*

✕ **3 The Wharf Tearoom** Wharf Hill, Llangollen LL20 8TA (01978 860702; www.horsedrawn boats.co.uk). Friendly café serving tea, coffee, scones, cakes, soup and light meals. Breakfast *until 11.30. Open daily 09.00-17.00.*

🍺 **4 The Sun Inn** 49 Regent St, Llangollen LL20 8HN (01978 860079; www.sunllan.com). Serving up to six changing real ales and real cider, this hostelry hosts live music *Wed-Sat.* Dog-friendly, garden. Traditional pub games, newspapers, real fires, sports TV and Wi-Fi. Camping nearby. *Open Wed-Sun 19.00-00.00 (Sun 23.00).*

🍺✕ **5 The Corn Mill** Dee Lane, Llangollen LL20 8PN (01978 869555; www.brunningandprice.co.uk/cornmill). A pub in a converted Corn Mill, with terraces above the mill race and the river rapids, serving an interesting range of real ale, real cider and food *daily 12.00-21.30 (Sun 21.00).* Dog- and child-friendly, garden. Newspapers and Wi-Fi. Camping nearby. *Open 12.00-23.00 (Sun 22.30).*

🍺✕ **6 The Chain Bridge Hotel** Berwyn Street, Llangollen LL20 8BS (01978 860215; www.chainbridgehotel.com). In a splendid position overlooking the river and the chain bridge, where monks from Valle Crucis once crossed the river. Food *L and E.* Restaurant meals *(Mon-Sat E and Sun L & E)* should be booked. Children welcome. Garden and Wi-Fi. B&B. *Open daily 11.00-23.00.*

WALKING AND CYCLING
Llangollen is a great centre for both activities. The Tourist Information Centre has a range of guides. From bridge 45 you can follow a path north to visit Castell Dinas Bran and Trevor Rocks; from bridge 48 you can take a circular walk to Valle Crucis Abbey, returning via bridge 48A, and visiting Horseshoe Falls and the canal's end. The towpath is good for cycling as far as Pontcysyllte, and after *walking* your bike over the aqueduct you can return to Llangollen along quiet lanes to the south of the A5 (avoid riding on this busy road!).

BOAT TRIPS
The Wharf Llangollen LL20 8TA (01978 860702; www.horsedrawnboats.co.uk). Horse-drawn trips have been available in Llangollen since 1884, visiting Pentrefelin and Berwyn. There are also trips on *nb Thomas Telford* over the Pontcysyllte Aqueduct and day boat hire. Gift shop and café.

Quarry (dis)
Monument
Garth
Gwer
Berthyr-Aur-
Wern-uchaf Wood
Llandyn Hall
Nythy-dryw
Bryn
Haulog
Offa's Dyke Path
Sort
Ceny
Esch Garth Pit
Trevor
Garth
Quarry
Llanddyn No 1 43
Bridge
Llandyn Cottage
84
42 Wenffrwd Bridge
Grid
TREVOR UCHAF
Tyno-uchaf
LLEN C
Towni Road
NARROW
41 Sun Trevor Bridge
Trevor Hall Wood
Trevor Hall
Bryn Sprys Oerog
44 Llanddyn No 2
Lift Bridge (open)
Langollen-fechant
85
Plas-ifa
Sor
40 Plas Ifan Bridge
Pipe Bridge
Bryn Sprys Oerog
23
NARROW
Maesmawr Road
River Dee (Afon Dyfrdwy)
Caregan Brayn
MS
39 Vale of Llangollen Bridge
108
539
38 Bryn Howel Bridge
railway
LLANGOLLEN CANAL
-coed
A5
CH
Bryn-How Farm
Plas-isaf
Llyn Farm
Pen-y-bryn Farm
Ty-ucha
Ford
Abercregan
Plas Isaf Bridge 37
34
Plas-y-Pentre Bridge
yn-pentr
Pen-y-coed
Bryn-dethol
Plas Isaf Bridge 37
VALE OF LLANGOLLEN
36
Bryn Ceirch Bridge
35
Millars Dd Bridge
Cysyllte Farm MS
wern all
Tyn Dwr
MS

Chirk and Pontcysyllte

The canal – little more than a narrow trough – leaves Llangollen, clinging spectacularly to the side of the valley above the Dee. Ducking under Rhos-y-coed Bridge, the waterway finally breaks out of the trees and, following a tricky turn to the right, the boater is immediately projected onto the vertiginous heights of the breathtaking Pontcysyllte Aqueduct. At the north end of the aqueduct there is a fascinating, short arm branching off to the left, which plays host to a boatyard. This arm, heading towards Ruabon, was originally intended as the canal's main line towards Chester and the Mersey, and the dry dock at Trevor Junction dates from this time. The line from Trevor to Llantysilio was envisaged purely as a navigable feeder. However the idea of a direct line to Chester was soon dropped and a connection made instead with the Chester Canal at Hurleston Junction. The waterway finally regains terra firma on a massive embankment, projecting out into the Dee valley, bordered by the village of Froncysyllte. To the north of the short Whitehouses Tunnel the navigation meets the railway before swinging due south passing Chirk Marina on its course for Chirk Aqueduct – an impressive structure by any canal enthusiast's standards, and accompanied by a very fine railway viaduct alongside. This is preceded by a tunnel with Chirk Station nearby. A long wooded cutting follows, while the railway disappears to the west. As Chirk Bank is reached, the waterway escapes its side-cutting and the boater is soon regaled with open views of Shropshire, stretching away into the distance. There are good *moorings* and a *turning place* in the restored basins beyond the *boatyard* at Trevor and *moorings* at the north end of Chirk Tunnel.

WALKING AND CYCLING

The alternative route of Offa's Dyke Path crosses Pontcysyllte Aqueduct. On the north side of the aqueduct three walks are indicated on a board. Cyclists must dismount when crossing the aqueduct. There is an excellent walk from the aqueduct along the towpath to bridge 27. Turn left to Newbridge then return through Ty Mawr Country Park along a path beside the River Dee.

NAVIGATIONAL NOTES

1   From Llangollen to Trevor the canal is very shallow, accentuating the flow downstream. It is not recommended for boats drawing more than 24". It is also, in places, very narrow. Just go slowly and keep a sharp watch for approaching boats.
2   Do not enter the Pontcysyllte Aqueduct if a boat is approaching from the opposite direction. Wait until it is clear.

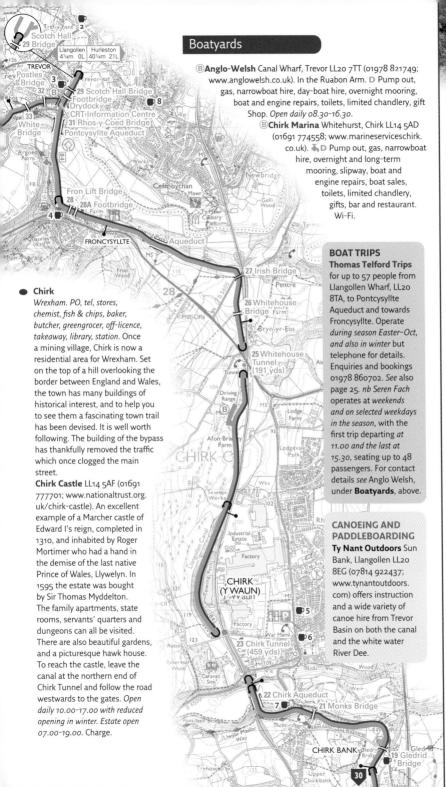

Boatyards

B Anglo-Welsh Canal Wharf, Trevor LL20 7TT (01978 821749; www.anglowelsh.co.uk). In the Ruabon Arm. D Pump out, gas, narrowboat hire, day-boat hire, overnight mooring, boat and engine repairs, toilets, limited chandlery, gift Shop. *Open daily 08.30-16.30.*

B Chirk Marina Whitehurst, Chirk LL14 5AD (01691 774558; www.marineserviceschirk.co.uk). D Pump out, gas, narrowboat hire, overnight and long-term mooring, slipway, boat and engine repairs, boat sales, toilets, limited chandlery, gifts, bar and restaurant. Wi-Fi.

BOAT TRIPS

Thomas Telford Trips for up to 57 people from Llangollen Wharf, LL20 8TA, to Pontcysyllte Aqueduct and towards Froncysyllte. Operate *during season Easter–Oct, and also in winter* but telephone for details. Enquiries and bookings 01978 860702. *See* also page 25. *nb Seren Fach* operates at *weekends and on selected weekdays in the season*, with the first trip departing *at 11.00 and the last at 15.30,* seating up to 48 passengers. For contact details *see* Anglo Welsh, under **Boatyards**, above.

CANOEING AND PADDLEBOARDING

Ty Nant Outdoors Sun Bank, Llangollen LL20 8EG (07814 922437; www.tynantoutdoors.com) offers instruction and a wide variety of canoe hire from Trevor Basin on both the canal and the white water River Dee.

Chirk

Wrexham. PO, tel, stores, chemist, fish & chips, baker, butcher, greengrocer, off-licence, takeaway, library, station. Once a mining village, Chirk is now a residential area for Wrexham. Set on the top of a hill overlooking the border between England and Wales, the town has many buildings of historical interest, and to help you to see them a fascinating town trail has been devised. It is well worth following. The building of the bypass has thankfully removed the traffic which once clogged the main street.

Chirk Castle LL14 5AF (01691 777701; www.nationaltrust.org.uk/chirk-castle). An excellent example of a Marcher castle of Edward I's reign, completed in 1310, and inhabited by Roger Mortimer who had a hand in the demise of the last native Prince of Wales, Llywelyn. In 1595 the estate was bought by Sir Thomas Myddelton. The family apartments, state rooms, servants' quarters and dungeons can all be visited. There are also beautiful gardens, and a picturesque hawk house. To reach the castle, leave the canal at the northern end of Chirk Tunnel and follow the road westwards to the gates. *Open daily 10.00–17.00 with reduced opening in winter. Estate open 07.00–19.00.* Charge.

Pontcysyllte Aqueduct, looking south

Chirk and Whitehouses Tunnels Neither of these tunnels is wide enough for two boats to pass, although each tunnel has a towpath running through it. Chirk Tunnel is 459yds long. Whitehouses Tunnel is 191yds long.

● **Chirk Aqueduct**
Opened in 1801, this is a splendidly massive brick and stone aqueduct carrying the canal in a narrow cast iron trough from England into Wales. The River Ceiriog flows 70ft below, and the great railway viaduct is beside and a little higher than the aqueduct.
Cycle Hire Station Road, Trevor LL20 7TP (01691 773532/07889 855908; www.hirecycle2go.co.uk). Adult and child bikes, trailers and child seats. *Open 09.30-17.30.*

● **Froncysyllte**
Wrexham. PO, tel, stores, takeaway. A village distinguished by its superb position on the side of the valley.

● **Pontcysyllte Aqueduct**
Easily the most famous and most spectacular feature on the whole canal system, this aqueduct cannot fail to astonish visitors. Apart from its great height of 126ft above the River Dee and its length of 1007ft, the excitement to be derived from crossing this structure by boat is partly due to the fact that, while the towpath side is fenced off with, albeit widely spaced, iron railings, the offside is completely unprotected from about 12in above the water level *so*

the only way for children to enjoy the voyage across this great aqueduct is from inside the boat. It is generally considered to have been built by Thomas Telford and, if so, is reckoned to be one of his most brilliant and successful works. The concept of laying a cast iron trough along the top of a row of stone piers was entirely new, and entirely Telford's: he realised that such a high crossing of the Dee valley was inevitable if time- and water-wasting locks were to be avoided, and it was obvious to the canal company that a conventional brick or stone aqueduct would be quite unsuitable. His plan for the aqueduct was greeted at first with derision; but the work went ahead, was completed in ten years and opened in 1805 at an estimated cost of £47,018. One can hardly imagine the utter amazement felt by people of that time as they witnessed boats moving easily across this tall, beautiful and unique structure. Today, the aqueduct remains as built, apart from renewals of balustrading and the towpath structure. The masonry is apparently in prime condition (note the very thin masonry joints, which were bonded by a mortar made from a mixture of lime and ox blood), and the dove-tailed joints in the iron trough, sealed with a combination of Welsh flannel and lead dipped in boiling sugar, hardly leak at all. The cast iron side plates of the trough are all wedge shaped, like the stones in a masonry arch. It is, without doubt, a masterpiece and a fitting centrepiece of this World Heritage Site.

Pubs and Restaurants (pages 26-27)

● ✗ **1 The Sun Trevor Hotel** Sun Bank, Llangollen LL20 8EG (01978 860651; www.suntrevor.co.uk). Above bridge 41. Beautifully situated pub with exceptional views of the valley, river and canal. Brasses, beams and a fine inglenook with a cosy curved settle are there to enjoy in a haunted building, which has its origins in the 14th C. Real ales. Food, using local ingredients, *daily 12.00-20.30.* Garden with children's play area. Mooring. *Open daily 11.00-23.00.*
● **2 The Duke of Wellington** Llangollen Road, Acrefair LL14 3SG (01978 512716). Traditional two-room local offering a friendly welcome and real ale. Garden. Traditional pub games, real fires and Wi-Fi. *Open Mon-Sat 12.00-23.00 (Fri-Sat 00.00) & Sun 12.00-22.00.*
● ✗ **3 The Telford Inn** Station Road, Trevor LL20 7TT (01978 820469). Imposing, multi-room pub beside Trevor Basin serving real ale and food *daily 12.00-21.00.* Small garden and play area; dog- and child-friendly. Real fires. *Open 11.00-23.00.*
● **4 The Aqueduct Inn** Holyhead Road, Froncysyllte LL20 7PY (01691 777118; www.facebook.com/AqueInn). Standing beside Telford's A5 road, with views of the canal but not the aqueduct itself, this comfortable pub dispenses real ale and good food *daily 12.00-20.00.* Small garden, dog- and family-friendly. Traditional pub games, real fires, sports TV and Wi-Fi. *Open 12.00-23.00.*

● **5 Stanton House** Holyhead Road, Chirk LL14 5NA (01691 774150). Traditional locals' pub serving real ale and food *L and E daily (not E in winter).* Outside seating, *regular* live music, sports TV and Wi-Fi. Traditional pub games. *Open Mon-Thu 11.00-00.00 (Fri-Sun 01.00).*
● ✗ **6 The Hand Hotel** Church Street, Chirk LL14 5EY (01691 773472; www.thehandhotelchirk.co.uk). Smart hotel, with resident ghosts, serving real ale. Food available in the Castle Room and Regency Restaurant Mon-Sat *L and E & Sun 12.00-14.30.* Children welcome. Garden with play area. Large-screen TV in public bar. Dog-friendly. Real fires and Wi-Fi. Camping & B&B. *Open Mon-Sat 10.30-23.00 (Thu-Sat 00.00) & Sun 12.00-22.30.*
● **7 The Bridge Inn** Chirk Bank, Chirk LL14 5BU (01691 773213; www.facebook.com/TheBridgeInnChirkTheTrap). Known locally as 'The Trap' this is the 'last pub in England', with a fine view of Chirk Aqueduct. Cosy welcoming bar with an open fire. Real ale. Food available *daily 12.00-20.00 (Sun 17.00).* Dogs welcome, patio with marvellous views. Real fires, sports TV and Wi-Fi. Traditional pub games. *Open 12.00-23.00 (Sun 22.00).*

Also try: ● **8 The Queens Hotel** Queen Street, Cefn Mawr LL14 3BD (01978 469889).

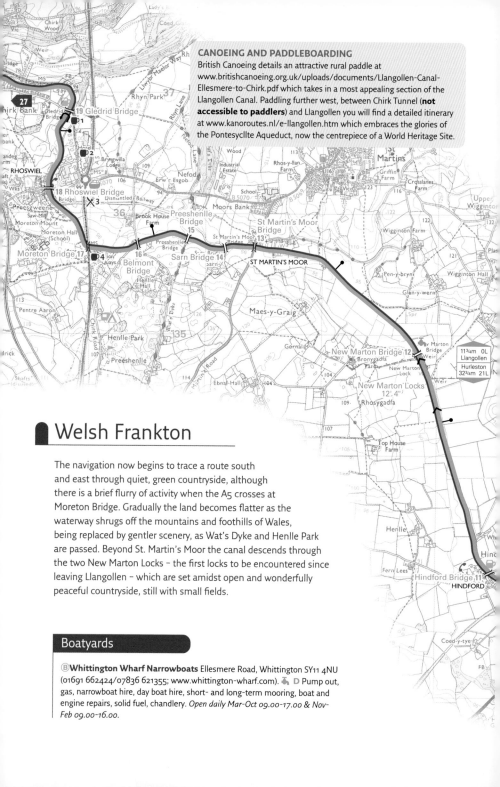

Welsh Frankton

The navigation now begins to trace a route south and east through quiet, green countryside, although there is a brief flurry of activity when the A5 crosses at Moreton Bridge. Gradually the land becomes flatter as the waterway shrugs off the mountains and foothills of Wales, being replaced by gentler scenery, as Wat's Dyke and Henlle Park are passed. Beyond St. Martin's Moor the canal descends through the two New Marton Locks – the first locks to be encountered since leaving Llangollen – which are set amidst open and wonderfully peaceful countryside, still with small fields.

Boatyards

Ⓑ**Whittington Wharf Narrowboats** Ellesmere Road, Whittington SY11 4NU (01691 662424/07836 621355; www.whittington-wharf.com). 🔧 D Pump out, gas, narrowboat hire, day boat hire, short- and long-term mooring, boat and engine repairs, solid fuel, chandlery. *Open daily Mar-Oct 09.00-17.00 & Nov-Feb 09.00-16.00.*

● **Weston Rhyn**
Shropshire. Tel, PO box, stores, takeaway, garden centre, garage. A tiny village on the Welsh border; the canal runs through it in a slight cutting.

Pubs and Restaurants

🍺✕ **1 The Poachers** Chirk Road, Glenrid LL14 5DG (01691 773250; www.poacherspocketpub. co.uk). Popular and friendly pub serving real ale. Good value, home-cooked meals *daily from 12.00*. Garden and outdoor play area. *Regular* live music and Wi-Fi. Moorings. *Open 12.00-23.00 (Sun 22.30).*

🍺✕ **2 The Lord Moreton** Gledrid, Chirk LL14 5DG (01691 778888; www.moretonpark.com/ lordmoreton). Large, tastefully appointed, modern pub serving real ale and excellent food available *all day*, including breakfast. Family-friendly, garden. Wi-Fi. B&B. *Bar open daily L and E.* Large canalside terrace, children welcome. *Regular* live music. Newspapers, real fires, sports TV and Wi-Fi. B&B. *Open 12.00-23.00 (Sun 22.30).*

✕ **3 BP Garage** (north of Moreton Bridge 17) The garage has a café serving breakfasts and lunches. There is also a small stores.

🍺✕ **4 The Waterside Bar** Weston Rhyn, Moreton SY11 3EN (01691 684300). Beside Bridge 17. Bar, two restaurants hotel, country club and spa. Food served *daily L and E.* Large canalside terrace, children welcome. *Regular* live music. Newspapers, real fires, sports TV and Wi-Fi. B&B. *Open 12.00-23.00 (Sun 22.30).*

🍺 **5 The Narrow Boat** Ellesmere Road, Whittington SY11 4NU (01691 661051). Pub with a nautical theme, situated in the old Canal Office. Real ale. Meals available *L and E (not Sun-Mon E).* Dog- and family-friendly, canalside garden. Moorings. *Open daily 11.00-15.00 & 18.00-23.00.*

WALKING AND CYCLING
The towpath is in poor condition between bridge 9 and Frankton Junction.

Ellesmere

At Frankton Junction the Montgomery Canal branches south towards Newtown: it is currently navigable to Crickheath Basin, just beyond Maesbury Marsh, and further restoration continues. Beyond the junction, the country once again becomes quiet and entirely rural, while the canal's course becomes very winding. However, Ellesmere is soon reached, and access is via a short arm. A fine old warehouse and a small canalside crane testify to the canal trading that used to be carried on from here. The main line of the canal to Hurleston Junction bears round sharply to the south east at the junction: the buildings here house the CRT office and maintenance yard. Beech House was once the canal company's office. The canal now enters the 87yd Ellesmere Tunnel and emerges into open parkland beyond. You will notice many oak trees alongside the canal around here – this is said to be the legacy of the Shropshire Union's policy of planting trees to provide the raw materials to replace their carrying fleet. Now the navigation runs right beside Blake Mere: this is a charming little lake, surrounded by steep and thickly wooded hills. Soon the hilly, sylvan landscape gives way to the open countryside that lies to the east of Ellesmere and contains several more beautiful meres. The canal skirts Cole Mere, which is below and mostly hidden from it by tall trees; there is a delightful timbered cottage at the west end.

WALKING AND CYCLING

There are woodland walks from the Meres Visitor Centre to the Castle Mound. The towpath is in very poor condition between Bridges 69 and 59. It is advisable to use the bridleway between Bridges 69 and 63.

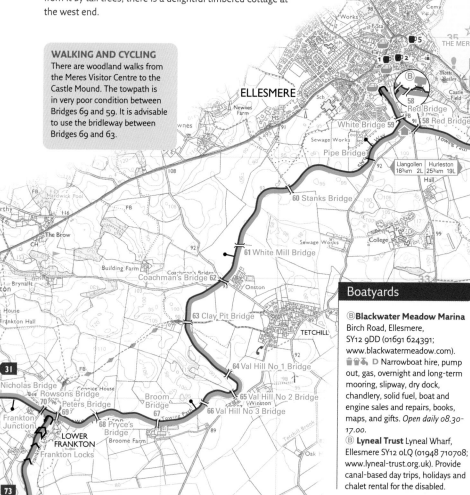

Boatyards

Ⓑ**Blackwater Meadow Marina** Birch Road, Ellesmere, SY12 9DD (01691 624391; www.blackwatermeadow.com). 🛁🛒⛽🛠 D Narrowboat hire, pump out, gas, overnight and long-term mooring, slipway, dry dock, chandlery, solid fuel, boat and engine sales and repairs, books, maps, and gifts. *Open daily 08.30-17.00.*

Ⓑ **Lyneal Trust** Lyneal Wharf, Ellesmere SY12 0LQ (01948 710708; www.lyneal-trust.org.uk). Provide canal-based day trips, holidays and chalet rental for the disabled.

73

- **Welshampton**
  Shropshire. Tel, PO box. 1 mile west of bridge 50.
- **Tetchill**
  Shropshire. A small farming village, quiet and unpretentious.
- **Ellesmere**
  Shropshire. PO, tel, stores, baker, butcher, delicatessen, chemist, DIY, takeaways, hardware, laundrette, garage. This handsome and busy 18th-C market town, with its narrow winding streets, is an attractive place to visit, with good access from the canal basin. There are many tall red-brick houses and several terraces of old cottages. It takes its name from the large and beautiful mere beside it.

Shropshire Wildlife Trust Mereside, Ellesmere SY12 0PA (01691 622981; www.shropshirewildlifetrust.org.uk). The Trust has a *daily presence* at The Boathouse Café (*see* below) *10.30-15.30*. They are a fund of local information including walks and wildlife. They also hold children's events *every Tue during school holidays.*
St Mary's Church SY12 9EG Standing on a hill overlooking the mere, the general appearance of this large red-stone church is Victorian, belying its medieval origins. It contains a medieval chest hewn out of a solid block of oak, many fine effigies and a beautiful 15th-C font.

NAVIGATIONAL NOTES

Passage through Frankton Locks is limited to *12.00-14.00 daily*. During the summer passage must be booked *before 10.00* on the day of travel and *48 hrs* notice given over the winter period. Bookings can be made on 0303 040 4040 during weekdays and via the Anderton Lift at weekends on 01606 786777 extension 8.

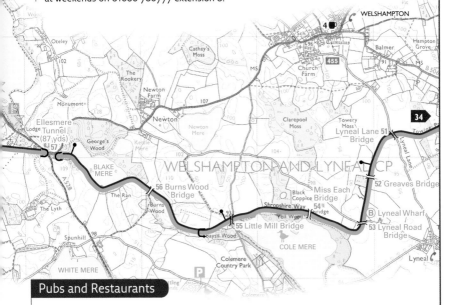

Pubs and Restaurants

● ✕ **1 The Black Lion Hotel** Scotland Street, Ellesmere SY12 0EG (01691 622937; www.facebook.com/blacklionellesmere). Smart pub with a Tudor bar and beams. Real ale and food available *L and E (not Sun L).* Heated patio, dog- and family-friendly. Real fires and Wi-Fi. B&B. *Open daily 11.00-23.00 (Fri-Sat 00.30).*
● **2 The Ellesmere Hotel** The High Street, Ellesmere SY12 0ES (01691 622055; www.ellesmerehotel.co.uk). Friendly town pub serving real ale and real cider. Carvery *Fri E. from 17.00. Regular* live music. Traditional pub games and sports TV. *Open Mon-Fri 16.00-23.00 and Sat-Sun 12.00-23.00.*
✕ ♀ **3 The Boathouse Restaurant & Café** Mereside, Ellesmere SY12 0PA (01691 623852; www.ellesmereboathouse.co.uk). The café is *open daily 08.30-17.00* serving breakfast (*until 11.00*) light meals and snacks, while the restaurant offers full meals. *Open daily 09.00-16.00. Breakfast served until 11.00.*
● ✕ **4 The Sun Inn** Welshampton, Ellesmere SY12 0PH (01948 710847; www.thesuninn.net). ¾ mile west of Bridge 50. Recently completely refurbished after a lengthy closure, a welcoming hostelry serving real ale and food that majors on local produce *daily 12.00-21.30*. Child- and dog-friendly, garden. *Regular* live music, real fires and Wi-Fi. B&B. *Open daily 11.00-00.00 (Sun 23.00).*

Also try: ● ✕ **5 The Red Lion Coaching Inn** 18 Church Street, Ellesmere SY12 0HD (01691 622632; www.redlion-ellesmere.co.uk).

Whixall Moss

Leaving Bettisfield, the canal heads for Whixall Moss and begins to wind this way and that, passing into Wales and then out again. Not a single bridge interrupts the long wooded straight, carrying the waterway over the uncharacteristically flat area of Whixall Moss, before its eventual junction with the Prees Branch. This leads to a marina and a nature reserve. Bridge 1 on the branch is grade II listed, and has been restored (*see* Navigational Note). The main line veers off to the north east along another straight embankment, and the canal now begins to traverse a very remote and under-populated area, passing no villages for miles. At Platt Lane the unnaturally straight navigation leaves the embankment, which has carried it across Whixall Moss and snuggles back into an accommodating contour.

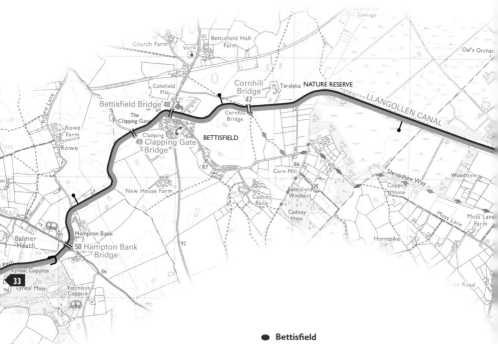

● **Platt Lane**
Shropshire. Tel. South east of bridge 43. A tiny settlement on the edge of the Moss.

● **Whixall Moss**
A raised bog rich in flora and insect fauna – including mosquitoes! Like other meres and bogs in the area, Whixall Moss came into existence at the end of the Ice Age, as huge blocks of ice were left behind when the remainder of the ice cap melted and drained off into what is now the Severn valley. The peat surface remains, in spite of the past cutting for garden use, and is now a SSSI, and an important site for rare insect and plant life, which survive on this delicate habitat. Details from Natural England (0300 060 3900; www.gov.uk/government/organisations/natural-england).

● **Bettisfield**
Wrexham. Tel. A quiet village with new housing.

● **Prees Branch**
Sometimes also known as the Edstaston Branch, this arm curved round to Quina Brook – it never did reach Prees. Its principal value in recent years lay in the clay pits just over a mile from the junction: the clay from here was used until a few years ago for repairing the 'puddle' in local canals. The arm had been disused for some years, but now the first 1/2 mile gives access to a marina constructed in the old pit. It is all very pleasant, and the canal arm has two lift bridges – one of which is a rare skewed example. Interesting plant communities exist along the unrestored section of the branch: enquiries may be made to Natural England at the number given above if you wish to explore.

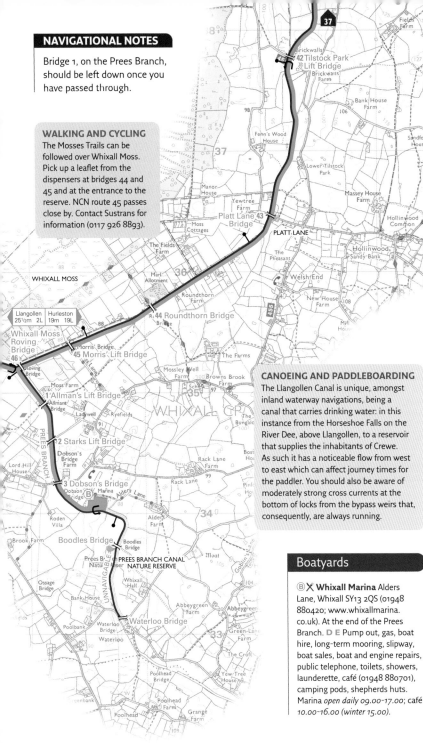

NAVIGATIONAL NOTES

Bridge 1, on the Prees Branch, should be left down once you have passed through.

WALKING AND CYCLING

The Mosses Trails can be followed over Whixall Moss. Pick up a leaflet from the dispensers at bridges 44 and 45 and at the entrance to the reserve. NCN route 45 passes close by. Contact Sustrans for information (0117 926 8893).

CANOEING AND PADDLEBOARDING

The Llangollen Canal is unique, amongst inland waterway navigations, being a canal that carries drinking water: in this instance from the Horseshoe Falls on the River Dee, above Llangollen, to a reservoir that supplies the inhabitants of Crewe. As such it has a noticeable flow from west to east which can affect journey times for the paddler. You should also be aware of moderately strong cross currents at the bottom of locks from the bypass weirs that, consequently, are always running.

Boatyards

Ⓑ ✕ **Whixall Marina** Alders Lane, Whixall SY13 2QS (01948 880420; www.whixallmarina. co.uk). At the end of the Prees Branch. D E Pump out, gas, boat hire, long-term mooring, slipway, boat sales, boat and engine repairs, public telephone, toilets, showers, launderette, café (01948 880701), camping pods, shepherds huts. Marina *open daily 09.00-17.00*; café *10.00-16.00 (winter 15.00)*.

Grindley Brook

The canal continues to meander through typically quiet and pretty countryside before arriving at a pair of busy road bridges beside a boatyard. This heralds the approach to the attractive market town of Whitchurch where a lift bridge marks the entrance to the Whitchurch Arm. The arm is being progressively extended and offers *moorings* a short walk from the town centre. After little more than a mile, the main line arrives at the top of the six locks at Grindley Brook: the first three locks being arranged in a staircase. Care should be exercised on the approach to these locks and anyone requiring assistance or advice should look for the friendly lock keeper, who will be there to help *Apr-Oct daily 08.30–18.30*. Boats should not stop in the flight and only moor once beyond the railway embankment, after negotiating the sharp bend. The canal now continues to descend through a series of isolated locks as the valley begins to open out.

● **Grindley Brook**
Shropshire. Stores, off-licence. The famous staircase locks have made this a canal monument.

● **Whitchurch**
Shropshire. All services. A fine town with some beautiful old houses of all periods in the centre. The streets are narrow and there is much to discover. It has its origins in Roman times as Mediolanum, 'the place in the middle of the plain', a stop on the route from Chester to Wroxeter. It was recorded in the Domesday Book as Westune, but was later to become White Church, or Whitchurch, for obvious reasons. There are lots of splendid pubs in the town, but unfortunately none near the canal. J. B. Joyce & Co was established here in 1690, and continued to make very fine tower clocks until their take-over by Smith of Derby Group. Sir Edward German was born in St Mary's Street in 1862 – he composed *Tom Jones and Merrie England*. If you visit on *Friday*, look out for farmhouse Cheshire cheese in the market.

BeWILDerwood Cheshire Bickley Moss, Whitchurch, Cheshire SY13 4JF (01829 830730; www.cheshire. bewilderwood.co.uk). Award-winning forest of family fun and outdoor adventure. Tree houses, wobbly wires, slippery slopes, crocklebogs, Twiggles and Boggles. Also story-telling and marsh walks. Café. *Open Wed-Sun 10.00–17.00.* Charge.

St Alkmund's Church High Street, Whitchurch SY13 1LB (01948 667253; www.stalkmunds.com). This striking church on the hill was built in 1713 by William and Richard Smith as the replacement for a late 14th-C building which 'fell ye 31 of July 1711'. This in turn had been built to succeed the Norman White Church which was attributed to William de Warren, one of William the Conqueror's lieutenants, who died in 1089. In 1862 the old pews were removed, and many human bones were found beneath them. These were re-buried and a new floor was laid. Those who know the Oxford Canal will recognise the present church's similarity to the magnificent church of the same vintage at Banbury. It has very large windows and a stunning interior. Indeed the whole church is on a grand scale and is well worth a visit. *Open daily 10.00–17.00.*

Whitchurch Heritage Centre & Museum and Archives 12 St Mary's Street, Whitchurch SY13 1QY (01948 664577; www.whitchurch-heritage.co.uk). A fascinating centre, with displays of Whitchurch clocks, plus the illustrations of Randolph Caldecott. *Open Tue and Thu 11.00–16.00.*

Pubs and Restaurants

● **1 The Black Bear** 49 High Street, Whitchurch SY13 1AZ (01948 663800; www.facebook.com/blackbearwhitchurch). Black and white, timber-framed hostelry, opposite the church and recently renovated. Real ale and real cider together with meals *daily 12.00-21.00 (Sun 20.00).* Dog-friendly, small garden. *Monthly* live music and real fires. *Open 11.00–23.00.*

● **2 The Old Town Hall Vaults** 1 St Mary's Street, Whitchurch SY13 1QU (01948 664682; www.facebook.com/oldtownhallvaultswhitchurch). Birthplace of Sir Edward German (1862–1936), composer of *Merrie England* and *Tom Jones*. Real ale. Home-made meals available *Mon-Sat 12.00-20.00 (Fri-Sat 11.00) & Sun 12.00-18.00.* Dog-friendly, courtyard. *Occasional* live music and real fires. *Open Mon-Sat 11.00-23.00 (Fri-Sat 00.00) & Sun 12.00-23.00.*

● ✗ **3 Reubens Bar & BBQ** 7 Pepper Street, Whitchurch SY13 1BG (01948 258030; www.reubensbarandbbq.com). A restored Victorian hotel dispensing real ale and food *Mon 17.00-21.00; Tue-Sat 10.00-21.00 & Sun 12.00-19.00.* Courtyard seating. Traditional pub games, *occasional* live music and Wi-Fi. B&B. *Open Mon 17.00-23.00; Tue-Sat 11.00-01.00 & Sun 12.00-19.00.*

● **4 The Old Eagles** 13 Watergate, Whitchurch SY13 1DP (01948 258841; www.facebook.com/ theoldeaglesofficialwhitchurch). Complete with an internal base-cruck frame, this pub is refuted to be the oldest building in the town, while the 'modern' Victorian exterior hides an original 14th-C structure. Real ale, a sheltered courtyard, traditional pub games, newspapers, a real fire and sports TV are available in what is effectively a one-room hostelry. *Occasional* live music. *Open 14.00-22.00 (Fri-Sat 23.30).*

● ✗ **5 The Horse and Jockey** Grindley Brook, Whitchurch SY13 4QJ (01948 662723; www.thehorseandjockey.pub). Large, welcoming, family-run pub near the bottom lock, with a cosy woodburning stove in the lounge, and a resident ghost. Real ale and real cider. Meals available *daily 12.00-20.00 (Sun 16.00).* Dog- and family-friendly, garden and play area. Traditional pub games, sports TV and Wi-Fi. Camping. *Open daily 12.00-23.00.*

✗ ♀ **6 The Lockside Café** Grindley Brook, Whitchurch SY13 4QH (01948 663385; www.facebook.com/ GrindleybrookLocksideCafe). Tea, coffee and hot and cold snacks served in the @29 Café where there is internet access. Licensed. Gifts and preserves. Dog-friendly, outside seating and mooring. *Open daily (including B Hols) 09.00-17.00 (Oct-Mar 16.30).*

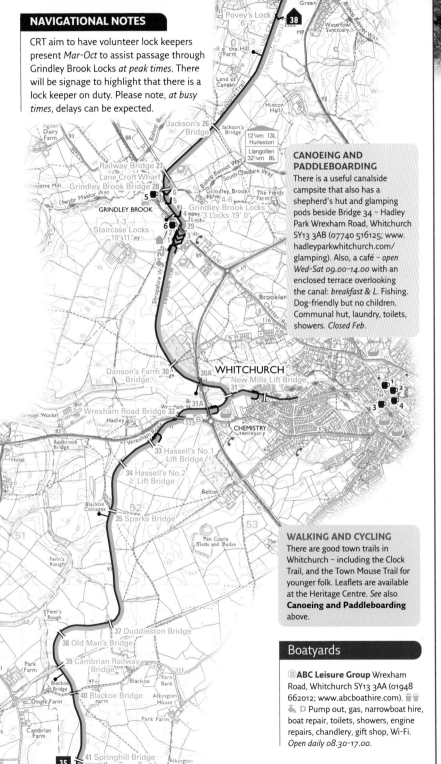

NAVIGATIONAL NOTES

CRT aim to have volunteer lock keepers present *Mar-Oct* to assist passage through Grindley Brook Locks *at peak times*. There will be signage to highlight that there is a lock keeper on duty. Please note, *at busy times*, delays can be expected.

CANOEING AND PADDLEBOARDING

There is a useful canalside campsite that also has a shepherd's hut and glamping pods beside Bridge 34 – Hadley Park Wrexham Road, Whitchurch SY13 3AB (07740 516125; www.hadleyparkwhitchurch.com/glamping). Also, a café – *open Wed-Sat 09.00-14.00* with an enclosed terrace overlooking the canal: *breakfast & L*. Fishing. Dog-friendly but no children. Communal hut, laundry, toilets, showers. *Closed Feb*.

WALKING AND CYCLING

There are good town trails in Whitchurch – including the Clock Trail, and the Town Mouse Trail for younger folk. Leaflets are available at the Heritage Centre. *See also* **Canoeing and Paddleboarding** above.

Boatyards

Ⓑ**ABC Leisure Group** Wrexham Road, Whitchurch SY13 3AA (01948 662012; www.abcboathire.com). 🛢 D Pump out, gas, narrowboat hire, boat repair, toilets, showers, engine repairs, chandlery, gift shop, Wi-Fi. *Open daily 08.30-17.00*.

Wrenbury

Making its ponderous way towards Marbury, the waterway descends through three locks: the middle one – Willeymoor – lies beside the eponymous Lock Tavern, whose only access is across the lock tail bridge. The A49 briefly intrudes above the last of the flight before the canal again enters remote and peaceful countryside. A further 1½ miles of the soft green Cheshire countryside leads to Marbury Lock: the village is a short walk to the south, along School Lane, and is well worth visiting. The tall obelisk visible to the south east is in distant Combermere Park. Wrenbury Wharf is a splendid place where there is a fine restored warehouse converted into a pub, a former mill now occupied by a *boatyard* and, set back a little, another *pub* – all grouped around the push-button lift bridge. The scale of these delightful bridges – a signature of this navigation– has appeared entirely sympathetic with that of the canal and, whilst most have generally been left open, those that required operation have surely provided added interest. The canal passes Wrenbury Hall, which is north west of bridge 17, and soon begins the descent of the three Baddiley Locks with Hurleston Junction now less than five miles distant.

NAVIGATIONAL NOTES

A Watermate key is required for the lift bridge at Wrenbury.

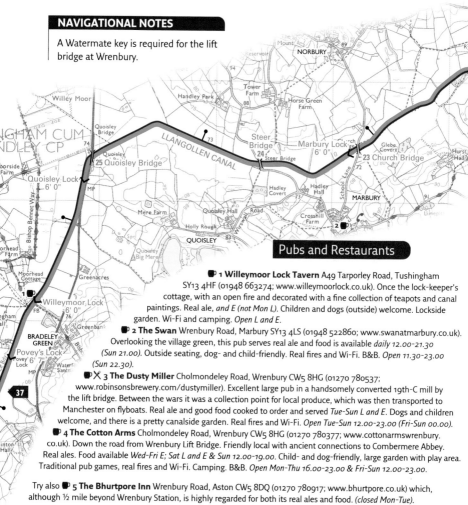

Pubs and Restaurants

🍺 **1 Willeymoor Lock Tavern** A49 Tarporley Road, Tushingham SY13 4HF (01948 663274; www.willeymoorlock.co.uk). Once the lock-keeper's cottage, with an open fire and decorated with a fine collection of teapots and canal paintings. Real ale, *and E (not Mon L)*. Children and dogs (outside) welcome. Lockside garden. Wi-Fi and camping. *Open L and E.*

🍺 **2 The Swan** Wrenbury Road, Marbury SY13 4LS (01948 522860; www.swanatmarbury.co.uk). Overlooking the village green, this pub serves real ale and food is available *daily 12.00-21.30 (Sun 21.00).* Outside seating, dog- and child-friendly. Real fires and Wi-Fi. B&B. *Open 11.30-23.00 (Sun 22.30).*

🍺✕ **3 The Dusty Miller** Cholmondeley Road, Wrenbury CW5 8HG (01270 780537; www.robinsonsbrewery.com/dustymiller). Excellent large pub in a handsomely converted 19th-C mill by the lift bridge. Between the wars it was a collection point for local produce, which was then transported to Manchester on flyboats. Real ale and good food cooked to order and served *Tue-Sun L and E.* Dogs and children welcome, and there is a pretty canalside garden. Real fires and Wi-Fi. *Open Tue-Sun 12.00-23.00 (Fri-Sun 00.00).*

🍺 **4 The Cotton Arms** Cholmondeley Road, Wrenbury CW5 8HG (01270 780377; www.cottonarmswrenbury. co.uk). Down the road from Wrenbury Lift Bridge. Friendly local with ancient connections to Combermere Abbey. Real ales. Food available *Wed-Fri E; Sat L and E & Sun 12.00-19.00.* Child- and dog-friendly, large garden with play area. Traditional pub games, real fires and Wi-Fi. Camping. B&B. *Open Mon-Thu 16.00-23.00 & Fri-Sun 12.00-23.00.*

Try also 🍺 **5 The Bhurtpore Inn** Wrenbury Road, Aston CW5 8DQ (01270 780917; www.bhurtpore.co.uk) which, although ½ mile beyond Wrenbury Station, is highly regarded for both its real ales and food. *(closed Mon-Tue).*

Boatyards

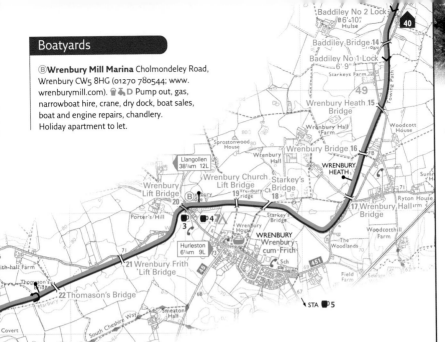

ⓑ **Wrenbury Mill Marina** Cholmondeley Road, Wrenbury CW5 8HG (01270 780544; www.wrenburymill.com). 📶♨D Pump out, gas, narrowboat hire, crane, dry dock, boat sales, boat and engine repairs, chandlery. Holiday apartment to let.

Marbury

Cheshire. Tel. An enchanting village ½ mile south of Marbury Lock. Centred on an ancient farm, the village boasts several other fine old and timbered buildings. 'Marbury Merry Days' are held in May, and the village wakes (holidays) once featured dancing bears, and puddings.

St Michael's Church SY13 4LN. This is a gem, and its setting is unrivalled: it stands on top of a small hill overlooking the beautiful Little Mere. The church was first mentioned in 1299: what remains today dates from the 15th-C. When you walk around the building look out for the many gargoyles: monkeys and grotesque faces expressing both pleasure and pain. The pulpit is the second oldest in Cheshire and, dating from the 15th-C, is in excellent condition. The grounds contain not just a graveyard but a charming garden: from here you will be able to see that the tower has developed an alarming tilt.

Wrenbury

Cheshire. PO, tel, stores, off-licence, station. About ¼ mile from the wharf – nearest access is via the footpaths from either Bridge 18 or 19. A quiet village recorded in the Domesday Book as Warenberie. Two miles to the south east are the remains of Combermere Abbey, established by Cistercian monks in 1133 who, in 1180, took the village church as a daughter chapel. By the church gates is the schoolmaster's cottage:

this stood next door to one of the earliest parish schools in Cheshire, founded in 1605. There are some thatched magpie cottages around the green and, remarkably, the railway station still operates. It is a further ¼ mile to the south east. The line goes from Crewe to Shrewsbury. Gas is available at the Village Stores, a shop that also sells coal and logs *open daily 07.30-20.00 (Sun 08.30).*

St Margaret's Church SCW5 8EY (01270 780890; www.wrenburychurch.org.uk/st-margarets-wrenbury). Overlooking Wrenbury village green, this large, battlemented 14th-C church is built from red Cheshire sandstone, with a late 15th-C west tower and an early 17th-C chancel and pulpit. The interior is very light and airy and contains a number of fine monuments. You will also notice the visible manifestation of an enduring dispute between two important local families: the Cottons of Combermere Abbey, and the Starkeys of Wrenbury Hall. They challenged each other's ownership of land and rights to church pews for over 400 years, to such an extent that an arbitrator, in 1748, allocated the south side of the church to the Cottons and the north to the Starkeys, in an effort to resolve matters. Next to the door is 'the dog-whipper's pew'. The job of the dog-whipper, later known as Beadle, was to throw out unruly dogs, and to keep dozing parishioners awake during particularly tedious sermons. The last holder of this esteemed position, Thomas Vaughan, died in 1879 and is buried by the door. Have a look in the churchyard for the most unusual cast iron grave plaques, dating from the early 1800s. These were an expression, in their time, of the very latest technology.

39

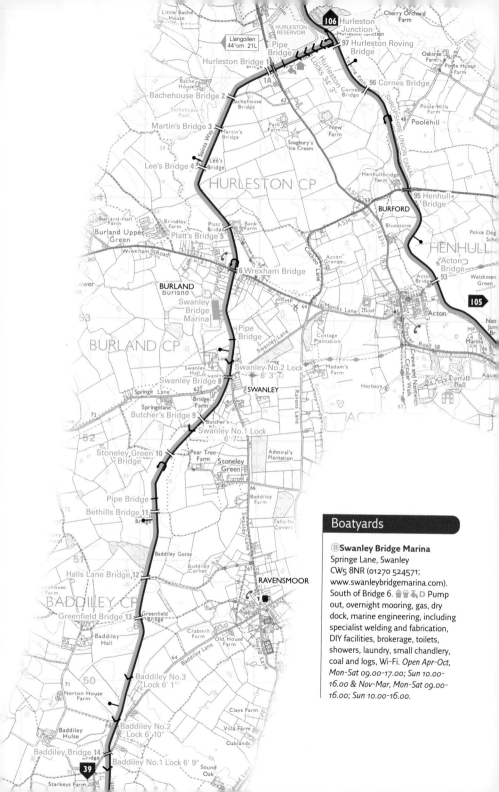

Boatyards

ⓑ **Swanley Bridge Marina**
Springe Lane, Swanley
CW5 8NR (01270 524571;
www.swanleybridgemarina.com).
South of Bridge 6. 🏠🏠⛽ D Pump
out, overnight mooring, gas, dry
dock, marine engineering, including
specialist welding and fabrication,
DIY facilities, brokerage, toilets,
showers, laundry, small chandlery,
coal and logs, Wi-Fi. *Open Apr-Oct,
Mon-Sat 09.00-17.00; Sun 10.00-
16.00 & Nov-Mar, Mon-Sat 09.00-
16.00; Sun 10.00-16.00.*

Hurleston Junction

The tall Georgian house surrounded by trees to the west of the bottom lock of the Baddiley Flight is Baddiley Hall, visible as the canal enters flat, rich farmland.

A few houses, some with attractive canalside gardens, are passed before the waterway reaches Swanley Locks. Running through a very shallow valley, the navigation exits into open countryside, looping round to the east before arriving at the four Hurleston Locks (note the unusual ground paddle gear on the third lock up) and its junction with the Shropshire Union Canal immediately beyond. The draw-off point for the canal water supplying Hurleston Reservoir is clearly visible above the top lock.

NAVIGATIONAL NOTES

Water is fed into the Llangollen Canal by the River Dee at Llantysilio, so there is a noticeable flow of water from west to east, slowing your journey to Llangollen. The flow can be particularly strong at the lock tails where bypass weirs discharge – this can make the approach from below difficult unless an allowance is made.

● **Hurleston Reservoir**
CW5 6AS. With a capacity of 85,000,000 gallons, Hurleston Reservoir receives its supply, via the Llangollen Canal, from the River Dee at Llantysilio. It is used both as drinking water (consumed in the Crewe and Nantwich conurbations) and as a supply for the Shropshire Union Canal.

Pubs and Restaurants

🍺✕ **1 The Farmer's Arms** Marsh Lane, Ravensmoor CW5 8PN (01270 623522; www.facebook.com/farmersarmsravensmoor). Welcoming creeper-clad inn serving real ale and home made food *Mon L; Tue-Sat L and E (not Sat E) and Sun 12.00-20.00*. Large garden and patio, dog- and child-friendly. Best access is probably from Bridge 12. *Open daily 12.00-23.00*.

CANOEING AND PADDLEBOARDING
Canal and River Trust, the navigation authority for the Llangollen Canal, produce an excellent set of introductory guidance notes to paddling on their waterways, covering everything from craft licensing to the waterways code for unpowered craft, available at: www.canalrivertrust.org.uk/enjoy-the-waterways/canoeing-and-kayaking-near-me.

Passing through the lift bridge just outside Wrenbury

The top (and only working) lock of the narrow Fourteen Locks flight

MONMOUTHSHIRE & BRECON CANALS

MAXIMUM DIMENSIONS

Length: 55'
Beam: 8' 6"
Headroom: 5' 11"
Draught: 2' 6"

MANAGER

Monmouthshire & Brecon Canal (Brecon to Solomons Bridge [47])
0303 040 4040
enquiries.walessouthwest@canalrivertrust.org.uk

Monmouthshire Canal
This is currently managed by three separate councils:
Solomons Bridge to below Ash Tree Bridge (32):
Torfaen: 01495 762200
Ash Tree Bridge to Barrack Hill Tunnel; Malpas to Harry Roberts Bridge (10): Newport: 01633 656656
Harry Roberts Bridge to Cwmcarn/Pontywaun:
Caerphilly: 01443 815588 or 01495 226622

MILEAGE

Monmouthshire Canal
PONTYWAUN to:
Risca: 1³/₄ miles
Fourteen Locks: 5¹/₄ miles
Malpas, junction with main line: 7 miles
CWMBRAN Five Locks: 13 miles
Pontymoile: 15¹/₂ miles

Navigable section
CWMBRAN Five Locks to:
Pontymoile : 2¹/₂ miles
Brecon & Abergavenny Canal:
Goytre Wharf: 8¹/₂ miles
Llanfoist: 14 miles
Gilwern: 17 miles
Llangattock Bridge: 20¹/₂ miles
Talybont: 29 miles
BRECON: 35³/₄ miles

Monmouthshire Canal
Locks: 50 (6 restored)
Brecon & Abergavenny Canal
Locks: 6

The Monmouthshire, Brecon and Abergavenny Canals Trust, The Fourteen Locks Canal Centre, Cwn Lane, Rogerstone, Newport NP10 9GN (01633 892167; www.mbact.org.uk) is concerned with the whole Monmouthshire & Brecon canals and is actively concerned with their regeneration.
The Islwyn Canal Association (01633 615668; www.islwyncanalassociation.com) is concerned with the Caerphilly section of the canal.

Canoeing and Paddleboarding: Category 1

In 1792 the Act of Authorisation for the Monmouthshire Canal was passed. This gave permission for a canal to be cut from the estuary of the River Usk at Newport to Pontnewynydd, north of Pontypool. In addition to this Main Line, there was to be an 11-mile branch from Malpas to Crumlin. Thomas Dadford Jnr was appointed engineer, and the canal was opened in 1796. When the Act for the Brecknock & Abergavenny Canal was passed in 1793, the canal was originally planned to connect Brecon with the River Usk near Caerleon, but the directors of the Monmouthshire Canal persuaded the promoters to alter their plans to include a junction with their own canal. And so the Brecknock & Abergavenny Canal, with Thomas Dadford Jnr again as engineer, was cut from Brecon to Pontymoile Basin, where it joined the Monmouthshire Canal. The Brecknock & Abergavenny Canal was fully opened in 1799. For a while the two canals were profitable, because the iron and coal cargoes justified the use of both canal and tramway. However, the greater speed and efficiency of the railways soon became apparent, and by the 1850s there were several schemes to abandon the canal. In 1865 the Monmouthshire bought the Brecknock & Abergavenny Canal Company, but already it was too late for this to be effective. Bit by bit the original Monmouthshire Canal was closed, but the Brecon line was kept open as a water channel. In 1962 the network was formally abandoned, and parts were filled in. In 1964 the slow task of restoration was begun, and boats were once more able to cruise from Pontymoile to Talybont. The present limit of navigation is Five Locks, although plans to extend south to Newport and Pontywaun to reclaim the Monmouthshire Canal are now coming to fruition.

Fourteen Locks

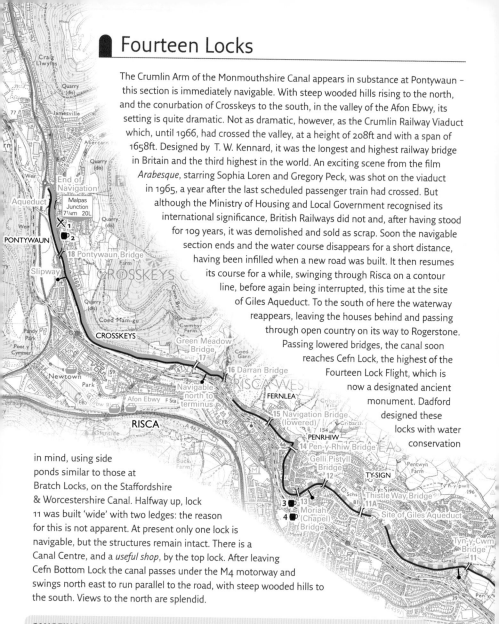

The Crumlin Arm of the Monmouthshire Canal appears in substance at Pontywaun – this section is immediately navigable. With steep wooded hills rising to the north, and the conurbation of Crosskeys to the south, in the valley of the Afon Ebwy, its setting is quite dramatic. Not as dramatic, however, as the Crumlin Railway Viaduct which, until 1966, had crossed the valley, at a height of 208ft and with a span of 1658ft. Designed by T. W. Kennard, it was the longest and highest railway bridge in Britain and the third highest in the world. An exciting scene from the film *Arabesque*, starring Sophia Loren and Gregory Peck, was shot on the viaduct in 1965, a year after the last scheduled passenger train had crossed. But although the Ministry of Housing and Local Government recognised its international significance, British Railways did not and, after having stood for 109 years, it was demolished and sold as scrap. Soon the navigable section ends and the water course disappears for a short distance, having been infilled when a new road was built. It then resumes its course for a while, swinging through Risca on a contour line, before again being interrupted, this time at the site of Giles Aqueduct. To the south of here the waterway reappears, leaving the houses behind and passing through open country on its way to Rogerstone. Passing lowered bridges, the canal soon reaches Cefn Lock, the highest of the Fourteen Lock Flight, which is now a designated ancient monument. Dadford designed these locks with water conservation in mind, using side ponds similar to those at Bratch Locks, on the Staffordshire & Worcestershire Canal. Halfway up, lock 11 was built 'wide' with two ledges: the reason for this is not apparent. At present only one lock is navigable, but the structures remain intact. There is a Canal Centre, and a *useful shop*, by the top lock. After leaving Cefn Bottom Lock the canal passes under the M4 motorway and swings north east to run parallel to the road, with steep wooded hills to the south. Views to the north are splendid.

CANOEING AND PADDLEBOARDING

The short section of the Crumlin Arm at Crosskeys has recently been dredged and is eminently suitable for both canoeing and paddleboarding. Launching is available at the current northern end of the navigable section in Pantywaun and at Darren Bridge 16. Also, at Bettws Lane Bridge 27 where there is a slipway and parking.

Cwmcarn Forest & Visitor Centre

Nantcarn Road, Cwmcarn, Crosskeys NP11 7FA (01495 272001; www.cwmcarnforest.co.uk). Off the A467. Superb views, sculpture exhibition, opportunities for mountain biking, walking, fishing, glamping pods, luxury lodges and camping. Visitor Centre *opens daily 09.00-17.00, (closes 16.30 Fri, Sept-Mar, closed 23rd Dec-2nd Jan)*. Gift and coffee shop. Charge for parking.

● Crosskeys

Caerphilly. PO box, tel. A village at the confluence of the rivers Ebbw and Sirhowey, its setting in a wooded valley is superb.

Risca

Caerphilly. PO, tel, stores, banks, chemist, off-licence, fish & chips, takeaways, garage, station. Lying in the valley below the canal, the town is making the transformation from the old economies of mining and, unusually, metal typesetting to newer, lighter industries. It was the scene, on 15 July 1880, of a dreadful mining accident, when a gas explosion killed 130 men and boys. It was though to have been caused by the use of the old Clanny lamp, which the miners preferred because it gave much better illumination than Sir Humphrey Davy's safety lamp. In 1892 there were 1050 men and 102 horses working in Risca colliery, and it was later one of the first to be lit by electricity, with underground traction using compressed air. It continued to grow, and by 1918, together with the nearby Blackvein Colliery, 2084 miners were employed. It closed in 1967 and the land is now an industrial estate.

Fourteen Locks Canal Centre Cym Lane, Rogerstone, Newport NP10 9GN (01633 892167; www.newport.gov.uk/en/Leisure-Tourism/attractions/Fourteen-Locks.aspx). An interpretative centre which demonstrates how vital canal transport was during the early stages of the Industrial Revolution, and tells the story of the Monmouthshire Canal. This superb flight of 14 locks, completed in 1799 by Thomas Dadford Jnr, raises the canal 168ft in under half a mile, and has now been designated an ancient monument. The top lock was restored during the summer of 2002, and the section to bridge 6A is navigable for boats up to 23ft (subject to water availability)– a slipway has been built in the pond below lock 21. There is a waymarked walk. Visitor centre, tea room with outside seating *open Mon-Sat 10.00-17.00 & Sun 10.00-16.30.* The centre is run by volunteers of the Monmouthshire, Brecon and Abergavenny Canals Trust (www.mbact.org.uk).

Pubs and Restaurants

1 Pizza Italiana Castle Lodge, Twyncarn Road, Pontywaun, Cwmcarn, NP11 7DU (07455 000859 www.pizzaitaliana1.co.uk) Wide range of Pizzas to eat in or takeaway. *Open Wed-Mon 15.00-21.30.*

2 The Philanthropic Twyncarn Road, Pontywaun, Crosskeyes NP11 7DU (01495 270448). Real ale in a traditional pub, with bar snacks *always available.* Newspapers. Children welcome. Garden. *Open daily 12.00-23.00.*

3 Prince of Wales Dixon Place, Risca NP11 6PY (01633 612616). Welcoming traditional pub with an unspoilt bar and a fine view over the town, and the rugby club, from the terrace. Food served *Sun-Tue L,* Fish & Chips *Fri all day.* Children and dogs welcome.

Live music *Sat.* Garden. *Open 12.00-01.00 (Sun 22.30).*

4 The Fox & Hounds Park Road, Risca NP11 6PW (01633 612937). Welcoming, old-fashioned pub serving real ale with traditional pub games and outside seating. Pool table. Quiz night *Thurs,* live music *Fri. Open Mon-Sat 12.00-00.00, Sun 22.30.*

5 The Rising Sun 1 Cefn Road, Rogerstone, Newport, NP10 9AQ (01633 895126; www.therisingsunnewport.co.uk). Just above the top lock, across the road from the canal. Family owned. Bar and restaurant with wide range of food available *Mon-Sat L and E; Sun all day until 17.30.* Children's play area. B&B. *Open Mon-Wed L and E & Thu-Sun all day.*

WALKING AND CYCLING

The towpath on the Monmouthshire Canal is in good condition for both walking and cycling, much of it forming NCN routes 47 or 465. At Pontywaun and Crosskeys there are great hill walks, with picnic sites and splendid views over the valley – the hill-fort on the top of Twmbarlwm, to the east of the canal terminus, is a popular venue, with a return down a valley with a stream. The 12-mile Raven Walk is a circular route crossing farmland and woodland high above the Sirhowey and Ebbw valleys and giving panoramic views of the Brecon Beacons to the north. Make sure you obtain a leaflet from the Cwmcarn Visitor Centre (*see* above), so that you can complete a brass rubbing from four separate posts on the way around (take a pencil!) - you may then receive a special Raven Walk Badge. A leaflet covering this route can be obtained by sending an sae and £1 to Caerphilly County Borough Council, Countryside and Landscape Services, Council Offices, Pontllanfraith, Blackwood NP2 2YW. There is a short waymarked trail at Fourteen Locks, and the Sirhowey Valley Walk, which explores the hills to the west, is signposted from here.

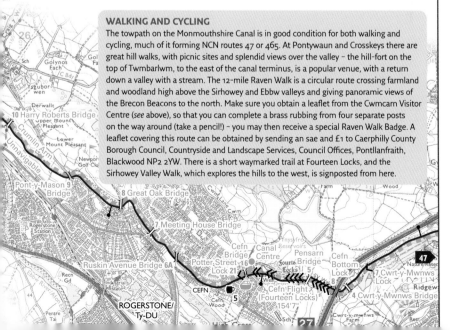

Six locks are passed to the south of the motorway before reaching the junction at Malpas, where the main line heads off to the north. The last of these, Gwastad, has been restored. Ahead, in under half a mile, and having passed Crindau Bridge, the line which once connected with the docks at Pillgwenlly in Newport ends at what was the entrance to Barrack Hill Tunnel, closed in the early 1930s. If you wish to visit Newport, you will have to complete the journey by following the signs for NCN47. A project to create a link between the current terminus at Barrack Hill Tunnel and the River Usk, complete with a marina, has been long in gestation but nevertheless remains a major objective of the Monmouthshire, Brecon and Abergavenny Canal Trust.

The main line heads north from Barrack Hill, crossing an aqueduct which, at one time, had a sundial built into the wall, to aid innumerate boatmen. The open expanse of Crindau Park lies to the west, with housing estates to the east, as Gwasted Lock, the first of many on the way to Cwmbran, is passed. At Bettws Lane Bridge there is a slipway, and you will also notice that a balance beam on the lock is hinged, a device to cope with a lack of space. You then pass some smarter gardens before gradually emerging into a stretch of open country, punctuated by a flurry of locks that continue the climb towards Cwmbran. Ty Coch locks are all in good order but are locked and the pounds to both the north and south are very weedy. All too soon houses reappear, the canal becomes shallow, and then piped, a short way beyond Bridge 40A. There is then one very short section in water before the course of the waterway disappears altogether. One of the most challenging restoration problems is the 500yds of canal bed built over to create Cwmbran Drive and Greenforge Way. An alternative route has been identified for approximately 400yds leaving a 100yd gap requiring an innovative engineering solution. Thankfully National Cycle Network route 49 follows the canal, so if you keep to the waymarked trail, you won't get lost.

● **City of Newport**
Gwent. All services. This is Wales' third-largest urban area, standing on the banks of the Severn, with the River Usk flowing through. Its original Welsh name was Casnewydd-ar-Wysg (pron: casneweth-ar-ooisg), meaning 'the new castle on the Usk', although there is now little to see of this 14th-C building, built by Hugh d'Audele or Ralph, Earl of Stafford, his son-in-law. Enlarged during the 15th C by the 1st Duke of Buckingham, it began to fall into disrepair when the 3rd Duke of Buckingham was beheaded. During the 19th C the Chartists rioted in Newport, led by Henry Vincent, who was arrested in May 1838 for making inflammatory statements and demanding greater rights for working people. His arrest brought 5000 marchers to the town who, upon hearing he was being held at the Westgate Hotel, went there and began chanting 'surrender our prisoners'. Soldiers stationed in the hotel opened fire: 20 marchers were killed and 50 wounded. The leaders were arrested and sentenced to be hung, drawn and quartered, although this was later reduced to transportation. The bullet holes can still be seen in the entrance pillars of the Westgate Hotel. A mosaic off John Frost Square commemorates the Chartists. City status was granted to Newport by the Queen, during her Golden Jubilee in 2002.
St Woolos Cathedral Stow Hill, Newport NP20 4EA (01633 267464; www.churchinwales.org.uk). There has been a church on this site since AD500. Left in ruins after being attacked by pirates, it was rebuilt

c.1080 by the Normans, with the tower being added during the 15th C.
Newport Transporter Bridge Brunel Street, Newport NP20 2JY (01633 656656; www.newport. gov.uk/heritage/Transporter-Bridge). The first recorded permanent river crossing of the Usk in Newport was in 1158, when a wooden bridge was built. Rapid industrial development in the late 19th C made the need for a new bridge a matter of urgency, and something had to be designed to cope with the passage of high-masted ships on the river, and the second-greatest tidal range in the world. The borough engineer at the time, R. H. Haynes, had heard about an 'aerial ferry' built by Ferdinand Arnodin, and suggested he design a similar structure for Newport. This was agreed and work began in 1902, with completion in 1906 at a cost of £98,000. It was in constant use until 1985, when the structure was found to be in a dangerous condition. Saved from demolition, it was re-opened in 1996 after four years of restoration costing £3 million. The largest remaining example of a transporter bridge left in the world, it is a magnificent sight. Visitor centre (free) *open daily throughout the year 10.00-16.00.* There are opportunities to walk over the top of the bridge, visit website for details. Bridge operating times: *Apr-Sep, Wed-Sun 10.00-17.00 & B Hols Easter, May and Aug.* Postcodes for location – west side: NP20 2JG and east side: NP19 0RB. Charge.

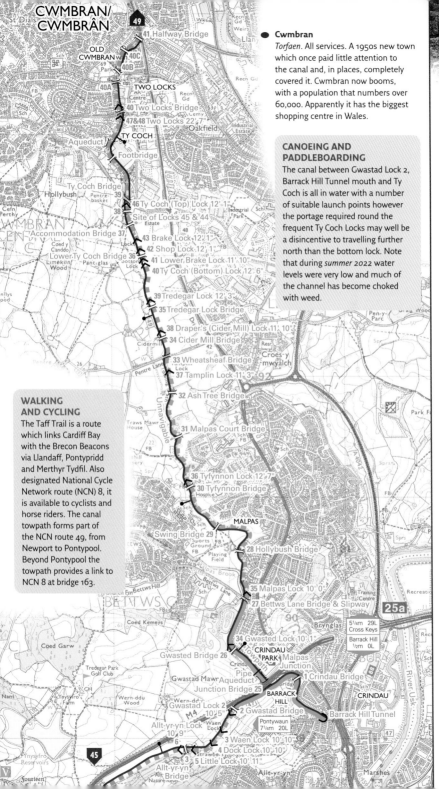

CWMBRAN/CWMBRÂN

49

41 Halfway Bridge

OLD CWMBRAN
40C
40B

TWO LOCKS
40A

40 Two Locks Bridge
47&48 Two Locks 22' 7"
Oakfield

TY COCH
Aqueduct
Footbridge

Ty Coch Bridge
Hollybush
39
38
46 Ty Coch (Top) Lock 12' 1"
Site of Locks 45 & 44
Accommodation Bridge 37,
43 Brake Lock 12' 1"
42 Shop Lock 12' 1"
Lower Ty Coch Bridge 36
41 Lower Brake Lock 11' 10"
40 Ty Coch (Bottom) Lock 12' 6"

39 Tredegar Lock 12' 3"
35 Tredegar Lock Bridge

38 Draper's (Cider) Mill) Lock 11' 10"
34 Cider Mill Bridge
33 Wheatsheaf Bridge
37 Tamplin Lock 11' 3"

32 Ash Tree Bridge

31 Malpas Court Bridge

36 Tyfynnon Lock 12' 7"
30 Tyfynnon Bridge

MALPAS

Swing Bridge 29

28 Hollybush Bridge

35 Malpas Lock 10' 0"
27 Bettws Lane Bridge & Slipway

25a

34 Gwasted Lock 10' 1"
CRINDAU PARK
Malpas Junction
Gwasted Bridge 26
1 Crindau Bridge
CRINDAU
Gwastad Mawr Aqueduct
Junction Bridge 25
BARRACK HILL
2 Gwastad Bridge
Barrack Hill Tunnel
Gwastad Lock 10' 5"
3 Waen Lock 10' 10"
4 Dock Lock 10' 10"
5 Little Lock 10' 11"
Allt-yr-yn Lock 10' 9" 6"

45

● **Cwmbran**

Torfaen. All services. A 1950s new town which once paid little attention to the canal and, in places, completely covered it. Cwmbran now booms, with a population that numbers over 60,000. Apparently it has the biggest shopping centre in Wales.

CANOEING AND PADDLEBOARDING

The canal between Gwastad Lock 2, Barrack Hill Tunnel mouth and Ty Coch is all in water with a number of suitable launch points however the portage required round the frequent Ty Coch Locks may well be a disincentive to travelling further north than the bottom lock. Note that during *summer 2022* water levels were very low and much of the channel has become choked with weed.

WALKING AND CYCLING

The Taff Trail is a route which links Cardiff Bay with the Brecon Beacons via Llandaff, Pontypridd and Merthyr Tydfil. Also designated National Cycle Network route (NCN) 8, it is available to cyclists and horse riders. The canal towpath forms part of the NCN route 49, from Newport to Pontypool. Beyond Pontypool the towpath provides a link to NCN 8 at bridge 163.

5¼am 29L Cross Keys
Barrack Hill ½m 0L

Pontywaun 7¼am 20L

47

Pontypool

To the north of Cwmbran the Monmouthshire Canal reappears, climbing short flights of locks at the evocatively named Forge Hammer, plus Three Locks, Pontnewydd and finally Cross Keys where, to the north of the road, navigation towards the Brecon & Abergavenny Canal begins. There is a *late-opening shop and cash point* at Upper Pontnewydd Bridge 44, while in the town there are *PO, tel, stores, a chemist and bank, takeaways and fish & chips*. This initial section, as far as Sebastopol, is under the care of Torfaen Borough Council. Overnight moorings are available at Five Locks Basin, where a sanitary station and charging point have recently been installed to encourage greater use. Heading north towards Pontypool the canal, which is quite shallow here, enters the short Cwmbran Tunnel, constructed to cope with the watershed from the adjacent mountains. One of the old Monmouthshire Canal Company mileposts stands beside the towpath, a memento of when the navigation extended its full course. Emerging from the tunnel, the land designated as Five Locks Nature Reserve is on the west bank. At Crown Bridge 48 there are *a stores, off-licence and fish & chips* opposite the pub. At Pontymoile the town centre is about one mile to the north west, through the lovely Pontypool Park. The old toll cottage at Pontymoile Basin, now available for rent as a holiday cottage, marks the junction of the Brecon & Abergavenny Canal with the Monmouthshire Canal. The cottage was built in 1813 for the tollkeeper who gauged boats which were moving from one canal to the other by measuring the height of the hull above the water. The nearby, boat-based, Marina Tearooms is *open Feb-Nov* for teas, coffee, breakfast and lunches.

● **Pontypool**
Torfaen. All services. Pontypool has been an industrial town since Roman times, concentrating on the production of iron. In 1720 tin plate was produced here for the first time in Britain and in the 19th C the town was a centre for japanning – the coating of objects with an extract of oils from coal, so producing a black varnish similar to Japanese lacquer. Japan ware remained popular well into the 19th C. Despite its industrial heritage, Pontypool has always remained a farming centre and so the hard industrial elements are softened by the traditions of a rural market town.
Pontypool Park Trosnant Street, Pontypool NP4 8AT. Originally the seat of the Hanburys, the famous iron and steel family, this Georgian mansion is now a school. The park is open to the public.
Torfaen Museum Park Buildings, Park Road,

Pontypool NP4 6JH (01495 752036; www.torfaenmuseum.org.uk). Situated in the stable block of Pontypool Park House. Tells the story of the Torfaen valley and its people. *Open Tue-Fri 10.00-17.00 Sat & Sun 14.00-17.00.* Charge.
The Shell Grotto and the Folly Tower Pontypool Park, Trosnant Street, Pontypool NP4 8AT (01495 766754; www.torfaen.gov.uk). Built by Capel Hanbury Leigh in the 1830s with internal decorations of shell, animal bones and crystals. *Open May–Sep, Sat, Sun and B Hols 14.00-17.00, groups by appointment at other times.* Free.
The Folly Tower Trosnant Street, Pontypool NP4 8AT. Commanding views over Gwent. The tower was demolished in 1940 by order of the Ministry of Defence as there were fears that it might guide the Luftwaffe bombers to the Royal Ordnance factory at Glascoed. Rebuilt in 1992. Opening details as for the Shell Grotto (above).

Pubs and Restaurants

◆✕ **1 The Open Hearth** Wern Road, Sebastopol Pontypool NP4 5DR (01495 763752; www.theopenhearth.wales). Canalside, between bridges 48 and 49, south of Pontymoile Basin. A fine collection of real ales await you at this friendly pub. An extensive collection of bottled beers decorates the lounge bar. An imaginative choice of food is available *L and E.* Garden. Children and dogs welcome. Regular live music and takeaway food. *Open all day.*
◆ **2 The Old Bridgend Inn** Commercial St, Cwmbran NP44 1AE (01633 483678). Good local pub serving well kept beers. Pub food served *daily E & Sun L.* Darts *Thu,* popular at *weekends.* Garden. *Open Mon-Thu 13.30-23.00, Fri-Sun 12.00-23.00.*
◆✕ **3 The Unicorn Inn** Albion Road, Pontypool NP4 6LE (01495 751304; www.theunicornpontypool.

com). Welcoming pub serving excellent food *all day Tue-Sat & Sun 12.00-16.00.* Children welcome *until 18.00* (20.00 if eating). Live jazz and blues *Sun 17.00-19.00.* Pool table, garden. *Open Sun-Thu 12.00-23.00, Fri- Sat 12.00-00.00.*
✕ **4 The Boatyard Tea Room** Fountain Road, Pontymoile, Pontypool NP4 8ER (07955 408683) Canal side café in an attractively fitted out, grounded canal boat serving breakfast, lunches, tea and cakes *Mon-Sun 09.00-14.30 closed Wed*
◆✕ **5 The Horse and Jockey** Usk Road, Pontypool, Torfaen NP4 0JB (01495 762723 www.horseandjocketjockey.co.uk) Beautifully restored pub just a short walk from the canal. Real ales and good food served *L and E.* Family friendly. Garden. *Open Tue-Sun 12.00-22.00 (Sun 21.00).*

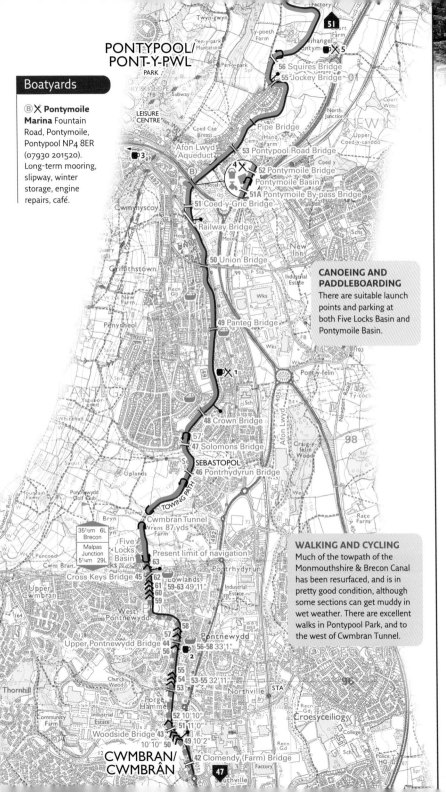

PONTYPOOL/
PONT-Y-PWL
PARK

Boatyards

Ⓑ ✕ **Pontymoile
Marina** Fountain
Road, Pontymoile,
Pontypool NP4 8ER
(07930 201520).
Long-term mooring,
slipway, winter
storage, engine
repairs, café.

LEISURE
CENTRE

Coed Cae
Breast

Afon Lwyd
Aqueduct

Ⓑ

Cwmmyscoy

Griffithstown

New
Farm

Penyrheol

51

Twyn-gwyn

Ty-poeth
Farm

Llanfihangel
Pontymoel

56 Squires Bridge
55 Jockey Bridge

Pipe Bridge
53 Pontypool Road Bridge
4 ✕
52 Pontymoile Bridge
Pontymoile Basin
51A Pontymoile By-pass Bridge
51 Coed-y-Gric Bridge

Railway Bridge

50 Union Bridge

49 Panteg Bridge

✕ 1

48 Crown Bridge
57
47 Solomons Bridge
SEBASTOPOL
46 Pontrhydyrun Bridge

TOWING PATH

Cwmbran Tunnel
Wrens 87 yds

35½m 6L
Brecon
Malpas
Junction
5¼m 29L

Five
Locks
Basin

Present limit of navigation

Cross Keys Bridge 45

Upper
Cwmbran

West
Pontnewydd

Upper Pontnewydd Bridge

Thornhill

CWMBRAN/
CWMBRÂN

5

NEW

North
Junction

New
Inn

Pont-y-
felin

98

Rowlands
59-63 49'11"
62
61
60
59

58
57
44
56

55
54 53-55 32'11"
62
52 10'10"
51 11'0"
49 10'2"

Woodside Bridge 43

42 Clomendy (Farm) Bridge

47

63

Pontnewydd

56-58 33'1"

Forge
Hammer

Croesyceiliog

CANOEING AND PADDLEBOARDING

There are suitable launch
points and parking at
both Five Locks Basin and
Pontymoile Basin.

WALKING AND CYCLING

Much of the towpath of the
Monmouthshire & Brecon Canal
has been resurfaced, and is in
pretty good condition, although
some sections can get muddy in
wet weather. There are excellent
walks in Pontypool Park, and to
the west of Cwmbran Tunnel.

Goytre Wharf

As the canal leaves Pontypool it twists and turns, clinging to the hillside on the west, while to the east wide views open up across the rolling pastures and woods of the Usk valley. The winding course and the frequent stone bridges make the canal interesting, for every bend offers a different view of the steep hills to the west and the valley to the east, while the canal itself remains entirely quiet, rural and isolated. Navigators should look out for the GWR boundary posts on the non-towing path side. There are no villages by the canal in this section, but services and pubs are never more than a short walk away at Mamhilad and at Penperlleni where there is *a shop (cash machine and gas)*. Main roads keep their distance, although they are generally clearly visible in the valley below the canal. After passing the long tunnel-like Saron's bridge, the seclusion is interrupted by long lines of moored boats, which are the prelude to Goytre Wharf – look out for Machine Cottage, where the weigh-bridge was once controlled, and the modelled figures in the lime-kilns. Just beyond the wharf the canal passes through a thick, wooded cutting before continuing its winding course with the open valley to the east.

Goytre Wharf Heritage, Activity & Study Centre
Goytre Wharf, Llanover, Abergavenny NP7 9EW (01873 880899; www.goytrewharf.com). Steeped in over 200 years of industrial history, Goytre Wharf occupies an 8-acre site and offers the visitor a rich diversity of walks, wildlife and the chance to absorb the feats of a bygone industrial era. Crafts and souvenirs, exhibitions and a natural amphitheatre, together with a tramroad exhibition, tourist information, children's play area and picnic area. Visitor moorings.

● **Mamhilad**
Torfaen. Tel. A little hillside hamlet scattered around the church of St Illtyd. The pleasantly kept churchyard is overshadowed by massive yew trees, the largest of which reaches some 38ft in circumference. This suggests that the tree could well be between 2000–3000 years old and would have therefore been standing when missionaries from the monastery of St Illtyd at Llantwit Major first visited in the 6th C.

● **Penperlleni**
Monmouth. PO, tel, stores (open 7 days), fish & chips, off-licence, garage. Main road village useful for supplies. The estate here was bought in 1794 by Colonel Henry Bird, who is depicted on the pub sign. Fish & chip shop *open Mon-Sat 17.00-23.00.*

Boatyards

Ⓑ✕ **ABC Leisure Group** Goytre Wharf, Llanover, Abergavenny NP7 9EW (01873 880516; www. goytrewharf.com). 🛁🚿♿ D. Pump out, gas, narrowboat hire, day hire craft, short- and long-term moorings, boat & engine sales and repairs, slipway, winter storage, telephone, toilets, showers, café, chandlery, books, map and gifts, holiday cottage rental and canoe hire. Wi-Fi. *Emergency call-out. Open daily 08.30-17.00.*

Pubs and Restaurants

🛈✕ **1 The Goytre Arms** Star Road, Penperlleni NP4 0AH (01873 880376; www.goytrearms.co.uk). ¼ mile east of bridge 72. The unusual inn sign depicts Colonel Henry Bird returning from the American War in 1794 with his new Indian wife. Real ale is served in the bar which once specialised in the making of coffins! Food served *Mon-Fri 16.00-21.00, Sat-Sun 12.00-21.00.* Children welcome. Garden and play area. Quiz *Fri* and pool table. *Open Mon 17.00-22.00, Tue-Sun 12.00-23.00 (Fri-Sat 23.30) & Sun 12.00-21.00.*

✕♇ **2 Penelope's Café** Goytre Wharf, Llanover NP7 9EW (01873 880899; www.goytrewharf.com/cafe). Café, bar and Italian restaurant located in the wharf. Café *Open Wed-Mon 10.00-16.00 (Sat-Sun 16.30).*

🛈✕ **3 The Horseshoe Inn** Old Abergavenny Road, Mamhilad NP4 8QZ (01873 880542; www. simonandsteve.com). ½ mile north of Bridge 65. It is worth the short walk uphill to this pleasant little (and possibly haunted) pub. A sign outside, referring to the view, reads, 'Relax, take in the view. God made this place when he finished his apprenticeship.' Real ale and real cider and meals available *Mon-Sun L and E.* Outside seating; children welcome. *Open Mon-Thu L and E & all day Fri-Sun.*

🛈 **4 The Star** Folly Lane, Mamhilad, Pontypool NP4 0JF (01495 785319). 200yds east of bridge 62. Cosy little pub serving a choice of real ale. Bar meals and snacks (using locally sourced ingredients) available *daily L and E.* Children and dogs welcome. Garden. *Open all day.*

WALKING AND CYCLING

A dense network of footpaths and minor lanes to the west of the canal give plenty of opportunities for circular rambles.

CANOEING AND PADDLEBOARDING

ABC Leisure Group Goytre Wharf Llanover, Abergavenny NP7 9EW (01873 880516; www.goytrewharf.com/canoe-hire). Canadian canoes are available for hire by the day or ½ day with lifejackets provided for non-swimmers and children under 18. *Open daily 08.30-17.00.* Free launching for your own canoe. For the facilities available at the boatyard *see page* 50. There are also good launch points at Park-y-Brain Upper Bridge 75, Preacher's Bridge 77, Ty-coch Bridge 84 and just east of Fro Bridge 122: all four have parking.

114

80 Mount Pleasant Upper Bridge
79 Mount Pleasant Lower Bridge
78 Mill Turn Bridge
PENCROESOPED
Aqueduct
77 Preacher's Bridge
76 Lapstone Bridge
75 Jenkin Rosser's Bridge
Aqueduct
GOYTRE WHARF ARM
Heritage Centre

27¼m	6L
Brecon	
Cross Keys	
8¼m	0L

74 Saron's Bridge
73 Penroel Bridge
72 Park-y-Brain Upper Bridge
Park-y-Brain Lower Bridge 71
PENPERLLENI
Birdspool Bridge 70
69 High House Bridge
68 Croes-y-Pant Bridge
Mortimers Bridge 65
Skinners Bridge 64
66 Brook Farm Bridge
Mamhilad Bridge 63
Pentre Bridge 67
TY-BACH
MAMHILAD
High Bridge 62
61 Troed-y-Rhiw Bridge
60 Govera Bridge
59 Keepers Bridge
58 Upper Wern Bridge
57 Lower Wern Bridge

49
53

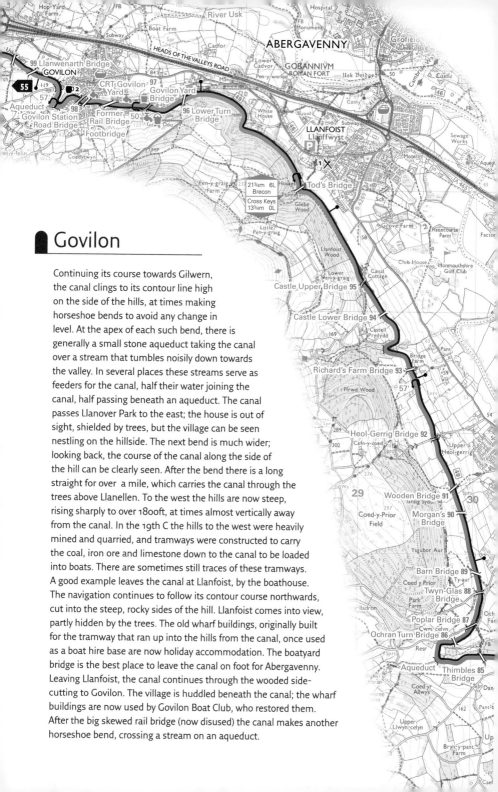

Hop Yard Farm · Subway · Boat Farm · Spr · Cadfor · River Usk · Hospital · FB · Monument

ABERGAVENNY · Grofield

HEADS OF THE VALLEYS ROAD · Lower Cadvor · GOBANNIVM ROMAN FORT · Pen-y-worlod · MS · Usk Bridge · Castle · 46

99 Llanwenarth Bridge · GOVILON
55 · 119 · 57 · CRT Govilon 97 · Govilon Yard · Govilon Yard Bridge
Aqueduct · 98 · 02 · Former Rail Bridge · 50 · 96 Lower Turn Bridge · White House · Subway
Govilon Station Road Bridge · Footbridge · Graig Ddu · LLANFOIST Llanffwyst · Sewage Works
Coedytwyn · MP · P · Motel

Pen-y-graig Farm · 23¾ · Houses · 1 · Tod's Bridge
21¾m 6L Brecon / Cross Keys 13¾m 0L · Glebe Wood
Little Pen-y-graig · Llanfoist Wood · Grove Farm · Racecourse Farm · Factory
Lower Pen-y-graig · Canal Cottage · Club House · Monmouthshire Golf Club
Castle Upper Bridge 95
Castle Lower Bridge 94 · Castell Prydydd · 169
Richard's Farm Bridge 93 · Bridge Farm · Pant · 59 · 57
Ffrwd Wood · 289 · 54
Heol-Gerrig Bridge 92 · Cefn-y-coed · Upper Heol-gerrig
302 · 276
29 · Wooden Bridge 91 · Graig Sychi · 30
Coed-y-Prior Field · Morgan's 90 Bridge
Ysgubor Aur
Barn Bridge 89 · Coed y Prior · Ty-aur
Twyn-Glas 88 Bridge · Park Farm
Poplar Bridge 87 · Cwm-celyn
Ochran Turn Bridge 86 · Resr
Aqueduct · Thimbles 85 Bridge
Coed yr Allwys
Upper Llwyn-celyn · Bryn-y-panc Farm

Govilon

Continuing its course towards Gilwern,
the canal clings to its contour line high
on the side of the hills, at times making
horseshoe bends to avoid any change in
level. At the apex of each such bend, there is
generally a small stone aqueduct taking the canal
over a stream that tumbles noisily down towards
the valley. In several places these streams serve as
feeders for the canal, half their water joining the
canal, half passing beneath an aqueduct. The canal
passes Llanover Park to the east; the house is out of
sight, shielded by trees, but the village can be seen
nestling on the hillside. The next bend is much wider;
looking back, the course of the canal along the side of
the hill can be clearly seen. After the bend there is a long
straight for over a mile, which carries the canal through the
trees above Llanellen. To the west the hills are now steep,
rising sharply to over 1800ft, at times almost vertically away
from the canal. In the 19th C the hills to the west were heavily
mined and quarried, and tramways were constructed to carry
the coal, iron ore and limestone down to the canal to be loaded
into boats. There are sometimes still traces of these tramways.
A good example leaves the canal at Llanfoist, by the boathouse.
The navigation continues to follow its contour course northwards,
cut into the steep, rocky sides of the hill. Llanfoist comes into view,
partly hidden by the trees. The old wharf buildings, originally built
for the tramway that ran up into the hills from the canal, once used
as a boat hire base are now holiday accommodation. The boatyard
bridge is the best place to leave the canal on foot for Abergavenny.
Leaving Llanfoist, the canal continues through the wooded side-
cutting to Govilon. The village is huddled beneath the canal; the wharf
buildings are now used by Govilon Boat Club, who restored them.
After the big skewed rail bridge (now disused) the canal makes another
horseshoe bend, crossing a stream on an aqueduct.

Pubs and Restaurants

✗♀ **1 Spice Lounge** Merthyr Road, Llanfoist NP7 9LP (01873 855720; www.spiceloungeonline.com). Contemporary Indian restaurant. *Open 17.00-23.30.*

🍺 **2 Tafarn y Bont** Church Lane, Govilon, Abergavenny NP7 9RP (01873 830720; www. tafarnybont.com). Once the Bridgend Inn, this cosy, well-kept hostelry serves real ale and food *Fri-Sat 18.00-20.00 & Sun 12.00-14.00.* Children and dogs welcome. Garden and open fires. Live music *Thu E*, bingo *Tue E. Open Tue-Thu 18.00-22.00; Fri-Sat 14.00-00.00 & Sun 12.00-18.00.*

✗ **3 The Hummingbird Coffee Shop** Llanover Business Centre, Llanover, Abergavenny NP7 9HA (www.thehummingbirdcoffeeshop.com) Coffee shop serving lunches and teas with a range of crafts and gifts. A short walk from bridge 81. *Open Tue-Sun 10.00-15.00.*

There are many pubs and restaurants in Abergavenny.

● **Llanover**
Monmouth. PO box, tel. The famous bell Big Ben in Westminster was named after the politician Benjamin Hall (Lord Llanover) who was responsible for the construction of the tower whilst Chief Commissioner of Works. He also initiated the tramway from Buckland House Wharf to Rhymney Ironworks, east of Talybont reservoir.

● **Llanellen**
Monmouth. PO box, tel. Although modern housing has greatly extended Llanellen into a suburb of Abergavenny, it is still an attractive village.

● **Llanfoist**
Monmouth. Tel, PO, takeaway. There is a good walk from the old stone wharf into the mountains, following the course of the old tramway. The *PO* is in the village hall, *open Mon-Thu 09.00-13.00 and Mon, Tue & Thu 14.00-17.30.*

● **Abergavenny**
Monmouth. All services. Abergavenny lies beside the fast-flowing River Usk, surrounded on all sides by mountains and hills; the Sugar Loaf, Blorenge and the Skirrids overlook the town. There is an annual event held at the end of March which involves the ascent of three peaks in one day. The Abergavenny Food festival is held annually over a *weekend* during *mid-September.*

Abergavenny Tourist Information Centre Town Hall, 61 Cross Street, Abergavenny NP7 5EH (01873 853254; www.visitabergavenny.co.uk). *Open Mon-Sat 10.00-16.00.*

Abergavenny Museum and Castle Lower Castle Street, Abergavenny NP7 5EE (01873 854282; www.abergavennymuseum.co.uk). The mound of the castle dominates the town. Built in the 11th C, the castle now houses the museum which presents the story of the market town from prehistoric times to the present day. *Opening times vary but closed Wed, Sep-Mar.*

St Mary's Church Monk Street, Abergavenny NP7 6EP (www.stmarys-priory.org). Originally the chapel of the Benedictine priory, the church was extensively rebuilt in the 14th C. It contains a fine carving of Jesse, hewn from a single oak trunk.

Abergavenny Leisure Centre King Henry VIII Comprehensive School, Old Hereford Road, Abergavenny NP7 6EP (01633 644800; www. monmouthshire.gov.uk). Swimming pool, squash courts and a sports hall amongst other facilities. *Open Mon-Fri 06.30-22.30 & Sat-Sun 08.15-18.30.*

Sugar Loaf A conspicuous landmark 2 miles north west of Abergavenny, so named because of its shape. The National Trust owns 2130 acres, including the 1955ft summit.

● **Govilon**
Monmouth. PO box, tel, stores, garage. Beside the aqueduct are steps leading down to Govilon, little of which can be seen from the canal.

WALKING AND CYCLING

There is a 3-mile section of scenic railway path between Llanfoist and Govilon, which makes for an excellent cycle ride. The route is part of NCN 46 which continues west through the dramatic Clydach Gorge. The surface is fine gravel, and climbs are gentle. Start from The Cutting, by the Post Office in Llanfoist.

Monmouthshire & Brecon Canals Govilon

(Map labels: LLANELLEN, Ham Cottage, Llanellen Court, Beili-glas, Green Court Cottages, Green Court, Ochram Brook, Ty-coch, 84 Ty-coch Bridge, 83 Beech Tree Bridge, LLANOVER PARK, Y Tylwch Teg, 82 Pwllyrhwyaid Bridge, 81 Llanover Bridge, LLANOVER, 80 Mount Pleasant Upper Bridge, Usk Valley Way, Cwrt Porth-hir, Sewage Works, 51, 31, Ty Uchaf)

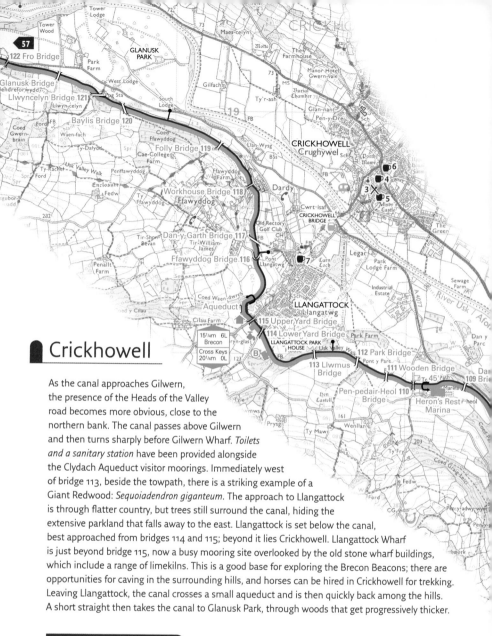

Crickhowell

As the canal approaches Gilwern, the presence of the Heads of the Valley road becomes more obvious, close to the northern bank. The canal passes above Gilwern and then turns sharply before Gilwern Wharf. *Toilets and a sanitary station* have been provided alongside the Clydach Aqueduct visitor moorings. Immediately west of bridge 113, beside the towpath, there is a striking example of a Giant Redwood: *Sequoiadendron giganteum*. The approach to Llangattock is through flatter country, but trees still surround the canal, hiding the extensive parkland that falls away to the east. Llangattock is set below the canal, best approached from bridges 114 and 115; beyond it lies Crickhowell. Llangattock Wharf is just beyond bridge 115, now a busy mooring site overlooked by the old stone wharf buildings, which include a range of limekilns. This is a good base for exploring the Brecon Beacons; there are opportunities for caving in the surrounding hills, and horses can be hired in Crickhowell for trekking. Leaving Llangattock, the canal crosses a small aqueduct and is then quickly back among the hills. A short straight then takes the canal to Glanusk Park, through woods that get progressively thicker.

Boatyards

Ⓑ**Castle Narrowboats** Church Road Wharf, Gilwern NP7 OEP (01873 830001; www.castlenarrowboats.co.uk). Pump out, narrowboat hire, day-boat hire, boat parts, chandlery, books, maps, and gifts. Castle Narrowboats operate two electric narrowboats with dedicated charging points along the canal. CRT sanitary station opposite.

Ⓑ**Road House Narrowboats** 50 Main Road, Gilwern NP7 oAS (01873 830240; www.narrowboats-wales.co.uk). Pump out, gas, narrowboat hire, overnight mooring, gifts, maps and books, B&B.

Ⓑ**Herons Rest Marina** Pen Pedair Heol Farm, Llangattock, Crickhowell NP8 1HS (07870 681174; www.hrmarina.co.uk) moorings, storage, repairs and brokerage.

Ⓑ**Beacon Park Boats** Hillside Road, Llangattock, Crickhowell NP8 1EQ (01873 858277; www.beaconparkboats.com) Pump out, narrow boat hire, day-boat hire (07966 461819).

Gilwern

Monmouth. PO, tel, stores, chemist, fish & chips (Wed-Sat 12.00-20.00), garage. The village is built along one main street which falls steeply away from the canal. There is a useful, well-stocked, gift shop across the road at bridge 103.

Llangattock

Powys. This little village, just down the lane from bridge 116, was once famous for its weaving and its limekilns. It also has a 12th-C church, founded in the 6th C. The hills behind the village are riddled with limestone caves and quarries.

Crickhowell

Powys. PO, tel, stores, butcher, chemist, bank, takeaways, off-licence, bakery, fish & chips, library, garage. The road down through Llangattock leads to the 13-arch medieval stone bridge over the Usk. In the centre of the town are the scant remains of the Norman castle. Apart from hill walking, there are opportunities for fishing and pony trekking.
Crickhowell Resource & information Centre
1 Beaufort Street, Crickhowell NP8 1BN (01873 811970; www.visitcrickhowell.co.uk). Tourist information, art gallery and internet café. *Open daily 10.00-16.30.*

Pubs and Restaurants

1 The Beaufort Arms 22 Main Road, Gilwern NP7 0AR (01873 832235). Downhill from bridge 103. Real ale is served, along with food *L and E (not Sun E)*. Children welcome. B&B. *Open Mon-Fri L and E & Sat-Sun 11.30-23.00 (Sun 16.00).*

2 The Corn Exchange Crickhowell Road, Gilwern NP7 0DG (01873 832404). A homely pub with some original features in the restaurant, where corn was once exchanged for goods. A variety of real ale is served together with food *Sun 12.00-15.00*. Family and dog friendly. Garden. *Open Mon-Fri 16.00-23.00 & all day Sat-Sun.*

✗ 3 Number 18 Café 18 High Street, Crickhowell NP8 1BD (01873 810337). Café located in Book-ish book shop *open daily Mon-Fri 10.00-16.30 (Sat 17.00) & Sun 10.00-16.00.* serving teas, coffee, appetising snacks, breakfast and light meals. Children welcome.

4 The Britannia Inn 20 High Street, Crickhowell NP8 1BD (01873 810553) Family-friendly establishment serving real ales and homemade bar meals *L and E*. Garden and pub games. Wi-Fi. *Regular* live music.

5 The Dragon Inn 47 High St, Crickhowell, Powys NP8 1BE (01873 810362; www. dragoninncrickhowell.com). Traditional old pub in the heart of the town, serving real ale and food *all day, every day*. Families welcome. B&B.

✗ 6 The Bear Hotel Crickhowell NP8 1BW (01873 810408; www.bearhotel.co.uk). The Bear has won many awards for its excellent food. Real ale. Meals served in both bar and restaurant *L and E (not Mon E or Sun E for restaurant)* small menu available *afternoons.* Children welcome, garden. B&B. *Open Mon-Sat 10.00-23.00 & Sun 11.00-22.30.*

7 The Horseshoe Inn Hillside Road, Llangattock, Crickhowell NP8 1PA (01873 268773). East of Bridge 116. Beside a stream and surrounded by trees, this pub serves real ale, along with food *Wed-Sun L and E*. Children welcome, garden. Wi-Fi. B&B. *Open Mon-Tue 18.00-00.00 and Wed-Sun 12.00-00.00.*

✗ 8 The Towpath Inn 49 Main Road, Gilwern, Abergavenny NP7 0AU (www.thetowpathinn.co.uk) Family-run, child- and dog-friendly canalside pub serving real ales and interesting food from a wood-fired kitchen. Garden. *Open Thu-Sun 11.00-22.00 (Sun 19.00).*

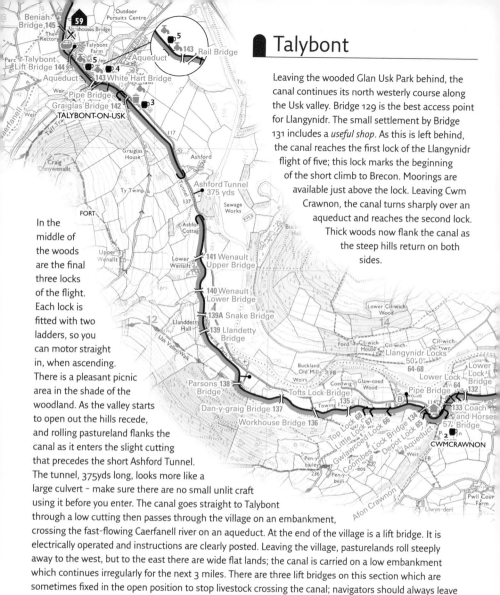

Talybont

Leaving the wooded Glan Usk Park behind, the canal continues its north westerly course along the Usk valley. Bridge 129 is the best access point for Llangynidr. The small settlement by Bridge 131 includes a *useful shop*. As this is left behind, the canal reaches the first lock of the Llangynidr flight of five; this lock marks the beginning of the short climb to Brecon. Moorings are available just above the lock. Leaving Cwm Crawnon, the canal turns sharply over an aqueduct and reaches the second lock. Thick woods now flank the canal as the steep hills return on both sides.

In the middle of the woods are the final three locks of the flight. Each lock is fitted with two ladders, so you can motor straight in, when ascending. There is a pleasant picnic area in the shade of the woodland. As the valley starts to open out the hills recede, and rolling pastureland flanks the canal as it enters the slight cutting that precedes the short Ashford Tunnel. The tunnel, 375yds long, looks more like a large culvert – make sure there are no small unlit craft using it before you enter. The canal goes straight to Talybont through a low cutting then passes through the village on an embankment, crossing the fast-flowing Caerfanell river on an aqueduct. At the end of the village is a lift bridge. It is electrically operated and instructions are clearly posted. Leaving the village, pasturelands roll steeply away to the west, but to the east there are wide flat lands; the canal is carried on a low embankment which continues irregularly for the next 3 miles. There are three lift bridges on this section which are sometimes fixed in the open position to stop livestock crossing the canal; navigators should always leave them as they find them.

Boatyards

Ⓑ**Country Craft Narrowboats**
The Old Lock House, Cwm Crawnon, Llangynidr NP8 1ND (01874 730850; www.countrycraftnarrowboats. co.uk). Pump out, narrowboat hire, toilets, showers.

CANOEING AND PADDLEBOARDING

The Brecon Beacons National Park, Brecon Canoe Club and the CRT have worked together to create the Beacons Water Trail – www.irp-cdn. multiscreensite.com/bd6fed78/files/uploaded/water-trail-leaflet.pdf – to encourage canoe touring on the River Usk and the canal. Initially, this included launch points along the canal to Talybont-on-Usk but has now been extended beyond Llangynidr. Launch points (all with parking) can be found at Yard Bridge 131, Lower Lock 64 and both immediately south and north of Ashford Tunnel to which canoeists have now been granted access. All have parking. *See note 2 (iii) covering tunnel safety on page 170.*

NAVIGATIONAL NOTES

Locks on this canal should be left empty with the bottom gates open.
Bridge 144 is an electrically operated lift bridge. The bridge should not be operated on school days between *07.45-08.45 and 15.15-16.15*. Boaters are requested to lower the bridge when three or more vehicles are waiting.

● **Llangynidr**
Powys. PO, tel, stores, off-licence, garage. Housing now sprawls up the hillside, linking the upper and lower parts of the village. There is a splendid stone bridge c.1600, which spans the Usk, and a pretty 19th-C church. Gas is available at the garage.

● **Cwm Crawnon**
Powys. Clustered round the canal as it climbs the Llangynidr locks, this hamlet is famous for the Coach & Horses, an attractive pub and restaurant.

● **Talybont-on-Usk**
Powys. PO, tel, stores, café, off-licence. When the railway and canal were both operating

commercially, Talybont must have been a busy village. Today it is a quiet holiday centre with facilities for fishing, pony trekking, mountain biking and hill walking, details of which can be obtained at the Talybont Venture Centre in the village. There is a useful stores and PO at bridge 144, selling groceries and gas, which also serves as an off-licence. The village also has an impressive line-up of three pubs. The leat to the old mill brought water from Afon Caerfanell which falls rapidly from Talybont reservoir in the hills to the south to join the Usk. The large wharf overlooks the village, which is clustered round the Caerfanell Aqueduct.

WALKING AND CYCLING
The Taff Trail is part of the Sustrans Welsh National Cycle Route (NCN 8), which stretches between Cardiff and Brecon, and it follows a section of the towpath to Brecon. There is an excellent circular walk taking in the towpath between Cwmcrawnon and Aberhowy Bridge (126) with the return made along the path by the Usk.

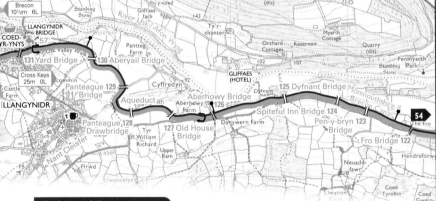

Pubs and Restaurants

🍴✕ **1 The Red Lion** Duffryn Road, Llangynidr NP8 1NT (01874 730223; www.theredlionpowys.co.uk). Homemade food available *daily L and E. Booking advisable for Sun L.* Walkers, cyclists, boaters, children and dogs welcome. Garden. B&B. *Open Tue-Sun 12.00-23.00.*

🍴✕ **2 The Coach & Horses** Cwm Crawnon Road, Llangynidr NP8 1LS (01874 730245; www.thecoachandhorsesinn.com). Canalside at bridge 133. Real ale, along with an interesting and well-priced menu, available *L and E.* Children and dogs welcome, garden. B&B. *Open Mon-Thu L and E and Fri-Sun 11.00-23.00.*

🍴✕ **3 The Travellers Restaurant & Rooms** Talybont-on-Usk LD3 7YP (01874 676333; www.travellersrestinn.com). Canalside pub at bridge 142 offering real ale and restaurant meals *L and*

E and Sun L. Children welcome, garden. B&B. Moorings. *Open Mon-Sun 11.00-23.00.*

🍴 **4 The White Hart Inn** Talybont-on-Usk LD3 7JD (01874 676227; www.whitehartinntalybont.co.uk). Canalside at bridge 143, and on the Taff Trail, this sociable pub serves real ale. Food, including curries and home-made pies, is served *L and E.* Children welcome. Canalside seating. Moorings. Inexpensive bunkhouse accommodation. *Open all day.*

🍴 **5 The Star Inn** Talybont-on-Usk LD3 7YX (01874 676635; www.starinntalybont.co.uk). Traditional village inn by the aqueduct. A choice of real ale and good pub food made from locally sourced ingredients *Tue-Fri E, Sat L and E, Sun 12.00-14.30.* Children welcome. Riverside garden. B&B. *Closed Mon, open B Hols 12.00-23.00, Tue-Fri 17.00-23.00 & Sat-Sun all day.*

Brecon

A sharp bend takes the canal into
the village of Pencelli where the mound
of the old castle dominates the village. There
is a slipway just beyond bridge 154. Leaving Pencelli,
the canal starts on a long horseshoe bend that carries it
through flat wooded country towards the crossing of the Usk.
A low embankment carries the canal across marshy ground towards
Llanfrynach, but it never goes near the village. Before bridge 158 the canal
crosses over the Nant Menascin on a small aqueduct. The best access point
for Llanfrynach is bridge 158, which is also the site of an old 18th-C canalside
warehouse. The name Llanfrynach suggests a religious settlement dedicated to Saint
Brynach, a local missionary in the 5th C. In 1775 mosaics and a villa bathhouse were
uncovered, dating back to the 5th C. Parts of these can now be seen in the National Museum
of Wales in Cardiff. Llanhamlach lies across the river. In addition to its 13th-C church, the area is
rich in prehistoric remains. The Usk now stays in sight all the way to Brecon, apart from one small
interruption. Bridge 162 takes the towpath to the west bank, where it remains to the terminus, and
then the canal turns sharply on to the Brynich Aqueduct. Engineered by Thomas Dadford Jnr in
1797, this four-arched stone structure takes the canal across the Usk to the east side of the valley.
To the west can be seen the old bridge that takes the B4558 across the river. Immediately beyond
the aqueduct is the last lock, restored in 1970. The canal now goes straight to Brecon, passing
through a tunnel-like bridge under the A470. The final mile of the route is high on the hillside,
overlooking the Usk all the way. The canal follows the road to the outskirts of the town, passing the
barracks, and then swings slightly to the west, along the backs of the houses. The entry into Brecon
is attractive, with many pretty houses and gardens flanking the canal. The navigation terminates in
the Theatre Basin, a joint venture by local bodies which has resulted in attracting grants from the
Welsh Office, Welsh Arts Council and the private sector. The development has seen the rebuilding
of the Brecknock Boat Company Wharf, filled in in 1881. A new canal bridge named after Thomas
Dadford has been constructed, giving access to the Theatre Basin. The basin provides mooring for
40 boats as well as a welcome turning area.

Pubs and Restaurants

1 The Royal Oak Pencelli LD3 7LX (01874 665396; www.theroyaloakpencelli.com). Canalside at bridge 153. Traditional village local serving real ale. Home-cooked food available *Mon-Sun L and E*. Children welcome, garden. Moorings. *Open all day every day from 12.00.*

2 The Three Horseshoes Groesffordd LD3 7SN (01874 665672; www.threehorseshoesgroesffordd.com). North of bridge 163. Inviting pub offering real ales locally sourced and home made food serve *daily L and E*. Outside seating in garden. Children and dogs welcome and games available. *Open Mon-Thu L and E & Fri-Sun 12.00-23.00.*

✗ 3 The George Hotel George Street, Brecon LD3 7LD (01874 620250; www.jdwetherspoon.com/pubs) Well refurbished 17th-C Inn serving typical Wetherspoon fayre. Children welcome. Paved courtyard. B&B.

✗ 4 The Wellington Hotel The Bulwark, Brecon LD3 7AD (01874 625225). Old established, comfortable central Hotel serving food *all day, every day*, together with a selection of real ales. B&B. Wi-Fi. *Open all day from 07.30.*

Also try: **5 Bar Rorkes** 4 Wheat Street, Brecon LD3 7DG (01874 611400); **6 The Clarence Inn** 25 Watton Street, Brecon LD3 7ED (01874 622810; www.clarenceinn.co.uk) or **7 The Bank Bar & Kitchen** 37 Watton Street, Brecon LD3 7EG (01874 623997; www.thebankbarbrecon.co.uk).

WALKING AND CYCLING

There is plenty of good walking around Brecon, as you would expect, with the Beacons presenting a challenge to the adventurous – you can get information from the TIC. Level circuits which link in with the towpath can easily be made south east of the town, and at Pencelli. Bike hire is available from Bikes and Hikes (07909 968135; www.bikesandhikes.co.uk), together with repairs and a range of outdoor activities. Located at Talybont Stores.

CANOEING AND PADDLEBOARDING

Canoeing, kayaking and paddleboarding opportunities are plentiful in this part of Wales somewhat loosely described as the Brecon Beacons: a rugged area simply filled with rivers, lakes, canals and reservoirs. An excellent starting point is www.breconbeacons.org/things-to-do/activities/watersports. www.breconcottages.com/guides/brecon-beacons-kayaking and www.beyonk.com/uk/canoeing-kayaking/in-brecon-beacons are further sources of inspiration and provide the equipment, training and locations. There are launch points at Chilson Bridge 146, the slipway at Pencelli Court Lift Bridge 155, Brynich Lock 69 and the terminal basin in Brecon. All have parking.

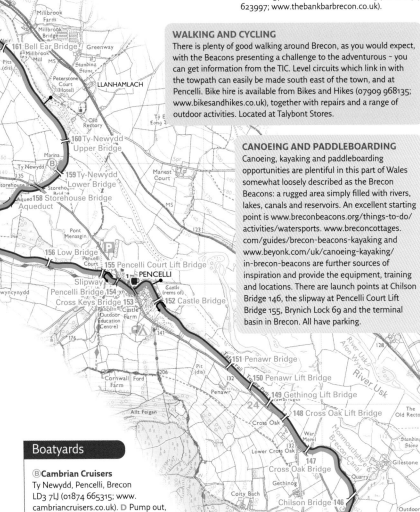

Boatyards

Ⓑ Cambrian Cruisers
Ty Newydd, Pencelli, Brecon LD3 7LJ (01874 665315; www.cambriancruisers.co.uk). **D** Pump out, gas, narrowboat hire. Moorings

Pencelli

Powys. This little village was at one time the head of a medieval lordship, but the only indication of this today is the castle mound. The castle farm occupies the site of the old castle which can now only be recognised by the footings of some of the walls laid down in the 13th C. The castle is not open to the public.

Llanfrynach

Powys. An attractive village built in a square round the pretty church. Nearby is the site of a Roman bathhouse.

Brecon

Powys. All services (except station). Built at the confluence of the Usk and Honddu rivers, Brecon has long been the administrative centre and market town for the Breconshire uplands. It dates back to the Roman period, and although little remains, the narrow streets that surround the castle give an idea of medieval Brecon. Today the town is famous as a touring centre and for its annual Jazz Festival which takes the town by storm *every August.* The cathedral and generous 18th-C architecture make it seem more English than Welsh. The Usk waterfront is especially attractive, dominated by the old stone bridge. Sarah Siddons and her brother Charles Kemble lived in the High Street.

Brecon Cathedral Cathedral Close, Brecon LD3 9DP. Originally the Priory Church of St John, founded by Bernard Newmarch, it was given cathedral status in 1923. Most of the building is 13th-C, although the nave is a century later. There is some fine glass, and side chapels dedicated to various medieval guilds.

Brecon Cathedral Heritage Centre (01874 623857; www.breconcathedral.co.uk). Situated in the beautiful Cathedral Close the centre houses an exhibition on cathedral life alongside a restored 16th-C tithe barn. *Opening times vary according to the season so telephone for details.* Charge. **Pilgrims Restaurant** (01874 625222) serving breakfast, coffee, teas and lunches *open 09.00-17.00 in summer & 10.00-16.00 in winter.*

Brecon Castle Most of the remains of the 11th-C castle now stand in the grounds of the Brecon Hotel and permission to view must be obtained from the hotel. A large motte and bailey, parts of the walls and two towers survive. The destruction of the castle during the Civil War was hastened by the inhabitants of Brecon, who did not want either side to occupy it.

Brecknock Museum & Art Gallery y Gaer, Glamorgan Street, Brecon LD3 7DW (01874 624121; www.ygaerpowys.org.uk). The collections include local history, natural history and a large archaeology section, from pre-Roman to medieval times. The museum also houses a fine collection of Welsh lovespoons. *Open all year, Mon–Fri 10.00-17.00, Sat 10.00-13.00 and 14.00-17.00, Sun 12.00-17.00.* Modest entry charge. You are advised to confirm opening times before visiting.

The Regimental Museum of the Royal Welsh Fusiliers The Barracks, Brecon LD3 7EB (01874 613310; www.rwfmuseum.org.uk). History of two famous regiments over 280 years. *Open throughout the year Mon-Fri 10.00-17.00 and Apr-Sep, Sat 10.00-16.00.* Charge.

Theatre Brycheiniog Canal Wharf, Brecon LD3 7EW (01874 611622; www.brycheiniog.co.uk). Host to a rich diversity of touring drama and music, overlooking the canal terminus. Also café, bar and ice creams.

Tourist Information Centre 11 Lion Yard, Brecon LD3 7BA (01874 620860; www.breconbeacons.org/brecon-tourist-information). *Open Mon-Sat 09.00-17.00 & Sun 10.00-16.00.*

BOAT TRIPS

Dragonfly Cruises and Day Boats Canal Wharf, Brecon LD3 7EW (07831 685222; www.dragonfly-cruises.co.uk). 2½ hour canal trip including a lock and an aqueduct on this 50-seater boat with wheelchair lift and 2 wheelchair places. Visit web site or telephone for times. Private charter available.

BRECON BEACONS NATIONAL PARK

Plas y Ffynnon, Cambrian Way, Brecon LD3 7HP (01874 624437; www.breconbeacons.org or www.beacon-npa.gov.uk). The park covers 519 square miles of mountain and hill country, embracing parts of the old counties of Herefordshire, Monmouthshire, Breconshire and Carmarthenshire. It includes three nature reserves, a forest reserve, opportunities for fishing, caving, pony trekking, sailing and boating, and several towns of interest to tourists, notably Brecon, Crickhowell, Talgarth and Hay-on-Wye. Virtually all the canal is within the park – a factor that greatly strengthened the case for its restoration and reopening. The canal is an excellent introduction to the park, crossing it roughly from south east to north west; in several places there are foot and bridle paths leading away into the mountains from the towpath. A good place to start any exploration is the Mountain Centre (LD3 8ER; 01874 623366), 1000ft up on Mynydd Illtud, above the village of Libanus, 5 miles south west of Brecon. There are rest and refreshment rooms, car parks and picnic sites overlooking the Brecon Beacons.

NEATH & TENNANT CANALS
SWANSEA CANAL

NEATH & TENNANT CANALS

Neath Canal (general)
Manager: John Smith
jsmith@stmodwen.co.uk

Neath Canal (North Resolven)
Parks & Cemeteries Manager Neath Port
Talbot County Borough Council
01639 686176

Tennant Canal
Manager: R. Williams
01792 644699
enquiries@leederproperties.co.uk

MAXIMUM DIMENSIONS
Length: 60'
Beam: 9'
Headroom: 6'

Canoeing and Paddleboarding: Category 1

MILEAGE
Tennant Canal
Junction with Glan-Y-Wern Canal *to:*
Neath Abbey: 3^1/$_4$ miles
ABERDULAIS JUNCTION: 6^1/$_2$ miles

Neath Canal
BRITON FERRY to:
Croft Bridge: 3 miles
Aberdulais Junction: 5 miles
Resolven: 8^3/$_4$ miles
YSGWRFA: 11^1/$_4$ miles

Locks:
Tennant Canal: 1
Neath Canal: 14

SWANSEA CANAL
Manager:
0303 040 4040
www.canalrivertrust.org.uk/contact-us/ways-
to-contact-us

MAXIMUM DIMENSIONS
Length: 69'
Beam: 7' 6"
Headroom: 7'

Navigation has been extended 5.5 miles between
Neath town centre and Abergarwed on the Neath
Canal, but remains very limited on the Tennant and
Swansea Canals.

Canoeing and Paddleboarding: Category 1

NEATH & TENNANT CANALS

The Neath Canal received Royal Assent in 1791 and work started immediately, initially with Thomas Dadford as engineer, who was soon followed by the less capable Thomas Sheasby. The navigation opened in 1795, and was extended to Giant's Grave in 1799, eventually reaching Briton Ferry in 1842. Fed by numerous branch canals and tramways it prospered, in spite of railway competition, due to its position on the west side of the Neath Valley and its denial of the right to build railway or tramway bridges over it. This finally all changed in 1875 and the canal then went into decline. Sadly the extensive restoration undertaken beyond Resolven in the early 90s has not been maintained and this section has now fallen into disrepair and is no longer navigable. The section between Abergarwed and Bridge Street in Neath town centre has been completely restored for navigation, including the construction of the longest single span aqueduct in the UK across the River Neath at Ynysbwllog. Notwithstanding, a breakdown in the feeder weir on the River Neath means that at certain times of the year water levels can be extremely low and thereby limit navigation. Although a canal or drainage ditch may have been dug between the rivers Neath and Tawe in the Middle Ages, the Tennant Canal has its origins in a navigation planned by Richard Jenkins, who wished to transport coal from his colliery at Glan-y-Wern to the River Neath. Acquired by George Tennant in 1817, remarkably it is still in the ownership of his descendants, the Coombe-Tennant family. Both canals have now lost their income from the sale of water and consequently there is little money to spend on maintenance.

SWANSEA CANAL

With the growth of collieries in the Tawe Valley, the expansion of the Ynysgedwyn Iron Works, increased copper smelting, improvements to Swansea harbour and the lack of a turnpike road, the demand for a canal in the Tawe Valley became irresistible. An Act was passed in 1794 sanctioning the building of such a waterway, and work began with initially Charles Roberts, and later Thomas Sheasby, as engineer.

Neath

When navigation on the Tennant Canal is permitted, it will begin at its junction with the Glan-y-Wern Canal, which crosses Crymlyn Bog, an SSSI. The mile or so of the main line to the basin at Port Tennant remains heavily overgrown. Heading east the waterway soon reaches Jersey Marine before passing under a series of railway bridges, entering a post-industrial landscape overshadowed by the M4 motorway. Bridge names give a clue to its busy past: Quarry, Gas Works, Abbey Wharf, Crown Copperworks and Skewen Tramroad are all passed on the approach to Neath. To the east the Afon Nedd brings tidal water inland, while gulls wheel overhead. Again the canal heads east, now passing the substantial remains of Neath Abbey. It then crosses the Clydach Aqueduct before being totally overshadowed by a web of roads and roundabouts.

● **Jersey Marine**
Neath Port Talbot, PO, stores, tel. By the tower Hotel you can see a tall camera obscura, built 150 years ago, with what was a handsome 'fives' court below.
● **Neath**
Neath Port Talbot. All services. Busy, bustling and friendly. A rich industrial past is revealed at Neath Abbey Ironworks, on the banks of the Afon Clydach. Owned by the Quaker families of Fox, Price and Tregelles, it dates from 1792 and produced about 80 tons of pig iron a week, which was then shipped to their Cornish foundry. Later the company was to become internationally renowned for its steam engines, locomotives and iron ships. The works closed in the 1880s.
Neath Abbey Baron Richard de Granville, a Norman, founded the abbey in 1130. A colourful history has included its use as a copper works, following the Dissolution. It is in the care of Cadw. *Open 10.00–16.00 daily.* Free.

Neath Castle First recorded in 1185, when the Welsh attacked it, the present structure probably dates from 1243–95, when the rest of the town was being built. *Open Mon-Sat, Oct-Mar 10.00-14.30 & Apr-Sep 10.00-16.00.* Free.
Society of Friends Meeting House Castle View, Neath SA11 3LY. Built in 1799 within the castle grounds on land donated by Lady Mackworth, it served the needs of the many Quaker entrepreneurs who were attracted by the area's industrial potential. Restored by the old Neath Borough Council, it is used for meetings and functions.
The Neath and Tennant Canal Trust contact www.neath-tennant-canals.org.uk for information on the canals. Telephone 01639 885319 for organised walks and talks. The Trust remains optimistic that the canals will eventually be restored to navigation and linked to Swansea Docks and the Swansea Canal.

CANOEING AND PADDLEBOARDING
Both canals are in private ownership and those making use of the waterways should seek authorisation from the owners/managers. The slipways and parking at Ynysbwllog and Aberdulais Basin provide convenient points of access but with portage required round Uchaf and Machin Locks, between these points. There are no locks below Aberdulais Basin where the towpath has recently been resurfaced and consequently *lifted*, however the many bridges between the basin and Briton Ferry may provide the easiest points for launching and recovery. Further east, there are launch points (both with parking) at the slipway beside the Vale of Neath Rail Bridge and the slipway at Ynysbwllog Bridge.

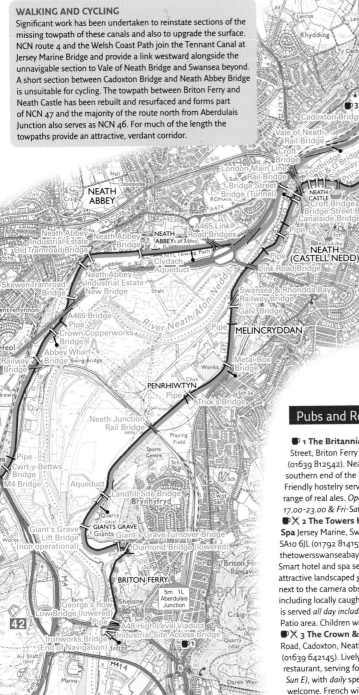

WALKING AND CYCLING

Significant work has been undertaken to reinstate sections of the missing towpath of these canals and also to upgrade the surface. NCN route 4 and the Welsh Coast Path join the Tennant Canal at Jersey Marine Bridge and provide a link westward alongside the unnavigable section to Vale of Neath Bridge and Swansea beyond. A short section between Cadoxton Bridge and Neath Abbey Bridge is unsuitable for cycling. The towpath between Briton Ferry and Neath Castle has been rebuilt and resurfaced and forms part of NCN 47 and the majority of the route north from Aberdulais Junction also serves as NCN 46. For much of the length the towpaths provide an attractive, verdant corridor.

Pubs and Restaurants

🍺 1 **The Britannia Inn** 18 Bethel Street, Briton Ferry SA11 2HQ (01639 812542). Nearest pub to the southern end of the Neath Canal. Friendly hostelry serving a limited range of real ales. *Open Sun-Thu 17.00-23.00 & Fri-Sat 17.00-00.00.*

🍺✕ 2 **The Towers Hotel & Spa** Jersey Marine, Swansea Bay SA10 6JL (01792 814155; www. thetowersswanseabay. com). Smart hotel and spa set in attractive landscaped gardens, next to the camera obscura. Food, including locally caught fresh fish, is served *all day including breakfast.* Patio area. Children welcome. B&B.

🍺✕ 3 **The Crown & Sceptre** Main Road, Cadoxton, Neath SA10 8AP (01639 642145). Lively village bar and restaurant, serving food *L and E (not Sun E),* with *daily* specials. Children welcome. French windows open onto a patio. Quiz on *Tue.* Open daily 12.00-23.00.

Aberdulais

The Tennant Canal continues towards Aberdulais, initially hemmed-in by roads and finally diving under a tangle of fly-overs, slip roads and roundabouts, to emerge at Aberdulais Lock and the squat and purposeful aqueduct, which carries the waterway to its junction with the Neath Canal at Aberdulais Basin. The aqueduct is currently de-watered and in a semi derelict condition, however a recent survey indicates it is actually in better condition than was first thought.

The Neath Canal keeps close to the south bank of the Afon Nedd, passing within 10ft of St Illtyd's Church, all in a pretty, wooded, setting. The restored Tyn-yr-Heol Lock north to the junction at Aberdulais. The conurbation is then finally left behind as the canal makes its way along the Vale of Neath, accompanied by the river and a busy road which, surprisingly, does little to intrude upon the waterway's quiet progress. Locks now appear at fairly regular intervals, raising the canal to the point where it can finally cross the river at Ynysbwllog through the impressive new aqueduct which was completed in March 2008. From there the canal passes under the main A465 using the new basins and under the well restored Ynysbwllog Bridge. In May 2011 the Welsh Waterways Festival, incorporating the IWA National Trail Boat Festival, was held at Ynysarwed Farm. More than 30 boats from all over the UK visited the canal and the event proved a great success. The Canal towpaths between Abergarwed and Neath now form part of the national cycle network. Beyond Resolven Lock and Ynysbiban Aqueduct the canal's course is abruptly interrupted by Commercial Road. Cross this and you are confronted with a vision of how splendid this navigation will one day be. With a fine pub nearby, a basin, a slipway and a lock, the whole canal from here to the terminus is beautifully restored, providing a fitting finale to your journey.

Pubs and Restaurants

● ✕ **4 The Whittington Arms** Park Street, Tonna, Neath SA11 3JF (01639 632577; www.thewhittingtonarms.co.uk) Family-friendly pub serves real ales. Wide range of good locally sourced food *L and E*, carvery *Sun*. Garden. *Open Tue-Sun 12.00-23.00.*

● ✕ **5 The Rock & Fountain** Glyn Neath Road, Aberdulais, Neath SA10 8HN (01639 642681). Welcoming pub serving real ale along with food *all day, every day*. Outside seating. Children welcome *until 20.00. Open daily 11.00-23.00.*

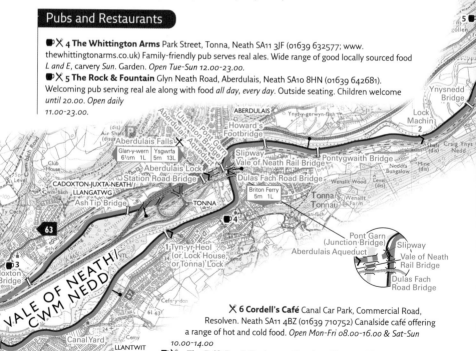

✕ **6 Cordell's Café** Canal Car Park, Commercial Road, Resolven. Neath SA11 4BZ (01639 710752) Canalside café offering a range of hot and cold food. *Open Mon-Fri 08.00-16.00 & Sat-Sun 10.00-14.00*

● ✕ **7 The Drift Bar & Restaurant** Resolven Miners Welfare, Resolven, Neath SA11 4AH (01639 710320) A beautifully converted bar and restaurant housed in an unprepossessing old, iconic building. The Miners Welfare is a historic institution, provided by the miners who worked the local drift mines, now serving a range of beers, wines and good food *Wed-Fri 17.00-21.00 & Sat 12.00-21.00 (Sun 16.00).*

WALKING AND CYCLING
The Vale of Neath is noted for its spectacular waterfalls, two of which are mentioned below. You can explore more of them with guidance from a booklet *Waterfall Walks*, which is available from local Tourist Information Centres. The walk to Melincourt Falls makes an excellent diversion.

Aberdulais Aqueduct Near Neath SA10 8EU (www.neath-tennant-canals.org.uk). This squat ten-arched aqueduct was built in 1823-4 by William Kirkhouse, George Tennant's engineer. At the eastern end a cast iron trough carries the canal over what was the Aberdulais Cut (*see* below). The sandstone used to build the aqueduct was quarried at Aberdulais Falls – Tennant was heavily criticised over this action, which forever changed the character of the falls.

Aberdulais Falls Near Neath SA10 8EU (01639 636674; www.nationaltrust.org.uk). Well-restored and run by the National Trust, this spectacular site has been utilised by a succession of industries, beginning with copper smelting in 1584. What can be seen today dates from 1830, when a tin plate works operated here. The artist J. M. W. Turner visited in 1796. The water from the falls, which once powered these industries, now turns a water wheel (a replica of that which turned in the 19th C and now the largest in Europe generating electricity), and a modern turbine, which generates 200kw and provides enough to supply 20 houses. *Open Mar-Oct, daily 10.00–17.00; and Nov-mid Dec, Fri-Sun 11.00–16.00.* Charge. Shop. Old School Room Café.

Aberdulais Cut Near Neath SA10 8EU (www.neath-tennant-canals.org.uk). Built in 1751, this was one of the earliest canals in Wales, and ran for 600yds transporting materials between Dylais Forge and Ynysygerwn tin plate works. It passed under one of the railway arches by The Railway pub. Its use as a navigation was superseded by the canal.

St Illtyd's Church Canalside at Llantwit. Before the Dissolution of the monasteries by Henry VIII, this was the parish church of Neath. It was established on the site of a hermit's cell dating from the 6th C, with the present building dating from 1859. The area in front of the church, on the canal bank, was once a coal wharf, served by tramway from the Gnoll Estate.

Tonna Workshops Located by Tyn-yr-heol Lock, this was once the canal company's registered office, clerk's residence and maintenance yard, with a forge and a carpenter's shop. There was at one time a loading dock opposite where stone, quarried above Tonna, was brought down by tramroad and transhipped onto barges, which then took it into Neath.

Ynysbwllog Aqueduct Construction of the canal reached Ynysbwllog in 1792, at which point the engineer Thomas Dadford handed over to Thomas Sheasby, who supervised the work until he was arrested for 'irregularities' in 1794. The canal to Abernant was finally completed in 1795. In 1813 it was reported that Sheasby's work on this aqueduct was substandard, and rebuilding of the five-arch structure took place. Remaining in less than perfect condition, it was washed away by floodwater in 1979. The aqueduct, believed to be the longest single-span aqueduct in Europe, was reopened in 2008 after extensive repair and renovation and in 2010 received a British Urban Regeneration commendation for its design and construction.

Melincourt Falls The falls can be reached by following the path which heads south east from above Ynysarwed Uchaf Lock. Beyond the road your route follows a tree-lined gorge, with the ruins of the old Melincourt Furnace hidden by trees above you on the opposite bank. Michael Faraday visited the falls in July 1819, and estimated their height to be some 70ft. He was taken there by a little 'welch damsel', and he paid her one shilling for guiding him.

● **Resolven**
Neath, Port Talbot. PO, tel, stores, baker, fish & chips, takeaways. The Farmer's Arms has now closed but the Council has refused a planning application for conversion to residential use. There is an excellent a new canalside café and the Miners Welfare Institution has been transformed into a bar and restaurant.

Rheola

Beyond Ty Banc the canal continues its steady climb towards Ysgwrfa Bridge. It is highly unlikely that restoration will proceed beyond this point, although there are those who think what is left of the watercourse could be reinstated. Beyond Crugiau Bridge two locks are climbed before you pass under Rheola Iron Aqueduct, which once carried the stream that now passes under the canal at Rheola Aqueduct. To the north is Rheola House, which was converted for use as a training centre by the British Aluminium Company and thus survived, while many other such houses were pulled down. Rheola Pond, where herons nest, lies to the north east. You then continue, closely accompanied by the busy main road, along the centre of the Vale of Neath, with fine views of the Rheola Forest on either side. It is easy to understand why this restored section won a highly acclaimed Civic Trust Award in 1992.

At Maesgwyn a 19th-C limekiln stands hidden amongst trees beside the lock – a demonstration that farming, as well as industry, was once well served by the canal. It is then just a short distance to Ysgwrfa Lock, which was at one time known as Pwllfa'r onn Lock, taking that name from a nearby colliery owned by the Neath Abbey Ironworks. Coal was loaded at a wharf below the lock, for transport to Neath. You are now at the end of the navigation, although this waterway originally climbed another five locks – Granary; Cae-dan-y-cwmwl (the field under the cloud); Pentremalwed; Lamb & Flag and Maesmarchog – before reaching its terminus at Glynneath. Part of this section can be followed, although the channel has been narrowed to accommodate a road.

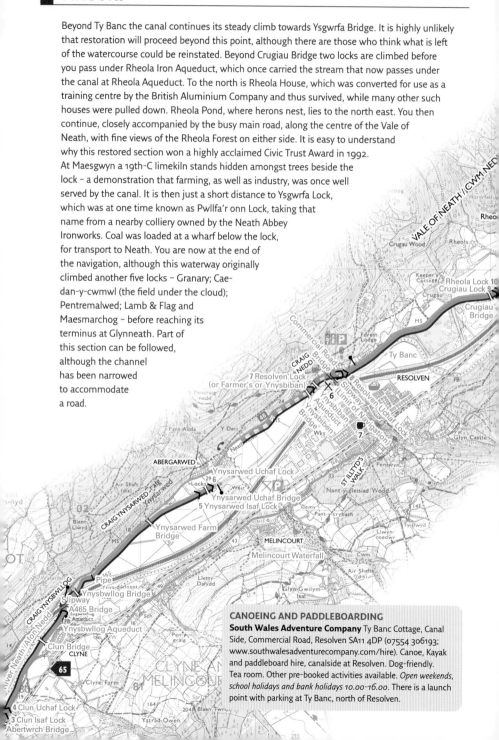

CANOEING AND PADDLEBOARDING
South Wales Adventure Company Ty Banc Cottage, Canal Side, Commercial Road, Resolven SA11 4DP (07554 306193; www.southwalesadventurecompany.com/hire). Canoe, Kayak and paddleboard hire, canalside at Resolven. Dog-friendly. Tea room. Other pre-booked activities available. *Open weekends, school holidays and bank holidays 10.00–16.00.* There is a launch point with parking at Ty Banc, north of Resolven.

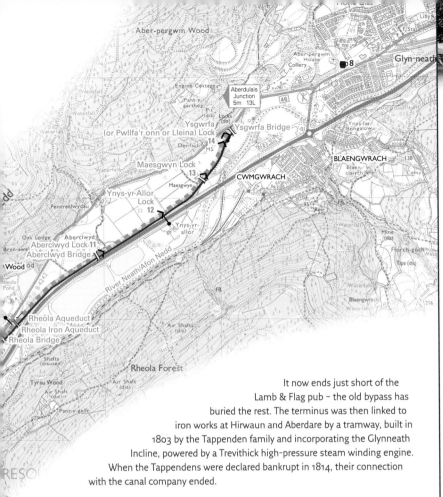

It now ends just short of the
Lamb & Flag pub – the old bypass has
buried the rest. The terminus was then linked to
iron works at Hirwaun and Aberdare by a tramway, built in
1803 by the Tappenden family and incorporating the Glynneath
Incline, powered by a Trevithick high-pressure steam winding engine.
When the Tappendens were declared bankrupt in 1814, their connection
with the canal company ended.

WALKING AND CYCLING
In the Rheola Forest, north of Blaengwrach, keen mountain bikers will be excited to find the route used
for the Dragon Downhill Course. It is about half a mile of single-track, and was classified as Extreme.
Visit www.dragondownhill.co.uk for more details, and do not take your motor vehicle into the forest.
There is also a low-level walking route between Resolven and Blaengwrach, on the southern side.

Pubs and Restaurants

🍺 **8 The Lamb and Flag** Wellfield Place
Glynneath, Neath SA11 5EP (01639 721995).
Friendly and welcoming pub. Refurbished to
a high standard and well worth the walk from
the end of the canal. Restaurant serving meals
all day. Real ale. Children welcome. Enclosed
garden. B&B. *Open daily 12.00-23.00.*

● **Rheola Forest**
This large forest has been used for two
stages of the Network Q Rally of Great
Britain, with Resolven as a base. Also
excellent for mountain biking, it has
recently been surveyed for the presence
of red squirrels.

Pontardawe

Although the *Nicholson guides* usually cover waterways in a linear fashion, most visitors to the Swansea Canal will arrive at Pontardawe, which is the perfect access point for the two separate sections seen here.

Exploring this canal to the north east, the initial section has been well restored, with an excellent towpath overlooked by the exceptionally tall spire of St Peter's Church on the opposite bank. Soon you round a corner to reach a lowered bridge – cross the road and you are now on the navigable section, which heads out of town beside an industrial estate, separating the canal from the Afon Tawe at this point. Now the conurbation is left behind as you skirt water meadows on your way to Ynysmeudwy Lock, which has yet to be restored and thus marks the limit of navigation. However the surroundings are splendid, and at the road bridge you can leave the canal for a visit to the Ynysmeudwy Arms. Ynysmeudwy Bridge was once known as Pottery Bridge, since in 1850 there was a pottery here making Victorian table ware and jugs. Only 112 people were employed, but a wide variety of items were made, all now eminently collectable! It is then well worth crossing the road to continue to the limit of the canal, since you will pass several abandoned locks and a canal which appears almost river-like, flowing in places little more than 6 inches deep over the overgrown bed of the waterway. Finally you reach the end, just south east of Godre'r graig, at a road.

Travelling south west from Herbert Street Bridge, in the centre of Pontardawe, again the waterway seems secure, but this is short-lived, and the canal disappears underground just before a new road. To follow its course you should go through the underpass and turn right onto a tarmac path, which passes a large store, a school, a leisure centre and playing fields before the clear water of the canal manifests itself again, and immediately carries on as if nothing had happened! Now the Afon Tawe meanders right beside the towpath, as you pass the atypical back gardens of canal-side houses. Just before Pont Coed Gwilym, beside Coedgwilym Park, a memorial tells of this section of the canal's restoration, beside a *slipway* where there is *Sun summer* canoe hire, and small craft can be launched. Beyond the bridge there is just a short section before the canal is again piped. The towpath is easily followed and soon you are amongst herons and ducks and passing the buildings of the imposing Clydach nickel refinery. The Tawe then

CANOEING AND PADDLEBOARDING

Two short sections of the canal are suitable for paddling: between the site of lock 7 and lock 8 and between Herbert Street Bridge and Lock 12.

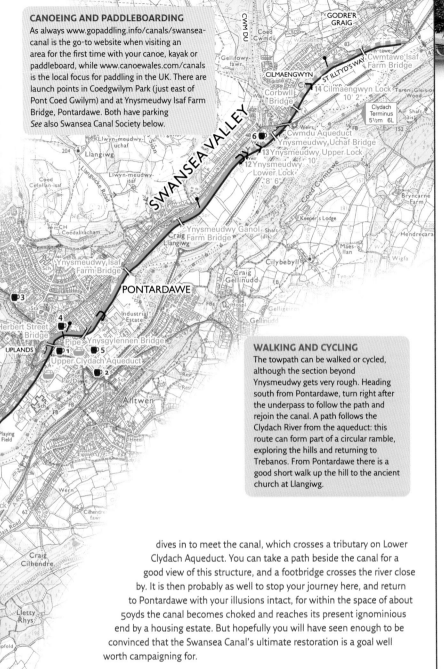

CANOEING AND PADDLEBOARDING
As always www.gopaddling.info/canals/swansea-canal is the go-to website when visiting an area for the first time with your canoe, kayak or paddleboard, while www.canoewales.com/canals is the local focus for paddling in the UK. There are launch points in Coedgwilym Park (just east of Pont Coed Gwilym) and at Ynysmeudwy Isaf Farm Bridge, Pontardawe. Both have parking *See* also Swansea Canal Society below.

WALKING AND CYCLING
The towpath can be walked or cycled, although the section beyond Ynysmeudwy gets very rough. Heading south from Pontardawe, turn right after the underpass to follow the path and rejoin the canal. A path follows the Clydach River from the aqueduct: this route can form part of a circular ramble, exploring the hills and returning to Trebanos. From Pontardawe there is a good short walk up the hill to the ancient church at Llangiwg.

dives in to meet the canal, which crosses a tributary on Lower Clydach Aqueduct. You can take a path beside the canal for a good view of this structure, and a footbridge crosses the river close by. It is then probably as well to stop your journey here, and return to Pontardawe with your illusions intact, for within the space of about 50yds the canal becomes choked and reaches its present ignominious end by a housing estate. But hopefully you will have seen enough to be convinced that the Swansea Canal's ultimate restoration is a goal well worth campaigning for.

Swansea Canal Society Coedgwilym Park, Clydach SA6 5NS (07876 412014; www.swanseacanalsociety.com). Beside Pont Coed Gwilym Bridge. Canoe hire *Easter-Oct* Sun 11.00-15.00. Charge.

Pontardawe

Neath, Port Talbot. PO, tel, stores, chemist, bank, baker, takeaways, fish & chips, off-licence. The 180ft-tall spire of St Peter's Church, erected in 1862, overlooks what was once an industrial town, where the Gilbertson's tin plate works and the chemical works of Jacob Lewis brought prosperity. But these are now gone, and the town provides a pleasant home for workers in nearby industries, while the surrounding countryside slowly recovers from the exposure to the highly toxic fumes these processes once produced. The main street, to the east of the canal bridge, is a lively place, with shops, pubs and restaurants around a fine new Arts Centre. The town's name means 'The bridge over the River Tawe', and it is this river which defines the valley: exploited for its mineral wealth and then abandoned when these resources were no longer needed, or were more cheaply obtained elsewhere. The channel of the Swansea Canal continues uninterrupted for a few miles to the north east; to the south west it ends abruptly by a new road. Beyond lie supermarkets, a school and a leisure centre.

Trebanos

Neath, Port Talbot. Tel, stores, off-licence. Takeaway, garage. Scene of brief media attention when protest camps where established, between 2006 and 2007, in opposition to the South Wales Gas Pipeline passing through the village.

Pontardawe Leisure Centre Parc Ynysderw, Pontardawe SA8 4EG (0800 043 4343; www.celticleisure.org). Swimming pool, fitness suite, squash courts. *Contact for opening times.*

The Arts Centre Herbert Street, Pontardawe SA8 4ED (01792 863722). A wide range of excellent entertainment, featuring jazz, folk, rock, storytelling, comedy, dance, drama and film.

Clydach

Swansea. PO, tel, stores, hardware, bank, chemist, off-licence, butcher, takeaways, library. Currently marking the southern limit of recognisable canal, the town is indistinguishable from its neighbour Trebanos, and is dominated by the nickel refinery.

Clydach Nickel Refinery This historic production facility, which stands right beside the canal, has produced high purity nickel pellets by the nickel carbonyl process for over 100 years on this site. It was an accidental discovery in a stable that led to one of the most elegant processes for refining metal. Ludwig Mond, born 1839 and a shrewd businessman and respected industrialist, pioneered this work in St John's Wood, London. Whilst conducting experiments with bleach, he stumbled upon a process for producing pure nickel, along with a previously unknown compound, which Mond named nickel carbonyl. After many teething troubles a pilot plant was built in Birmingham and began producing 3000 pounds of nickel a week. After unsuccessfully trying to sell his process, he set up this plant in Clydach in 1900, since here it could easily be supplied with anthracite fuel, had a good water supply, good transport links with the port of Swansea and a reliable labour force. Nickel ore was brought in from Canada and deliveries of 99.95 pure pellets were produced in 1902. The company later merged with the International Nickel Company of Canada, and production continues to this day.

Cwm Clydach

Ty'n y Berllan Craig Cefn Parc, Clydach (029 2035 3000; www.rspb.org.uk). 2 miles north of Clydach at the New Inn, on the B4291. This RSPB mixed woodland reserve is home to redstarts, breeding pied flycatchers and buzzards. There are two nature trails.

Swansea Tourist Information Centre Barham Centre, Mount Pisgah, Parkhill Swansea SA3 2EQ (01792 468321; www.visitswanseabay.com). *Open Mon-Sat 09.30-17.30 & B Hols 10.00-16.00.*

Pubs and Restaurants (pages 68-69)

There are plenty of pubs to choose from in Pontardawe.

🍺✕ **1 The Dillwyn Arms Hotel** The Cross, Pontardawe SA8 4EB (01792 863310; www.dillwynshotel.com). A community pub and restaurant, serving real ale, and food *L and E*. Outside seating. Children welcome. B&B. *Open 12.00-00.00 daily.*

🍺 **2 The Pontardawe Inn** 123 Herbert Street, Pontardawe SA8 4ED (01792 447562; www.pontardaweinn.co.uk). Ancient, community pub made up of four separate rooms serving real ale and real cider, together with food *L and E (not Sun E)*. Family-friendly. Traditional pub games and *regular* live music. Beer garden. *Open all day.*

🍺 **3 Travellers Well** 76 Commercial Road, Rhydyfro, Pontardawe SA8 4SS (07757 561568). Serving bar snacks and a rotating selection of guest ales, this welcoming hostelry is *open all day from 15.00 Mon-Thu and 12.00 Fri-Sun*. Traditional pub games and garden.

🍺 **4 The Castle Hotel** High Street, Pontardawe SA8 4HU (01792 869961). Old-fashioned pub, which does not serve food. Outside seating. Children welcome *until 19.00*. Live music at the *weekend*. B&B.

🍺 **5 Pink Geranium Hotel** 31 Herbert Street, Pontardawe SA8 4EB (01792 862255). This pub is for the over 25s, and has live music *Fri and Sat*. Outside drinking area. B&B. *Open all day from 10.00.*

🍺✕ **6 Ynysmeudwy Arms** Ynysmeudwy Road, Pontardawe SA8 4QJ (01792 864847) Friendly, modernised pub serving generous portions of food *L and E, Mon-Fri; all day Fri-Sat & Sun L*. Children welcome. Garden.

Also try 🍺 **7 Carpenters Arms** High Street, Clydach SA6 5LN (01792 844902); the 🍺 **8 Colliers Arms** Swansea Road, Trebansws SA8 4BU (01792 864847).

MONTGOMERY CANAL

MAXIMUM DIMENSIONS

Length: 72'
Beam: 6' 10"
Headroom: 7'
Draught: 2'

MANAGER

0303 040 4040
enquiries.westmidlands@canalrivertrust.org.uk

MILEAGE

FRANKTON JUNCTION to:
Carreghofa: 11½ miles
Welshpool: 21½ miles
Garthmyl: 27¾ miles
ABERBECHAN: 32½ miles

Locks: 25 (to Freestone Lock)

RESTORATION

The future of the Montgomery Canal as a navigable waterway now thankfully seems secure, although there are concerns about the preservation of rare flora and fauna on some sections. The restored and navigable sections are as follows:

From Frankton Junction to to Crickheath Bridge 85 where there is a winding hole.

From Ardd-Lin Bridge 103 to just south of Berriew Bridge 129.

Canoeing and Paddleboarding: Category 1

The Montgomery Canal has much to offer walkers and boaters alike, with its characteristic rurality and peacefulness. It is both rich in wildlife and in reminders of its industrial past. The villages dotted along the canal are mostly quiet and picturesque self-contained communities with pleasant country pubs, in which boaters and walkers can relax and explore. Welshpool is a good shopping centre and, of course, the impressive Powis Castle is well worth visiting. The initial development of this canal was sparked by the publication of the plans for the Ellesmere Canal, which inspired a separate company to plan a canal from Newtown northwards to join the Llanymynech branch of the Ellesmere Canal at Carreghofa. The canal was authorised in 1793, and by 1797 the line was open from Carreghofa to Garthmyl. The Montgomery Canal was mainly agricultural; apart from the limestone, it existed to serve the farms and villages through which it passed, and so was never really profitable. The lack of capital and income greatly delayed the completion of the western extension to Newtown, which was not finally opened until 1821, having been financed by a separate company. So what eventually became known as the Montgomery Canal was in fact built by three separate companies over a period of 30 years. The downfall of the canal became inevitable with World War I when a pattern of regular and heavy losses started, from which the company was never able to recover. In 1921 the company gave up canal carrying and sold most of its boats to private operators. Locks began to close at weekends and standards of maintenance started to slip. From 1922 onwards many changes in the company ownership of the Shropshire Union Canal system began and, although the network remained open despite these changes, trade declined rapidly. Many traders were driven away by the lack of maintenance, which meant that most boats could only operate half full. In 1936 the breach of the Montgomery Canal at the Perry Aqueduct, just one mile south of Frankton Junction, precipitated the eventual closure of the line. Although the company set out to repair the damage they changed their minds, and with trade at a standstill there were no complaints. In 1944 an Act was passed making the closure official. The situation remained this way for many years, and with many road bridges lowered, it was thought that the waterway would fade away gracefully. But today the canal is dotted with restoration works, and considerable lengths are once again open to navigation. Look out for the distinctive paddle gear found on most locks, fitted by George Buck.

Frankton Junction

At Welsh Frankton, what was the original main line of the canal heads south towards Newtown, while the Llangollen Canal continues to the west (*see page 31*). Leaving the junction at Lower Frankton, the canal descends the four Frankton Locks: a staircase of two, and then two singles. Below the third lock, on the offside, are the remains of the dry dock where, in 1929, Cressy (later to be owned by Tom Rolt) was converted to leisure use. A plaque on the tail of the lock supplies further details. At Lockgate Bridge 71 there is a *parking area* and some *picnic tables* which encourage walkers to visit the area, and *moorings* and a *sanitary station* are provided in a short remnant of the Weston Branch; the remainder is now a linear nature reserve. The canal then falls through Graham Palmer Lock and curves through open fields to Perry Aqueduct. During February 1936, a 40yd breach occurred in the east bank, north of the aqueduct. This was a major factor in the closure of the canal and resulted in its eventual demise in 1944. The canal passes the unnavigable Rednal Basin, which you can explore on foot and Heath Houses, where there is a fine restored warehouse by the canal. Open arable farmland and woods surround the navigation as it approaches Queen's Head, where there is a *winding hole, moorings, a paddlesports centre and a welcoming pub*. The three Aston Locks, adjacent to Aston Nature Reserve, lower the canal as it approaches Llanymynech.

● **Heath Houses**
Shropshire. A beautiful red-brick and timber warehouse stands by the elegant turn-over bridge, which takes the towpath to the east bank, where it remains until Newtown. To the north a short unnavigable arm leads to the completely intact Rednal Basin. On 7 June 1865 a railway disaster occurred 600yds north of the canal on the Great Western line, which crossed over just east of bridge 74. A way gang was lifting the line and, as a warning to any oncoming trains, placed a green flag on top of a pole. A large excursion train consisting of 32 coaches and two brake vans hauled by two engines, failed to see this crude warning. The train speeded on until the working men were seen, but by this time it was too late to shut off steam. Four coaches were destroyed, 11 damaged and 12 people were killed.

● **Queen's Head**
Shropshire. Tel. An expanding canalside settlement intersected by the old main road and the busy A5. The pub is a focal point for canal visitors, with the village spreading south eastwards from the bridge.

British Ironwork Centre Whitehall Aston, Oswestry SY11 4JH (0800 688 8386; www.britishironworkcentre.co.uk). ½ mile north of Queen's Head, along A5. Fascinating display of both old and new items, from a family company dedicated to preserving and creating quality ironwork. This varied collection includes an impressive selection of animal sculptures. *Open Tue–Sat 09.00–16.00.* Free.

WALKING AND CYCLING
Although the canal is not yet fully open to navigation, the towpath makes a fascinating walk. You will, however, have to cross main roads here and there, and make one or two short diversions, until the waterway is completely restored.

CANOEING AND PADDLEBOARDING
Shropshire Paddlesports Queen's Head, Oswestry SY11 4EB (07973 743103; www.shropshirepaddlesport.org). Community-based canoe and kayaking club located opposite the pub at Queen's Head. 'Go Paddling' sessions *Sat 09.00–12.00.*

Pubs and Restaurants

●✕ **1 The Queen's Head** Queen's Head, Oswestry SY11 4EB (01691 610255; www.the-queens-head-oswestry.co.uk). A smart canalside pub with a conservatory eating area, popular with motorists. Real ale is served, and there are home-cooked bar and restaurant meals available *Wed–Sun 12.00–21.00 (Sun 17.30)*. Outside seating, dog- and family-friendly. Wi-Fi. *Open Wed–Sun 12.00–23.00 (22.00)*.

Evenall Gorse

Rodenhurst Bridge 3

Nicholas Bridge 2

Rowsons Bridge 70

Frankton Farm

Frankton Coppice House

Bee V Junction

Peters Bridge

Val Hill No 3 Bridge 66

Towing Path

Gronwyn Bridge 7m 8L

LOWER FRANKTON

Frankton Locks

68 Pryce's Bridge

Broome Farm

67 Broom Bridge

CANOEING AND PADDLEBOARDING

The Montgomery Canal provides some excellent opportunities to take to the water in a small, unpowered boat. There is good parking, somewhere to launch and a picnic area on the derelict Weston Branch Canal beside Bridge 71. Many of the locks have portage points and movement of powered craft is limited.

Lockgate Bridge 71

Weston Branch (disused)

Hordley Bridge

Lockgate Bridge 81

Graham Palmer Lock

87 HORDLEY

Wildern

Berghill

Lower Berghill Farm

37

38

Shropshire Way

Hawk's Wood

Hawkswood Farm

Perry Aqueduct

Rednalmill Bridge

Frankton in the rain

Montgomery Canal

Green Wood

Cottage Wood

Woodhouse

Keepers Bridge

Berrywood

73

Woodhouse Drive

Red

74 Heath House Bridge

Rail Bridge

Swing Bridge

Rednal Basin

HEATH HOUSES

Pen-yr-estyn

Station Farm

Rednal Moss

Sutton

Sutton Farm

WEST

wyford

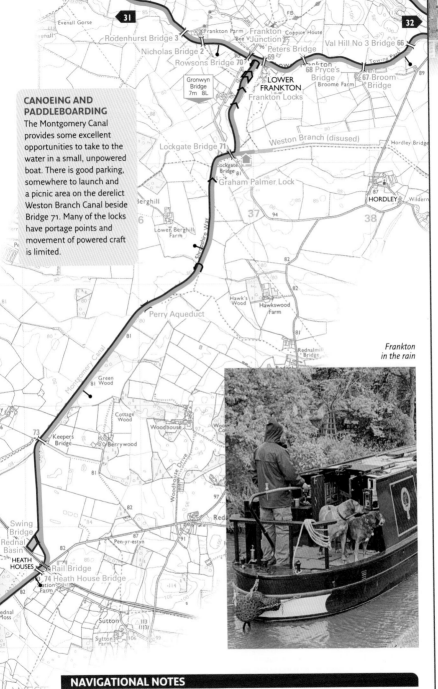

NAVIGATIONAL NOTES

Pre-booked passage through Frankton Locks is available *daily Apr-Oct 09.00-12.00* via the CRT online booking service or by phoning 0303 040 4040. *In winter 48hrs notice* is required. Bookings can also be made on 01606 786777 extension 8.

The canal continues southwards. After the three Aston Locks the level remains constant for a while, crossing fields on low embankments or through shallow cuttings. At Maesbury Marsh a fine crane, built by Ormerod & Crierson of Manchester and thought to be the only surviving example of such a 15cwt crane, stands opposite the pub and marks the wharf, restored and used as a *sanitary station (including toilets and showers)*. Beyond here, at Gronwyn Bridge, the remains of the old tramway from Morda can be seen. Once the new Crickheath length opens in 2022, the half-mile section leading up to Schoolhouse Bridge 86 – together with the reconstruction of the bridge itself – will be the 'front line' of the restoration. It will also be the last obstruction before the Welsh border at Llanymynech. Note the fine limekilns by bridge 91, and the prominent chimney to the north, as the canal approaches Llanymynech. This marks the remains of a Hoffman Continuous Kiln – built at the beginning of the 20th C – which, unlike the more common bottle kiln, was a multi-chamber device, producing a non-stop output of fine agricultural and building lime. The waterway then begins to meander as it approaches Pant.

Cambrian Heritage Railways Oswald Road, Oswestry SY11 1RE (01691 688763/07527 728131; www.cambrianrailways.com). Ultimately this heritage line, which is the subject of on-going restoration, will run from Gobowen in the north through to Pant. Currently activity is split between two sites – Oswestry and Llynclys – and trains operate from both. There is a museum at their station in Oswestry. Telephone for timetable details and special events or visit the website.

● **West Felton**
Shropshire. PO, tel, stores (with cashpoint), off-licence. A pleasant rural village which can be reached from Aston Locks. The PO is open on Mon and Wed morning and Fri afternoon.

● **Woolston**
Shropshire. A tiny collection of houses by St Winifred's Well.

St Winifred's Well A 7th-C princess, St Winifred was brought back to life by St Bueno after being decapitated by an angry suitor at Holywell in Flintshire. In the 12th C her body was brought to Shrewsbury from its grave in Denbighshire, and this well is said to mark a resting place on that journey, and where a spring miraculously appeared. It has been visited by pilgrims for centuries. The pretty timbered building has been restored by the Landmark Trust for holiday lets (01628 825925) so, when you visit, please *respect the privacy* of any visitors who may be staying in the cottage.

● **Maesbury Marsh**
Shropshire. PO box, tel. A superb canal village clustered around the wharf and pub, now engulfed by new housing. The church is a curious white corrugated iron structure which appears to be well used. The stores and a café are just south of Bridge 80.

● **Llynclys**
Shropshire. Tel. This village is drowned out by traffic on the A483, but the pub is just about close enough for those who leave the canal at Crickheath Wharf (bridge 85) and follow the footpath to the north west across farmland.

● **Pant**
Shropshire. PO, tel, stores, off-licence. Pant grew up around the limestone quarries, one of the main reasons for the existence of the canal. The limekiln bank on the offside of the canal before bridge 91 has been excellently restored and is probably among the best examples to be seen along the Montgomery Canal. Shop open daily 07.00-21.00.

WALKING AND CYCLING

There is a good walk from Maesbury Marsh to St Winifred's Well, then across country to Park Mill Bridge and back to Maesbury. Cyclists will find the towpath hard going south of bridge 82, and almost impassable between bridges 85 and 92 due to a number of stiles and kissing gates.

● **Llanymynech**
Powys. PO, tel, stores, off-licence, takeaways, fish & chips.
Offa's Dyke and the Anglo-Welsh border run through the village, their line actually passing through the bar of the Lion Hotel; it is possible to drink with one foot in each country. The church, St Agatha's, is very interesting, a 19th-C French-style Norman building with a lateral bell tower and huge clock face. Such Norman revival buildings were rare in the 19th C.

Llanymynech Heritage Area SY22 6HB (0345 678 9000; www.shropshire.gov.uk). A short walk from the village along the towpath, this intriguing area is reached. It gives an insight to the industrial history and significance of Llanymynech in the production of limestone. There are some fine old kilns to be explored here. The Visitor Centre (01691 830506), with café, is *open Suns & B Hols 13.30-16.30.*
Llanymynech Rocks Nature Reserve The limestone cliffs reach 500ft, and the abandoned limestone quarry is now part of the nature reserve.

NAVIGATIONAL NOTES

A windlass is required to operate bridge 81.

BOAT TRIPS

nb George Watson Buck from the wharf beside the Visitor Centre and Llanymynech Heritage Area (www.llanylime.co.uk/about/canal-boat-trips), *Easter–Sep, Sun 13.30–16.30, Bank Holidays* and other special occasions. Teas and snacks available.

Pubs and Restaurants

● 1 **The Navigation Inn** Maesbury Marsh, Oswestry SY10 8JB (01691 672958; www.thenavigation.co.uk). Warm and friendly 18th-C canalside inn incorporating a listed canal warehouse, dating from around 1785. Real ale, real cider and food available *Thu-Sat (not Thu L) & Sun 12.00-15.00.* Canalside garden, real fire and Wi-Fi. *Open Thu-Sat (not Thu L) & Sun 12.00-18.00.*

✗ 2 **Canal Central Café** Coed Y Rae Lane, Spiggots Bridge, Maesbury Marsh SY10 8JG (01691 652168; www.canalcentral.co.uk). Breakfast, lunch and homemade cakes. Self-catering accommodation with balcony overlooking the canal. Tearoom and shop selling books, cards and gifts. Camping and caravanning. Miniature-gauge railway. Wi-Fi. *Open Fri-Sun 10.00-16.00.*

● 3 **The White Lion** Llynclys SY10 8LJ (01691 831999; www.facebook.com/thelionllynclys). An old pub with an eclectic mix of rooms, serving real ale and excellent home-cooked food *daily 12.00-21.00 (Sun 20.00).* Family-friendly, garden. Traditional pub games and camping. *Open daily 12.00-23.00.*

● ✗ 4 **The Cross Guns Inn** Rockwell Lane Pant SY10 9QR (01691 839631). Friendly establishment serving real ale and food *daily 12.00-20.00.* Child- and dog-friendly, garden. Traditional pub games, real fires and Wi-Fi. *Open 12.00-23.00.*

● ✗ 5 **The Cross Keys Hotel** North Road, Llanymynech SY22 6EA (01691 831585; www.crosskeyshotel.info). Impressively constructed from limestone blocks, this pub serves real ale. Dog- and family-friendly *(until 21.00).* Traditional pub games, *occasional* live music, real fires, sports TV and Wi-Fi. B&B. *Open Mon-Fri 15.00-22.00 (Fri 00.00) & Sat-Sun 12.00-00.00..*

● ✗ 6 **The Dolphin Inn** Carregoffa Cottages, Llanymynech SY22 6ER (01691 839672; www.thedolphininn.co.uk). Reached by crossing the stile past bridge 92 and walking through the car park to the street. Friendly and sociable pub serving real ale and food *L and E.* Dog- and family-friendly, garden. Newspapers, real fires, sports TV and Wi-Fi. B&B. *Open Tue-Wed L and E; Thu L and E; Fri-Sat 12.00-23.00 & Sun 12.00-18.00.*

● ✗ 7 **The Bradford Arms Hotel & Restaurant** The Street, Llanymynech SY22 6EJ (01691 930582). Comfortable hotel with luxury accommodation and well-priced, innovative food, all prepared on the premises, *L and E.* Real ale. Dogs welcome, garden. Traditional pub games, real fires and Wi-Fi. B&B. *Open daily L and E.*

The two locks at Carreghofa, in a beautiful setting, continue the descent, while the line of the old Tanat feeder, which used to join the canal between the locks, can still be seen to the west of the road bridge. The lock cottage here is inhabited. The toll house, built in 1825, has also been restored by volunteers and this makes a good resting place for walkers of the towpath and of Offa's Dyke, which follows the canal to the east here, after crossing at Llanymynech. South of the Vyrnwy Aqueduct a wooden crane stands beside a sturdy stone wharf building; the canal follows the course of the hills to the west, often running through woods in an embanked side-cutting. It then continues south through rolling countryside on the western side of the Severn and dominated by hills to the west. Before the two pretty Burgedin Locks lower the canal further, the disused Guilsfield Arm can be seen running away to the west. From the locks there are superb views of the Breidden Hills to the east, and the Long Mountain, which reaches a height of 1338ft. Henry Tudor camped here in 1485, gathering strength for his battle against Richard III at Bosworth, in which Henry was victorious and took the English throne.

● **Vyrnwy Aqueduct**
Opened in 1796, the stone aqueduct across the river Vyrnwy is one of the canal's original features. Its building was fraught with problems; one arch collapsed during construction, and after completion subsidence distorted the whole structure, necessitating the addition of iron braces in 1823. The distortion also caused continual leakage problems; in 1971 repairs were undertaken to try yet again to stop the leaks, and further restoration has subsequently been carried out. To the north a long embankment precedes the aqueduct, partly of earth and partly of brick arches, which makes it altogether a much longer structure than it appears at first sight.

● **Offa's Dyke**
Offa's Dyke, which runs from Chepstow to Prestatyn, passes near the canal at several points in the area. Although the dyke is at times only fragmentary, its 168-mile course has been designated a long-distance public footpath. The dyke was constructed by Offa,

King of Mercia, between AD750 and AD800 to mark the boundary of Wales. The impressive structure consisted of a long mound of earth with a ditch on one side, though in parts it is hardly recognisable as such.

● **Four Crosses**
Powys. Stores, takeaway, garage. Once a busy main road village, now returned to its past slumbers with the construction of a bypass. The mix of old and new housing is built around Offa's Dyke. *The stores are in the garage and are open 07.00-23.00 daily.*

● **Guilsfield Arm**
This 2-mile arm runs close to the village of Guilsfield and is reached by crossing the road just before bridge 104. It is now a nature reserve, providing a haven for wildlife.

● **Arddleen**
Powys. PO box, tel. A small settlement to the west of the canal – known also as Arddleen – marks a significant obstacle in full restoration of the canal.

CANOEING AND PADDLEBOARDING
From a canoeist and paddleboarder's perspective, www.kanoroutes.nl/e-montgomery.htm gives a very good overview of the Montgomery Canal and helps the paddler to understand the current, fragmented restoration of this attractive rural waterway. 'Joining the dots' is the objective of the very active Shropshire Union Canal Society and this absorbs countless volunteer hours. Wildlife thrives along the navigation and it is one of the most important canals in the country for nature. Much of it is a Site of Special Scientific Interest (SSSI) and the Welsh section is of international importance, designated a Special Area of Conservation for its aquatic plants. One of several SSSIs around our waterways, the 'Monty' as the canal is colloquially known, is the best location in the world for floating water plantain. Otters and water voles are regularly spotted along its length and paddling is the best way of ensuring a sighting. Several nature reserves border the navigation, filled with wild flowers and insects, including dragonflies and damselflies. New canoe launch pads are being installed by locks and road crossings. Small craft can also be launched from the slipway at Welshpool Wharf.
Details of launch points and the availability of parking can be found at www.canalrivertrust.org.uk/refresh/media/thumbnail/24049-slipways-on-montgomery-canal.pdf.

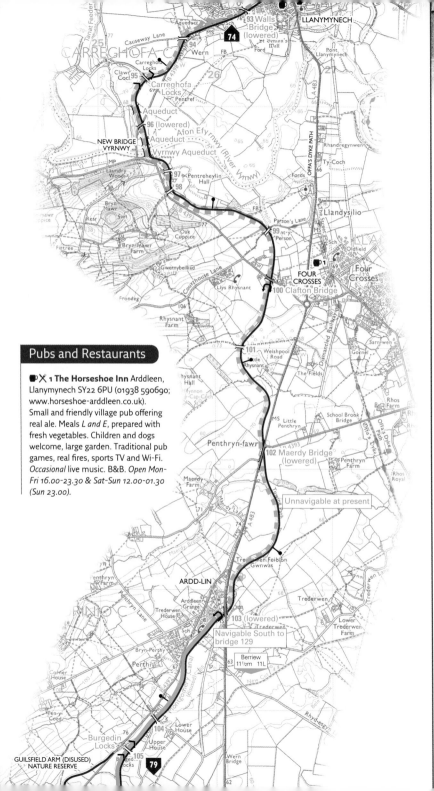

Pubs and Restaurants

📷✗ 1 **The Horseshoe Inn** Arddleen,
Llanymynech SY22 6PU (01938 590690;
www.horseshoe-arddleen.co.uk).
Small and friendly village pub offering
real ale. Meals *L and E*, prepared with
fresh vegetables. Children and dogs
welcome, large garden. Traditional pub
games, real fires, sports TV and Wi-Fi.
Occasional live music. B&B. *Open Mon-
Fri 16.00-23.30 & Sat-Sun 12.00-01.30
(Sun 23.00).*

Unnavigable at present

Navigable South to
bridge 129

Berriew
11½m   11L

Pool Quay

Continuing south the canal clings to the steep hills to the west of the Severn Valley, often in a wooded side-cutting. There is a *car park and picnic tables* at bridge 106. Four locks around the Pool Quay area and one in the centre of Welshpool begin the canal's rise towards Newtown. The stretch of canal between Pool Quay and Welshpool is known as the Prince of Wales length, restored by the Prince of Wales Trust and the Shropshire Union Canal Society. There are many reminders of the industrial history of the canal along here, especially at Pool Quay, once the highest navigable point on the Severn, and later a transhipment point between river and canal. The footprint of the Wern corn mill remains, and the clay pit is now a nature reserve. Between the lock south of bridge 111 and Abbey Bridge (112) Offa's Dyke long-distance footpath follows the towpath. There is a cast iron milepost half-way along this stretch, similar to the one south of bridge 110. These were placed by the Montgomery Waterway Restoration Trust in 1983 and 1984 respectively. Before Welshpool there are two draw bridges, Abbey Bridge (112) and Moors Farm Bridge (114).

The Wern
At the Red Bridge (106) there is parking and a picnic site. The water from the lock overflow and bypass weir once powered the corn mill here, an ingenious use of the otherwise wasted 25,000 gallons of water released each time the lock operated. The sump level (or bottom level) of the canal is at The Wern, and this meant that the water-powered mill was in an excellent position for receiving the surplus water. Only the foundations of the mill remain with a small pool and sluice visible. The information boards here show what the mill would have looked like. Today the overflow weir provides water for the small but pleasant nature reserve created on the site of The Wern clay pits. This was the major source of puddling clay used to line the canal.

Pool Quay
Powys. Tel. This was a former river port at the limit of viable merchant transport up the River Severn from Bristol. Travelling northwards toward Welshpool the white-washed lock keeper's house, dating from 1820, is one of several interesting buildings here. Further along are the relics of buildings serving the grinding mills and maltings that were based in the village. The Powis Arms pub is well worth visiting – the beam in the bar was marked by navigators stranded here when the River Severn was in drought. An 18th-C red-brick warehouse once stood nearby, now replaced with new houses. Across the road is a now overgrown area beside the river, once known as Swan Wharf. This was a transhipment point where, amongst many other goods, fine oaks, for which the area was once famous, were stored prior to being loaded for carriage downstream to the naval dockyards at Bristol.

Buttington
Powys. 1/2 mile east of bridge 115. The church is a medieval building, restored in 1876. The village has twice suffered from attempted invasions – in AD894 by the Danish army which was evicted from here by King Alfred the Great, and in 1916 by a presumptuous German Zeppelin, whose crew mistakenly believed that the Welsh would offer less resistance than the English. Today the only air traffic floating overhead are the hot air balloons that regularly pass this area at sunset from Oswestry.
Buttington Wharf Just to the north of Buttington Bridge (115). A former kiln-bank, now a picnic site. The charging holes of the three kilns are still visible. There are good *moorings* here.

Breidden Hills
East of Buttington are the three impressive peaks of the Breidden Hills which dominate the flat landscape of the Shropshire Plain. The Breidden Crag (1324ft), increasingly defaced by quarrying, is best climbed from Criggion. An 18th-C pillar on the summit commemorates Admiral Rodney, who defeated a French fleet off Cape St Vincent, Dominica, in 1782. The excellent view from the summit across the Shropshire Plain highlights the meandering nature of the River Severn, particularly around the village of Melverley, which is constantly under threat of flood waters.

WALKING AND CYCLING
There are circular walks from Red Bridge (106) around the nature reserve at The Wern clay pits, which was created in 1987. Offa's Dyke long-distance footpath, which stretches 180 miles between Chepstow and Prestatyn, follows the towpath between bridges 111 and 112. If you follow the lane west from Bank Lock, then turn left across country at Coppice East Farm, you will return to the canal at Abbey Lift Bridge. You can complete the circuit along the towpath, stopping for a pint at the Powis Arms (The Quay).

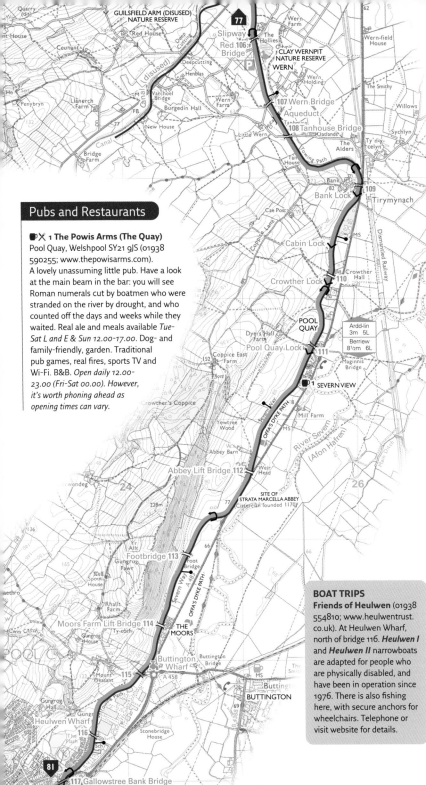

Pubs and Restaurants

⛴✕ 1 The Powis Arms (The Quay)
Pool Quay, Welshpool SY21 9JS (01938
590255; www.thepowisarms.com).
A lovely unassuming little pub. Have a look
at the main beam in the bar: you will see
Roman numerals cut by boatmen who were
stranded on the river by drought, and who
counted off the days and weeks while they
waited. Real ale and meals available *Tue-
Sat L and E & Sun 12.00-17.00*. Dog- and
family-friendly, garden. Traditional
pub games, real fires, sports TV and
Wi-Fi. B&B. *Open daily 12.00-
23.00 (Fri-Sat 00.00). However,
it's worth phoning ahead as
opening times can vary.*

BOAT TRIPS

Friends of Heulwen (01938
554810; www.heulwentrust.
co.uk). At Heulwen Wharf,
north of bridge 116. *Heulwen I*
and *Heulwen II* narrowboats
are adapted for people who
are physically disabled, and
have been in operation since
1976. There is also fishing
here, with secure anchors for
wheelchairs. Telephone or
visit website for details.

Welshpool

As you enter Welshpool, there are few remains which give a hint of the importance of the canal to the town, for there were once limekilns, dry docks and wharfs, a gas works and factories. The metal bridge, 118, was built to carry the Welshpool & Llanfair Light Railway on its way through the town. Note the old Canal Agent's office by the museum – often the door is open and you can speak to the man at the desk. The town is a useful stop for boaters, with *moorings* and typical town centre facilities. By the side of the lock is a waterwheel pit and the last remains of the wheel bearings – unusually this canal usually had surplus water, which could be used to power mills. The canal runs at the foot of the landscaped grounds of Powis Castle, flanked by the A483, and then dives under the new Whitehouse Bridge, edging away from the River Severn for a few miles. Four locks continue the rise towards Newtown, the two at Belan *(picnic site, parking and interpretation)* recently restored, and then two singles north of Berriew. The stretch towards Brithdir is an excellent area for bird watchers, with sightings of a broad range of species from kingfishers to herons and, high in the sky, buzzards, which can be seen circling the hilltops. At Brithdir there is a nature reserve adjacent to the lock. Beyond this, the antiquated Luggy Aqueduct carries the canal towards Berriew.

● **Welshpool**

Powys. All services. The canal runs through the east of the town, passing attractive gardens and a traditional wharf and warehouse c.1880, now housing a museum *(see below)*. There are excellent moorings here with three jetties and a slipway, south of bridge 118. The town stretches away to the west – look out for the restored octagonal cockpit just off the main street, thought to be the only one in Wales which survives on its original site.

Powysland Museum and Montgomery Canal Centre The Canal Wharf, Welshpool, SY21 7AQ (01938 553001; en.powys.gov.uk/article/8562/Y-Lanfa-Powysland-Museum). Illustrates the archaeology, history and literature of the local area, and includes a canal exhibition and a display featuring the Montgomeryshire Yeomanry cavalry. *Open Mon-Sat 09.30. Closing times vary so telephone for details.* Charge.

Powis Castle *NT.* Access from High Street, Welshpool SY21 8RF (information line 01938 551944; www.nationaltrust.org.uk). The seat of the Earl of Powis, this impressive building has been continuously inhabited for over 500 years. It is a restored medieval castle with late 16th-C plasterwork and panelling, and has on display fine paintings, tapestries, early Georgian furniture and relics of Clive of India. The castle is in the centre of beautiful 18th-C terraced gardens and a park. Programme of events, fine plant shop, excellent tearooms. Castle, gardens and museum *open daily throughout the year but times vary* so telephone or check the website for details. Charge.

The Flash Leisure Centre Salop Road, Welshpool SY21 7DH (01938 555952; www.freedom-leisure. co.uk/centres/flash-leisure-centre). Swimming pool with a flume, bowls hall, fitness suite, sauna and sports hall. Café. *Open daily 06.15-21.45 (Sat-Sun 15.45).* Charge.

Tourist Information Centre 1 Vicarage Gardens, Church Street, Welshpool SY21 7DD (01938 552043; www.visitwelshpool.org.uk/welshpool-in-bloom). *Open Mon-Sat 09.30-16.30 & Sun 10.00-16.00.*

● **Welshpool & Llanfair Light Railway**

The Station, Llanfair Caereinion, Welshpool SY21 0SF (01938 810441; www.wllr.org.uk). This delightful narrow-gauge railway originally opened in 1903, and is now restored and run by enthusiasts. Telephone or visit website for timetable. *Open Tue-Sun 09.30-17.00.*

● **Brithdir**

Powys. A small main road settlement on the busy A483 with an isolated pub and scattered houses and farms. To the south is the Luggy Aqueduct, a small iron trough carrying the canal over the fast-flowing Luggy Brook, built in 1819 by George Buck, who was also responsible for the distinctive paddle gear found at the majority of locks.

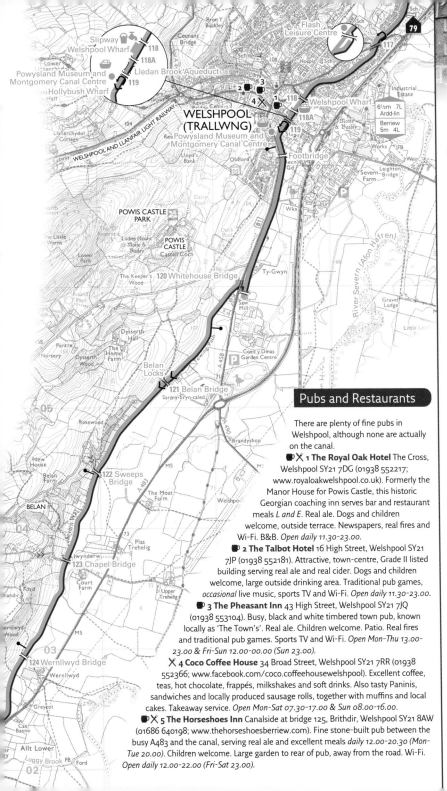

Pubs and Restaurants

There are plenty of fine pubs in Welshpool, although none are actually on the canal.

1 The Royal Oak Hotel The Cross, Welshpool SY21 7DG (01938 552217; www.royaloakwelshpool.co.uk). Formerly the Manor House for Powis Castle, this historic Georgian coaching inn serves bar and restaurant meals *L and E*. Real ale. Dogs and children welcome, outside terrace. Newspapers, real fires and Wi-Fi. B&B. *Open daily 11.30–23.00.*

2 The Talbot Hotel 16 High Street, Welshpool SY21 7JP (01938 552181). Attractive, town-centre, Grade II listed building serving real ale and real cider. Dogs and children welcome, large outside drinking area. Traditional pub games, *occasional* live music, sports TV and Wi-Fi. *Open daily 11.30–23.00.*

3 The Pheasant Inn 43 High Street, Welshpool SY21 7JQ (01938 553104). Busy, black and white timbered town pub, known locally as 'The Town's'. Real ale. Children welcome. Patio. Real fires and traditional pub games. Sports TV and Wi-Fi. *Open Mon-Thu 13.00–23.00 & Fri-Sun 12.00–00.00 (Sun 23.00).*

4 Coco Coffee House 34 Broad Street, Welshpool SY21 7RR (01938 552366; www.facebook.com/coco.coffeehousewelshpool). Excellent coffee, teas, hot chocolate, frappés, milkshakes and soft drinks. Also tasty Paninis, sandwiches and locally produced sausage rolls, together with muffins and local cakes. Takeaway service. *Open Mon-Sat 07.30–17.00 & Sun 08.00–16.00.*

5 The Horseshoes Inn Canalside at bridge 125, Brithdir, Welshpool SY21 8AW (01686 640198; www.thehorseshoesberriew.com). Fine stone-built pub between the busy A483 and the canal, serving real ale and excellent meals *daily 12.00–20.30 (Mon-Tue 20.00)*. Children welcome. Large garden to rear of pub, away from the road. Wi-Fi. *Open daily 12.00–22.00 (Fri-Sat 23.00).*

Berriew

Continuing south west the canal passes Berriew, crossing the attractive River Rhiw on a fine aqueduct (*where there are toilets, picnic tables, parking and an interpretation board*) and then swings back towards the River Severn, as the valley is narrowed by the hills sweeping in from the east. The A483 follows the canal very closely. However, there are some fine glimpses of the River Severn between the trees to the east and the rolling hillsides to the west, all covered with broad-leaved woodland. Two locks, at Berriew and Brynderwyn, continue the rise towards Newtown, lifting the canal above the level of the Severn, whose waters flow swiftly alongside from Tan-y-fron to Newtown. The two lock keeper's cottages are fine white-washed houses and at Brynderwyn, a former coal wharf, there is a late 19th-C warehouse still standing. Just past bridge 135 there is a llama paddock, at the base of the wooded hills to the east of the canal, looking decidedly out of place in the more traditional farmscape. It is part of Penllwyn Holiday Lodges, where a lake has been created, adjoining the cut. Several of the bridges beyond Tan-y-fron have their dates of construction cast into them: Glanhafren Bridge (143) was built in 1889 and is comparatively ornate with cast iron balustrades, and bridge 147 has elegant white iron railings displaying the date 1853 and Brymbo. Bridge 142 is one of the few remaining swing bridges on the canal.

Berriew

Powys. PO, tel, stores. butcher. The village of Berriew lies to the west, climbing the steep slopes of the fast-flowing river which cascades over rocks beneath the houses. In the centre of the village is a handsome 18th-C single-span stone arch across the river; the black and white painted timber-framed and stone houses are ranged on either side. The village is very picturesque, with a unity of style, and has been voted the Best Kept Village in Wales numerous times; but this has not spoilt it, for it is still quiet, pretty and self-contained. The church – a Victorian restoration of a medieval building, dedicated to St Bueno (who miraculously brought St Winifred back to life: *see* St Winifred's Well in the Llanymynech section) – is the centre point of the village, set attractively amongst trees. The vicarage is dated 1616. A two-arched brick aqueduct carries the canal over the beautiful wooded valley of the River Rhiw. Originally built of stone, the aqueduct was reconstructed in 1889 and although it appeared quite sound when the navigation was closed, the canal was piped across it, because of leakage, before the latest renovation work.

Andrew Logan Museum of Sculpture Berriew, Welshpool SY21 8AH (01686 640689; www. andrewloganmuseum.org). Next to the Talbot Hotel by the river Rhiw. Works of popular poetry and metropolitan glamour by the founder, in 1972, of the Alternative Miss World Contest. Inspired by the excesses of Busby Berkeley, his works are wild, bizarre and exciting, and not at all what you would expect in this village. An enlivening and enriching experience? – George Melly called it 'Fabergé for the Millennium' – you will either love it or hate it. Café and extraordinary gift shop. *Open May-Oct 10.00-13.00 (Sat-Sun 16.00) and some weekends during the rest of the year* – telephone for details and to arrange a private visit. Charge.

Garthmyl

Powys. Tel. An old village beside the canal. The original wharf buildings can still be identified, looking rather incongruous as the wharf has long vanished. The concentration of remains, such as kiln banks, warehouses and a maltings, is probably due to the fact that the canal terminated here until the extension of the navigation between 1815 and 1821.

THE QUAY TO THE MARCHES

Prior to the building of the Montgomery Canal, the River Severn was a natural artery for trade, navigated above Shrewsbury as far as Pool Quay. Of course such river transport was unreliable, and low water levels would result in long delays. The beams in the Powis Arms (The Quay) were marked for each day the boatmen were stranded for lack of water. It was from Swan Wharf, opposite the pub, that Montgomeryshire oak was shipped downstream to the naval dockyards at Bristol. In 1712 the *Duchess*, owned by George Bradley, was transporting 40-ton loads to Bristol and back. Until the Montgomery & Ellesmere Canal linked with the main inland waterways network in 1833, Pool Quay remained an important transhipment point.

WALKING AND CYCLING

There is an excellent walk from the aqueduct into the village of Berriew. Turn left and left again at The Talbot, then right by Faenor Isaf. Follow the path over stiles and through gates to emerge at a road. Turn left to reach the canal, where you turn left again to return to the aqueduct.

CANOEING AND PADDLEBOARDING

The part-derelict section of canal from Aberbechan, north to Welshpool, is covered at www.ukriversguidebook.co.uk/rivers/wales/north/montgomery-canal-aberbechan-to-welshpool while the shorter paddle, from Aberbechan to Berriew, is described at www.canoedaysout.com/trip/1019. The southern section is the last section scheduled for restoration and south of Garthmyl there are lowered road crossings to be portaged alongside more natural obstacles. This is a challenging stretch of the 'Monty' for the paddler and most can be seen from the main A483 road, giving the opportunity to opt out in favour of the attractive, restored waterway between Garthmyl and Ardd-Lin.

Pubs and Restaurants

1 The Lion Hotel Berriew, Welshpool SY21 8PQ (01686 640452; www.lionhotel-berriew.co.uk). In the centre of the village by the church. Superb 17th-C traditional black and white painted country hotel, which retains original wattle and daub wall panels in the lounge. Real ale. Home-made food served L and E Tue-Sun (not Sun E). Dog-and child-friendly, patio. Real fires and Wi-Fi. B&B. *Open Tue-Sun 12.00-23.00.*

2 The Talbot Inn Berriew, Welshpool SY21 8PJ (01686 640881; www.talbot-hotel.com). Black and white timber-framed pub, close to the aqueduct, serving real ales and food Tue-Sun L and E. Dog- and child-friendly, garden. Traditional pub games and Wi-Fi. B&B. *Open 12.00-00.00 (Mon 16.30).*

3 Lychgate Cottage Tearoom & Delicatessen Berriew SY21 8PG (01686 640750/07989 302563). Using locally sourced ingredients wherever possible, this delightful establishment offers light lunches, snacks, savoury pasties, soup, baguettes and sandwiches, homemade cakes, sweets and puddings. Takeaway service. *Open Tue-Sat 09.00-16.30 (Sat & winter 16.00).*

4 The Upper Rectory Restaurant Berriew SY21 8AN (01686 640930; www.upperrectory.co.uk). This restaurant offers a unique experience in superb French-influenced cuisine, focusing on locally sourced, fresh, seasonal produce. During the summer months most of the vegetables, herbs & salads are picked from their own garden. They also use their own free range eggs and chickens. B&B and a shepherds hut situated in an adjacent meadow. *Open Fri-Sun 19.00-23.30.*

Newtown

The canal continues south west towards Newtown along the wooded west side of the Severn valley. Canal and river flow side by side, the river providing the water for the canal via a feeder at Penarth and at one time by a pumping station at Newtown. Five single locks raise the canal to its summit level just outside the town. Aberbechan aqueduct is triple-arched and spans Bechan Brook, where there are the remains of a corn mill and maltings, hidden between the trees. Bridge 153 south of the aqueduct has the place and date of construction – Brymbo 1862 – cast into it. The canal is dry south of Freestone Lock and the course ends short of its original terminus. The once busy basin and the last half mile or so have vanished under housing, although street names recall what was once there. The entry to Newtown must now be made on foot – it is a pleasant walk.

● **Abermule**
Powys. PO (part time) stores, off-licence. The best feature of the village is the iron bridge carrying the road jointly over the canal and the River Severn. After a plain girder bridge across the canal it develops into a beautiful elegant single-span arch leaping across the river. Into the curve of the arch are cast the words 'This second iron bridge constructed in the county of Montgomeryshire 1852'. By the stores there is a water pump and the mobile post office *opens Mon 14.30-15.30 & Thu 09.00-10.00.*

Pwll Penarth Newtown, Powys SY16 3BA (01938 555654; www.montwt.co.uk/nature-reserves/pwll-penarth). Once the settling beds for a sewage farm, this is now a Montgomeryshire Wildlife Trust haven for wildlife, where you may see grey wagtails, kingfishers, skylarks and lapwings, along with otters. In the autumn salmon can be seen jumping the fish pass. Access directly from the towpath near Freestone Lock.

● **Newtown**
Powys. All services. Built around the Severn which sweeps through the town in a gentle curve. Prosperous as a woollen manufacturing town from the 18th C; the industry has now ceased. Its growth in the early 19th C prompted the building of the canal as a means of supplying coal and raw materials.

CANOEING AND PADDLEBOARDING
Canadian canoes or 'sit-on' open top kayaks can be hired from Kingfisher Kayak & Canoe Hire Glan Hafren Hall, Abermule, Newtown SY15 6NA (07474 562669/547769; www.kingfisherkayakhire.com) for use on both the canal and the River Severn, *available Mar-Oct.* They will collect you for free, from a designated pick up spot, and return you to your car. Bookings by phone or email: info@kingfisherkayakhire.com.

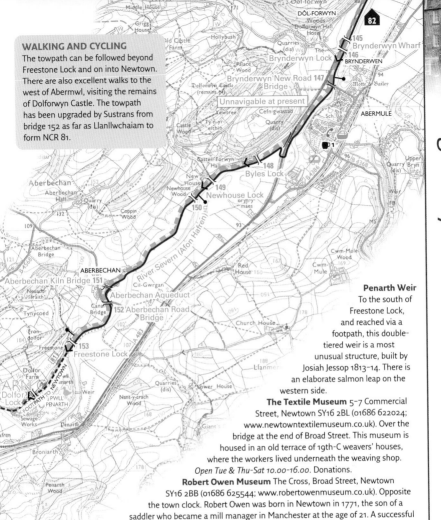

WALKING AND CYCLING
The towpath can be followed beyond Freestone Lock and on into Newtown. There are also excellent walks to the west of Abermwl, visiting the remains of Dolforwyn Castle. The towpath has been upgraded by Sustrans from bridge 152 as far as Llanllwchaiam to form NCR 81.

Penarth Weir
To the south of Freestone Lock, and reached via a footpath, this double-tiered weir is a most unusual structure, built by Josiah Jessop 1813–14. There is an elaborate salmon leap on the western side.

The Textile Museum 5–7 Commercial Street, Newtown SY16 2BL (01686 622024; www.newtowntextilemuseum.co.uk). Over the bridge at the end of Broad Street. This museum is housed in an old terrace of 19th-C weavers' houses, where the workers lived underneath the weaving shop. *Open Tue & Thu-Sat 10.00–16.00. Donations.*

Robert Owen Museum The Cross, Broad Street, Newtown SY16 2BB (01686 625544; www.robertowenmuseum.co.uk). Opposite the town clock. Robert Owen was born in Newtown in 1771, the son of a saddler who became a mill manager in Manchester at the age of 21. A successful capitalist, he was an advocate of co-operative ideas. As a result of his writing, many became socialists and set up co-operative ventures. One of these, the Rochdale Pioneers, was the precursor of today's Co-operative Movement. *Open Mon-Fri 11.00–15.00 & Sat (Jul-Aug only) 11.00–15.00. Other times on request. Free.*

W. H. Smith High Street, Newtown SY16 2NP (01686 626280). All you would expect, housed in a fine recreation of the early shop, with a small museum upstairs.

Tourist Information Centre The Cross, Broad Street, Newtown SY16 2BB (01686 610066; www.newtown.org.uk/news/view/tourist-information-centre-newtown). *Open Mon-Fri 11.00–15.00.*

Pubs and Restaurants

Access to Abermule village is via Brynderwyn Bridge (147) and follow the road, turning right at the roundabout, for about ½ mile.

◆✕ **1 The Abermule Inn** Abermule SY15 6ND (01686 639110). Real ale and an interesting menu is served, much of it based around the meat from a local Wagyu herd of Kobe beef: cattle of Japanese origin that are fed a daily helping of the pub's beer, together with a rice wine massage. Food available *Mon-Thu E & Fri-Sun L and E.* Family-friendly, garden and patio. Traditional pub games, newspapers, real fires, sports TV and Wi-Fi. Caravanning and camping. *Open Mon-Thu 16.00–23.30 & Fri-Sun 12.00–23.30.*

There are plenty of pubs and hotels in Newtown.

Montgomery Canal Newtown

SHROPSHIRE UNION CANAL

MAXIMUM DIMENSIONS

Autherley to Nantwich, and Middlewich Branch
Length: 72'
Beam: 7'
Headroom: 8'

Nantwich to Ellesmere Port
Length: 72'
Beam: 9'
Headroom: 8'

MANAGER

0303 040 4040
enquiries.westmidlands@canalrivertrust.org.uk

Canoeing and Paddleboarding: Category 1

MILEAGE

AUTHERLEY JUNCTION (Staffordshire & Worcestershire Canal) to:
Norbury: 15½ miles
Market Drayton: 27 miles

HURLESTON JUNCTION (Llangollen Canal): 40¾ miles
Barbridge Junction (Middlewich Branch): 42 miles
Chester Junction with Dee Branch: 58 miles

ELLESMERE PORT JUNCTION with Manchester Ship Canal: 66½ miles
Locks: 47

Middlewich Branch
Middlewich (Trent & Mersey Canal) to:
Barbridge Junction: 10 miles
Locks: 4

THE CHESTER CANAL

In 1772 an enabling Act was passed for a canal from the River Dee in Chester to join the Trent & Mersey Canal at Middlewich, with a spur to Nantwich. The building of the Trent & Mersey was the cause of this new venture, for it was seen as a threat to the future of the River Dee Navigation and the port of Chester. The new canal was designed to bolster Chester as an alternative port to Liverpool, and so was planned as a barge canal, with locks 80ft by 14ft 9in. Work started in Chester in the middle of 1772 and progressed slowly. There were engineering and financial problems, and the main line of the new canal was altered to terminate at a basin and warehouses just outside Nantwich: the proposed line to Middlewich was now to be a branch. The Nantwich–Chester link was completed in 1779, but the spur to Middlewich was not built until 54 years later. When the Nantwich–Chester Canal was finished, arguments with the Dee River Company delayed the building of the river lock. By this time competition with the Trent & Mersey was out of the question. Although regular freight and fast passenger services were run, the canal was wholly uneconomic and in 1787 the company collapsed. In 1790 it was revived and the canal repaired, for the directors saw the publication of the plans of the Ellesmere Canal as their last chance to complete the line to Middlewich.

THE BIRMINGHAM & LIVERPOOL JUNCTION CANAL

The future prosperity of the Ellesmere & Chester was limited by the lack of an outlet to the south, without which its trade could never be more than local. So the company was much cheered by the plans for the Birmingham & Liverpool Junction Canal which received its Act in 1825. The line from Nantwich to Autherley, on the Staffordshire & Worcestershire Canal, would give a direct link between Liverpool and the Midlands, and thus with the canal network as a whole. After serious engineering difficulties the canal was opened in 1835, shortly after the opening of the long-planned branch from the Chester Canal to the

Trent & Mersey at Middlewich, providing access to Manchester and the Potteries. Railway competition was close at hand by this date, and so the Birmingham & Liverpool Junction and Ellesmere & Chester companies worked closely together to preserve their profits. Ellesmere Port was greatly enlarged, and by 1840 steam haulage was in use on the Wirral line and on the Mersey itself. In 1845 the two companies merged, and then shortly after were reformed as the Shropshire Union Railways & Canal Company.

THE SHROPSHIRE UNION CANAL

The Shropshire Union Railways & Canal Company was formed under the shadow of railway expansion. Its initial plans were to build railways instead of canals, on the principle that it would halve the construction costs to lay a railway along the bed of an existing canal. By 1849 this plan had been abandoned, for the slow development of railways in Wales had shown the company that canals could still be profitable. Throughout the mid 19th C the Shropshire Union network remained profitable, and did not experience the steady decline of other major canal systems. The London & North Western Railway Company was a major shareholder in the Shropshire Union, and they were happy to let the canals remain as they provided the company with a significant tentacle into Great Western Railway territory. As a result the Shropshire Union was allowed to expand steadily; in 1870 the company owned 213 narrowboats, and in 1889 there were 395. By 1902 this fleet had increased to 450 boats. A few branches were threatened with closure on the grounds of unprofitability, but all remained open. The flourishing trade continued until World War I, which started a pattern of regular heavy losses from which the company was never able to recover. In 1921 the company gave up canal carrying, and sold most of its fleet of boats to private operators. Locks were closed at weekends, and standards of maintenance began to slip. In 1922 the Shropshire Union Company was bought out by the London & North Western Railway, which then was swallowed in turn by the newly-formed London Midland & Scottish Railway. Despite these changes the network remained open, although trade declined rapidly. Many traders were driven away by the lack of maintenance, which meant that most boats could only operate half empty. In 1936 a breach occurred on the Montgomery Canal one mile south of Frankton Junction; the company set out to repair the damage and then changed its mind. (The Weston line had been similarly abandoned after a breach in 1917.) With trade at a standstill there were no complaints, and in 1944 an Act was passed making closure official. This Act also officially abandoned 175 miles of the old Shropshire Union network. Out of this mass closure only the main line and the Middlewich Branch remained, although the Llangollen Branch (*see* page 23) luckily also escaped closure, being originally retained as a water supply channel. The Montgomery Canal also survives and is now the subject of an exciting restoration project (*see* page 71).

MEETING ONESELF COMING BACK

When first constructed the Shroppie relied very heavily on Belvide Reservoir – beside the A5 – for its supplies of water. In its original form the reservoir proved woefully inadequate and its capacity was doubled in 1836 to give a total of 70 million cubic metres of water. Thirty-four years later Barnhurst Sewerage Farm opened at Autherley Junction and, when it later became a treatment works, its entire discharge became available to feed both the Shroppie and the Staffs & Worcs Canal. Today there is rarely a problem of water shortage on the Shroppie, which can largely be attributed to the regular habits of the good people of Wolverhampton.

Autherley Junction

The Shropshire Union Canal leaves the Staffordshire & Worcestershire Canal at Autherley Junction, and runs straight along the side of the former Wolverhampton Aerodrome at Pendeford, now covered with houses. Passing the Wolverhampton Boat Club (visiting boaters welcome), the canal soon enters a short cutting, which is through rock and narrow in places. This is a barren area for pubs and thirsty boaters and walkers, not intending to visit the boat club, are best advised to make for Brewood to quench their thirst. Emerging briefly into the green and quiet countryside that is found along the whole length of this navigation, the canal (having shrugged off the noisy intrusion of the M54 motorway) again plunges into a deep, long cutting that is typical of this particular stretch. The start of this length is beautifully framed by the arch of bridge 8, beguiling the boater into a tree-lined avenue.

NAVIGATIONAL NOTES

The canal is very narrow south of bridges 5 and 6, and between bridges 8 and 9.

● **Autherley Junction**
An important and busy canal junction, where in 1830 Thomas Telford brought his Birmingham & Liverpool Junction Canal (now part of the Shropshire Union system) to join the much older Staffordshire & Worcestershire Canal (built by James Brindley and opened in 1772). There is a former canal toll office here, also a boatyard and a boatclub. The stop lock has a fall of only about 6in: it was insisted upon by the Staffordshire & Worcestershire Company to prevent the newer canal stealing water from them. Autherley Junction is sometimes confused with Aldersley Junction, 1/2 mile to the south, where the Birmingham Canal Navigations join the Staffordshire & Worcestershire Canal from the east after falling through the Wolverhampton flight of 21 locks.

WALKING AND CYCLING
The Shropshire Union Canal offers a delightfully rural cycling and walking corridor from Wolverhampton all the way to the Mersey Estuary. Apart from the historic city of Chester, there is virtually no urban intrusion and little impact from industry or trunk roads and motorways. There is good disabled access to the towpath off Wobaston road, to the north of Bridge 4 and in Wheaton Aston at Bridge 19.

Boatyards

Ⓑ**Napton Narrowboats** Autherley Junction, Oxley Moor Road, Wolverhampton WV9 5HW (01902 789942; www.napton-marina.co.uk/bases/autherley/index.php). 🛁🪣D Pump out, gas, narrowboat hire, overnight mooring, short term mooring, slipway, limited chandlery, provisions, books and maps, boat repairs, solid fuel, gifts. *Emergency call out-24hr. Open daily 09.00-17.00.*

Ⓑ**Oxley Marine** The Wharf, Oxley Moor Road, Wolverhampton WV10 6TZ (01902 789522; www. oxleymarine.co.uk). 🛁 D Pump out, gas, overnight and long-term mooring, winter storage, slipway, boat and engine sales and repairs, DIY facilities, *emergency call out.* 🍺 1 Licensed bar *open daily 19.00-23.00.* Snacks.

CANOEING AND PADDLEBOARDING
As always, the Go Paddling website presents an excellent overview of the waterway from the canoeist and paddleboarders' perspective – www.gopaddling.info/canals/shropshire-union-canal – majoring on the remoteness and associated tranquillity of this canal. For those that find paddling a thirsty occupation, waterside pubs crop up with reliable regularity, many offering good food and somewhere to camp. For a detailed overview of paddling opportunities, Canal & River Trust's planning site is a useful tool: www.canalrivertrust.org.uk/local-to-you while a selection of suitable launch and recovery sites are detailed at www.canalrivertrust.org.uk/media/original/24055-slipways-on-shropshire-union-canal.pdf.

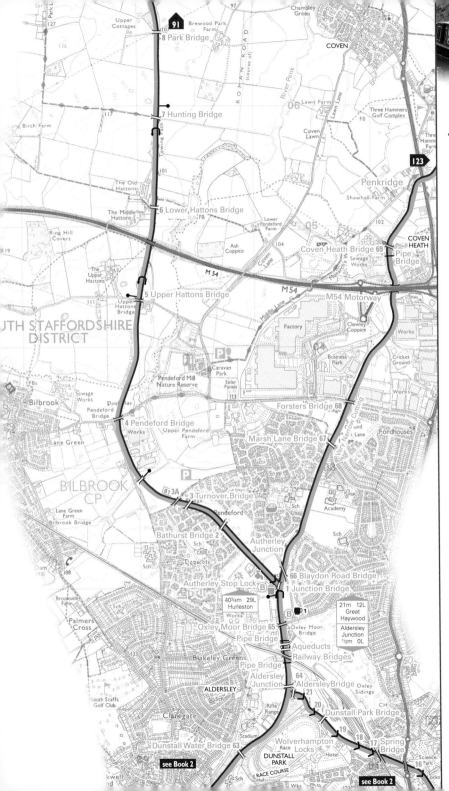

Upper
Cottages

127

136

Upper
Cottages

107

91
8 Park Bridge

Brewood Park
Farm
(course of)

97

Chambley
Green

COVEN

ROMAN ROAD

River Penk

Lawn Farm

Lawn Lane

Three Hammers
Golf Complex

FB

117

7 Hunting Bridge

Long Birch Farm

Towing Path

Coven
Lawn

06

Three
Hamm

123

101

Penkridge

Shawhall Farm

The Old
Hattons

The Middle
Hattons

6 Lower Hattons Bridge

FB

Lower
Pendeford
Farm

05

COVEN
HEATH

Ring Hill
Covert

119

M 54

Ash
Coppice

Coven
Lane

104

102

Coven Heath Bridge 69
Pipe
Bridge

Sewage
Works

The
Upper
Hattons

Upper
Hatton's
Bridge

5 Upper Hattons Bridge

111

M 54

Middle Lane

M 54

M54 Motorway

Clewley
Coppice

Works

UTH STAFFORDSHIRE
DISTRICT

Factory

Business
Park

Cricket
Ground

Bilbrook

FBs

Sewage
Works

Don Bay

Pendeford
Bridge

Caravan
Park

Pendeford Mill
Nature Reserve

Solar
Panels

113

Very Narrow Cutting

Forsters Bridge 68

Works

Fordhouses

Lane Green

4 Pendeford Bridge

Works

Upper Pendeford
Farm

Marsh Lane Bridge 67

Academy

BILBROOK
CP

3A
3 Turnover Bridge

Pendeford

Sch

Lane Green
Farm
Bilbrook Bridge

Bathurst Bridge 2

Sch

Dovecote

Sch

Autherley
Junction

Sch

Dam
Mill

108

Brookside
Farm

Palmers
Cross

Autherley Stop Lock

B

Authexley Stop Lock
Works

40¾/4m   29L
Hurleston

66 Blaydon Road Bridge
1 Junction Bridge

B   1

21m   12L
Great
Haywood

Oxley Moor Bridge 65
Pipe Bridge

Oxley Moor
Bridge

Aldersley
Junction   ½m   0L

Blakeley Green

133

Pipe Bridge

Aqueducts
Railway Bridges

South Staffs
Golf Club

Pipe Bridge
Aldersley
Junction

64

Aldersley Bridge

Oxley
Sidings

ALDERSLEY

21

Claregate

20

Dunstall Park Bridge

Rifle
Range

19

18

17   Spring
Bridge

Dunstall Water Bridge 63

Stadium

Wolverhampton
Locks

DUNSTALL
PARK

Hotel

Hotel

Wks

16

Science
Park

see Book 2

RACE COURSE

Sch

see Book 2

89

Brewood

Mottey Meadows
National Nature Reserve
103
Dirty Lane Bridge 20
93
Tavern Bridge 19
Tavern Bridge
WHEATON ASTON
5
Wheaton Aston Lock
6
Sewage
Works
Wheaton Aston Bridge 18
Brook House
Farm
PLEY, STRET
EATON AS

Leaving the balustraded Avenue Bridge
(10), which leads westward to Chillington Hall,
the canal curves in a bold cutting past the village
of Brewood (moorings by bridge 14) and its attractive
wharf – and moves north west along a very straight
embankment. The head bank of the big Belvide Reservoir
can be seen on the west side; its feeder stream enters the canal
just south of Stretton Aqueduct. This solid but elegant cast iron
structure carries the canal over the A5. Crossing the aqueduct by boat
tends to give the canal traveller an air of great superiority over the teeming
motorists below. After another long, wooded cutting the canal reaches
Wheaton Aston Lock. This lock marks the end of the long pound from Autherley
and the beginning of the 17-mile level that lasts almost to Market Drayton. Very
reasonably priced *diesel* can be obtained from Turners Garage (01785 840286) – on the
off-side, immediately north of Bridge 19 – which also holds an amazing stock of boat and
bicycle parts and sells a variety of *solid fuel*. Free range eggs are for sale west of Bridge 19.

Brewood

Staffs. PO, tel, stores, chemist, takeaway, off-licence, butcher, baker, library. The name (pronounced Brood) derives from Celtic Bre, meaning hill, thus giving wood on the hill. It originally consisted of a Roman fort on Beacon Hill to defend Watling Street. Dean Street, below the church, is a gem with a great diversity of façades jostling for attention side by side. Most obvious are the tripartite windows of Dean Street House, although lower down the street are Old Smithy Cottages, built c.1350 and once a hall house open to the roof. The village church is a tall, elegant building which has been greatly restored but still contains a 16th-C font and several 16th-C effigies and 17th-C monuments commemorating the Giffard family of Chillington Hall. Speedwell Castle, on the market square, has a most strikingly ornate façade and is a delightful building (some would say folly) erected by an apothecary around 1740. He is reputed to have won handsomely on a horse named Speedwell and used his winnings to build this dwelling. The chemist shop, nearby, has an 18th-C exterior and in 1828 was the birthplace of Thomas Walker, an eminent Victorian engineer, who built the Severn railway tunnel. The entire market square is allegedly riddled with underground vaults and passages interconnecting Speedwell Castle with the pubs and hotels ringing the square.
Chillington Hall Codsall Wood, Wolverhampton WV8 1RE (01902 850236; www.chillingtonhall.co.uk) 1½ miles west of the canal, south west of Brewood, has been the home of the Giffard family since the 12th C. The existing hall was built in the 18th C, and the wooded park in which it stands was designed by Capability Brown. Telephone or visit website for opening times (restricted).
Belvide Reservoir A large nature reserve open to naturalists by permit only. The West Midland Bird Club is developing the reserve to include displays and hides, enabling enthusiasts to have a greater opportunity to observe the many species of birds. They can be contacted at www.westmidlandbirdclub.com/belvide.

Stretton

Staffs. 1 mile north east of Stretton Aqueduct off the A5. The church was rebuilt in the 19th C but retains its original chancel and fragments of medieval glass in the east window.
Stretton Hall Built in 1620 to designs by Inigo Jones. Most interesting features are the vast fireplace with steps up to it for chimney sweep boys, and the remarkable staircase suspended by chains from the roof. The house is private.

Lapley

Staffs. 3/4 mile north east of bridge 17. The central tower of the church dominates the village. It is an interesting building with fine Norman windows, an old Dutch font and traces of medieval paintings on the nave wall. The church as we see it now was completed in the 15th C.

Wheaton Aston

Staffs. PO, tel, stores. chemist, off-licence, garage. Overrun by new housing. The village green around the church (rebuilt in 1857) is a memento of a more pleasant past. The garage beside the canal can repair boat engines and also sells chandlery. There is wheelchair access on both sides of the canal at bridge 19.

Pubs and Restaurants

🍺 **1 The Bridge Inn** 22 High Green, Brewood ST19 9BD (01902 903966; www. thebridgebrewood.com). Real ale, real cider and food *daily 12.00 (Sun 17.00).* Dog- and child-friendly, garden. Quiz *Mon. Occasional* live music, real fires and Wi-Fi. *Open Mon-Sat 12.00-23.00 (Fri-Sat 00.00)* & *Sun 12.00-22.00.*

🍺✗ **2 The Oakley Arms** Kiddemore Green Road, Brewood ST19 9BQ (01902 859800; www.brunningandprice.co.uk/oakley). Originally a Victorian country house and estate, much of the interior was destroyed by fire in 2015 before conversion into an attractive dining pub overlooking a lake. Real ale and excellent food available *Mon-Sat 12.00-21.30 (Fri-Sat 22.00)* & *Sun 12.00-21.00.* Terrace, dog- and family-friendly. Real fires and Wi-Fi. *Open daily 11.00-23.00 (Sun 22.30).*

✗ **3 Lazy Days** 25 Stafford Street, Brewood, Stafford ST19 9DX (01902 850038; www.facebook.com/people/Lazy-Days-Brewood/100076178193251). Friendly establishment serving breakfast, light lunches, appetising snacks and afternoon teas *Tue-Sat 09.00-15.00.*

✗🍷 **4 The Curry Inn** 13 Church Road, Brewood ST19 9BT (01902 850989; www.curryinnbrewood.co.uk) Indian restaurant and takeaway *open daily 17.30-23.00 (Fri-Sat 00.00).*

🍺 **5 The Hartley Arms** 56 Long Street, Wheaton Aston ST19 9NF (01785 840232; www.hartleyarms.co.uk). Real ales, real cider and homecooked food available *Mon-Sat L and E & Sun 12.00-16.00. Fortnightly* quiz. Garden, family-friendly. Sports TV and Wi-Fi. *Open 12.00-23.00*

🍺 **6 The Coach & Horses** 36 High Street, Wheaton Aston ST19 9NP (01785 840232). Community pub dispensing real ale. Terrace, dog- and child-friendly. *Tue* Quiz. Traditional pub games, sports TV and Wi-Fi. *Open 12.00-23.00 (Fri-Sat 00.00).*

Boatyards

Ⓑ**Countrywide Cruisers** The Wharf, Brewood ST19 9BG (01902 850166; www. countrywide-cruisers.co.uk). Just north of bridge 14. 🚽🏪⛽ Pump out, narrow boat hire, gas, overnight and long-term mooring, boat sales and repairs, boat building, engine repairs, boat fitting out, solid fuel, books, maps, toilet. *Open daily 08.00-18.00.*

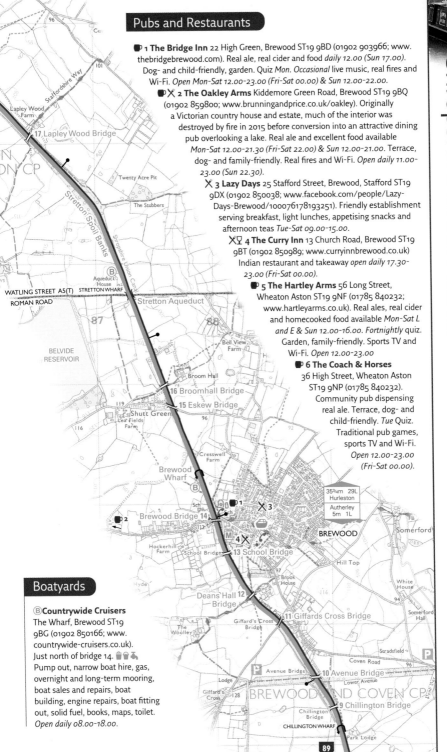

Church Eaton

The canal now proceeds along the very long pound, alternately in cuttings and on embankments. Both offer interest: the cuttings for their rich vegetation, and the embankments for the excellent views over quiet, unspoilt grazing land.

Pubs and Restaurants

🍺✕ **1 The Royal Oak** High Street, Church Eaton ST20 0AJ (01785 823078; www.royaloakchurcheaton. co.uk). Community-owned pub serving real ales and excellent food *Wed-Fri E; Sat L and E & Sun 12.00-19.00.* Family-friendly, garden. Traditional pub games, real fires, sports TV and Wi-Fi. Camping. *Open Mon-Fri 16.00-23.30 & Sat-Sun 12.00-23.30 (Sun 21.30).*

High Bridge, Grub Street Cutting

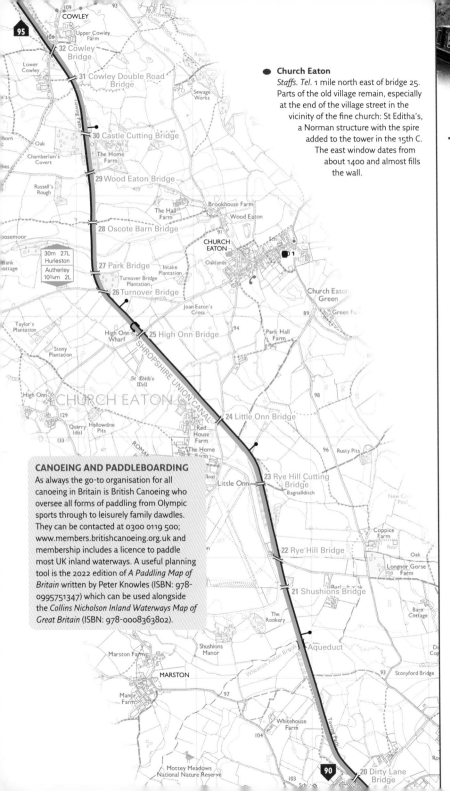

● **Church Eaton**
Staffs. Tel. 1 mile north east of bridge 25.
Parts of the old village remain, especially
at the end of the village street in the
vicinity of the fine church: St Editha's,
a Norman structure with the spire
added to the tower in the 15th C.
The east window dates from
about 1400 and almost fills
the wall.

CANOEING AND PADDLEBOARDING
As always the go-to organisation for all
canoeing in Britain is British Canoeing who
oversee all forms of paddling from Olympic
sports through to leisurely family dawdles.
They can be contacted at 0300 0119 500;
www.members.britishcanoeing.org.uk and
membership includes a licence to paddle
most UK inland waterways. A useful planning
tool is the 2022 edition of *A Paddling Map of
Britain* written by Peter Knowles (ISBN: 978-
0995751347) which can be used alongside
the *Collins Nicholson Inland Waterways Map of
Great Britain* (ISBN: 978-0008363802).

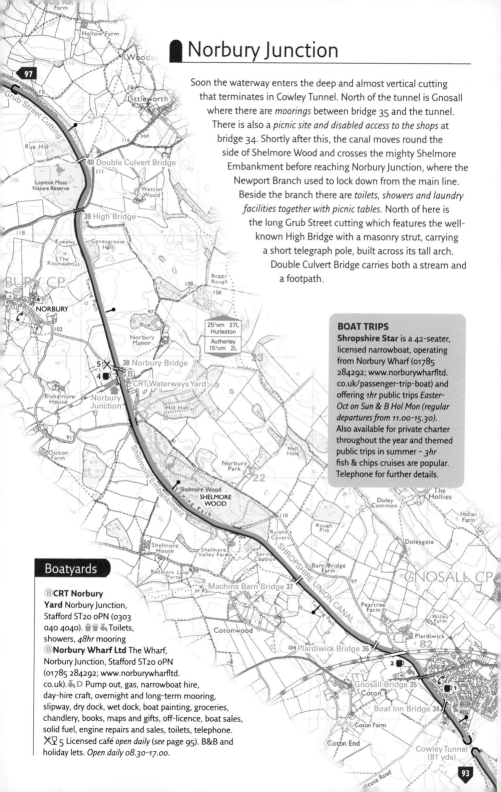

Norbury Junction

Soon the waterway enters the deep and almost vertical cutting that terminates in Cowley Tunnel. North of the tunnel is Gnosall where there are *moorings* between bridge 35 and the tunnel. There is also a *picnic site and disabled access to the shops* at bridge 34. Shortly after this, the canal moves round the side of Shelmore Wood and crosses the mighty Shelmore Embankment before reaching Norbury Junction, where the Newport Branch used to lock down from the main line. Beside the branch there are *toilets, showers and laundry facilities together with picnic tables*. North of here is the long Grub Street cutting which features the well-known High Bridge with a masonry strut, carrying a short telegraph pole, built across its tall arch. Double Culvert Bridge carries both a stream and a footpath.

BOAT TRIPS

Shropshire Star is a 42-seater, licensed narrowboat, operating from Norbury Wharf (01785 284292; www.norburywharfltd. co.uk/passenger-trip-boat) and offering *1hr* public trips *Easter-Oct on Sun & B Hol Mon (regular departures from 11.00-15.30)*. Also available for private charter throughout the year and themed public trips in summer – *3hr* fish & chips cruises are popular. Telephone for further details.

Boatyards

Ⓑ**CRT Norbury Yard** Norbury Junction, Stafford ST20 0PN (0303 040 4040). 🚽🚿♿Toilets, showers, *48hr* mooring
Ⓑ**Norbury Wharf Ltd** The Wharf, Norbury Junction, Stafford ST20 0PN (01785 284292; www.norburywharfltd. co.uk).♿D Pump out, gas, narrowboat hire, day-hire craft, overnight and long-term mooring, slipway, dry dock, wet dock, boat painting, groceries, chandlery, books, maps and gifts, off-licence, boat sales, solid fuel, engine repairs and sales, toilets, telephone. ✕♡5 Licensed café *open daily (see page 95)*. B&B and holiday lets. *Open daily 08.30-17.00*.

- **Cowley Tunnel**
This short tunnel was originally intended to be much longer – 690yds – but most of it was opened out at an early stage during construction (in 1831) because of dangerous faults in the rock, and now only 81yds remain. The tunnel is unlined, and to the south of it a steep narrow cutting through solid rock stretches a considerable distance – an awe-inspiring sight.

- **Gnosall**
Staffs. PO, stores, off-licence, chemist, takeaways, fish & chips, laundrette. The main feature of interest in the village is the church of St Laurence, 1 mile east of the canal. It is a 15th-C building with original Norman tower arches. The east window has fine decorated tracery framing modern stained glass. *The stores are open daily 06.00-22.00.*

- **Shelmore Embankment**
The construction of this great embankment, 1 mile long, just south of Norbury Junction, was the source of endless grief and expense to the Birmingham & Liverpool Junction Canal Company in general and to Thomas Telford, the engineer, in particular. It was an enormous task anyway to shift the millions of cubic feet of earth to build the bank; but while the contractors struggled to complete it, the bank slipped and collapsed time and again. By early 1834, Shelmore Embankment was the only unfinished section of the whole canal. It was not until 1835, after 5½ years' solid work on it and well after Telford's death, that the embankment was completed by William Cubitt and the B & LJ Canal was opened as a through route. There are flood gates at each end, to close off the channel in case of a breach. These were closed each night during World War II as a precaution against bombing.

- **Norbury Junction**
This was once the outlet for the Shrewsbury, Newport and Trench branches on to the rest of the Shropshire Union Canal system. There was a long flight of locks from the junction down to Newport, but these are now closed, except for the top lock which is used as a dock.

- **Loynton Moss**
Norbury, Stafford ST20 0PQ (01889 880100; www.staffs-wildlife.org.uk/reserves/loynton-moss). There is a floating bog with an interesting plant community managed by Staffordshire Wildlife Trust (01889 880100; www.staffs-wildlife.org.uk). It can be accessed by a footpath immediately north of bridge 39 which links into a circular walk with interpretation boards. **Keep to the footpath** as the moss is potentially dangerous. There are viewpoints around the site.

Pubs and Restaurants

⬤❌ **1 The Boat Inn** Wharf Road, Gnosall, Stafford ST20 0DA (01785 822208; www.boatinngnosall.com). Canalside pub serving real ale and food *Tue-Sat L and E & Sun 12.00-16.00.* Dog- and family-friendly, garden. Traditional pub games and real fires. *Open Mon-Thu L and E (not Mon L) & Fri-Sun 12.00-23.00 (Sun 20.00).*

⬤❌ **2 The Navigation** Newport Road, Gnosall, Stafford ST20 0BN (01785 824562; www.facebook.com/NavigationInnGnosall). Real ales together with a good selection of food available *Mon-Fri L and E & Sat-Sun 12.00-20.00 (Sun 19.00).* Child- and dog-friendly, garden. Traditional pub games, *occasional* live music, real fires and Wi-Fi. *Open Mon-Thu 12.00-00.00 (Wed 20.00) & Fri-Sun 12.00-01.00 (Sun 23.00).*

⬤❌ **3 The Royal Oak** Newport Road, Gnosall, Stafford ST20 0BL (01785 822828). Comfortable bar and lounge where you can enjoy real ale and homemade food *Mon-Fri L and E & Sat-Sun 12.00-21.00 (Sun 20.00).* Dog-and family-friendly, garden. Traditional pub games, *regular* live music, real fires and Wi-Fi. *Open daily 12.00-00.00.*

⬤❌ **4 The Junction Inn** Norbury Junction, Stafford ST20 0PN (01785 284288; www.thejunctioninnnorbury.co.uk). Canalside, at Norbury Junction. Superbly situated canal pub serving real ales and food *Mon-Fri L and E & Sat-Sun 12.00-21.00.* Dog- and family-friendly with a wide range of facilities for children; garden. Traditional pub games, real fires and Wi-Fi. *Open daily 11.00-23.00 (Sun 22.30).*

❌⬤ **5 The Old Wharf Tearoom** Norbury Junction, Stafford ST20 0PN (01785 284292; www.norburywharfltd.co.uk). Attractive waterside café with an interesting display of Measham teapots. Inexpensive selection of light snacks and refreshments. Gift shop. *Open daily 08.30-17.00. Last hot food orders 16.00. Reduced winter opening hours.*

WALKING AND CYCLING
Between Norbury Junction and Nantwich the navigation passes through several spectacular cuttings and many more of lesser magnitude. During the wetter months of the year the towpath can become waterlogged making it impassable for the cyclist and unpleasant for walkers. Probably the worst section is through Woodseaves Cutting between bridges 56 and 59 and a diversion through Woodseaves village and back to the canal at Tyrley Wharf should be considered. CRT are progressively draining and upgrading the towpath so the situation will improve.

99

Westcott

ott Mill

Sewage Works

SOUDLEY

53 Hallemans Bridge

Hanwood Farm

93

KNIGHTON RESERVOIR

Drumble

117

118

Bungalow Farm

Hopshort

GOLDSTONE

Little Soudley

52 Fox Bridge

120

116

120

123

109

Shawbroom

FB

51 New Brighton Bridge

Ellerton Wood Farm

Soudley Park

111

KNIGHTON WOOD

ADBASTON CP

Hazeldines Bridge

Canal Feeder

49

48 Park Heath Bridge

Knighton Grange

arlake

Soudley Bridge 50

Towing Path

Knigh Mou

SHROPSHIRE UNION CANAL

Ellerton Wood

87

100

ane

90

92

Park Heath Farm

100

47 Black Flat Bridge

Palins Farm

hill Farm

97 Park Heath

Knighton Bridge 46

wks

Newport Road 45 Bridge

Thorneypits

94

114

The Rookery

Ellerton Grove

Mill Pond

93

Water Brook

Stone Plantation

Bat Pl

The Links

Kingswell Cottages

Links Farm

94

Ellerton Grange

98

105

Ellerton

Ellerton Hall

Flashbrook Manor

FB

Banqueting Farm

FB

CANOEING AND PADDLEBOARDING

The Shropshire Union Canal, as the name implies, was formed from the amalgamation of the Chester Canal and the Birmingham & Liverpool Junction Canal under the shadow of Victorian railway expansion. The main line was both the last trunk narrow canal route built and the last major civil engineering project undertaken by Thomas Telford. The significance of these joint swan songs, from the paddlers point of view, is that the navigation tends to take the most direct route between two points, rather than meander along specific contours for extended periods of time. The result is that the construction employed large earthworks with extensive cuttings and embankments and, by and large, locks are conveniently grouped together in flights, giving long stretches of uninterrupted paddling. So, leaving Autherley Junction (and apart from the stop lock – originally built to separate the water of two adjoining, rival canal companies) the canoeist and paddleboarder will meet just a single lock over a distance of almost 27 miles, before encountering their first, relatively short and compact lock flight at Tyrley, just outside Market Drayton. However, along the way there is the opportunity to sample a range of deep, gloomy cuttings and some impressive earthworks, both bearing Thomas Telford's distinctive signature. Banks tend to be untypically high in the cuttings so the more normal bridge holes, mooring spots and village wharfs provide suitable locations to launch and disembark. Wheaton Aston has useful parking beside the waterway down the short track leading south from the village to the lock and there is plenty of scope to park and launch at Norbury Junction. Many of the bridges shown on the mapping, where a minor road crosses the navigation, are also suitable but the A5 and its aqueduct should be discounted.

Shebdon

The canal moves out of Grub Street cutting, leaving behind the unusual double-arched bridge, containing a small telegraph pole, and, passing the village of High Offley on a hill to the north, continues in a north westerly direction through the quiet open farmland that always accompanies this canal. Along this stretch there used to be two remote canalside *pubs* – both amazed the traveller by their very survival, situated as they were on quiet roads and an even quieter waterway. Today *only one survives* remaining, untouched, in testimony to a past era. The great Shebdon Embankment is heralded by an aqueduct; at the far end is a large ex-chocolate factory (now producing dried milk delectables such as Bird's Custard, Marvel dried milk and Angel Delight), whose goods used to be carried to and from Bournville (on the Worcester & Birmingham Canal) by narrowboat.

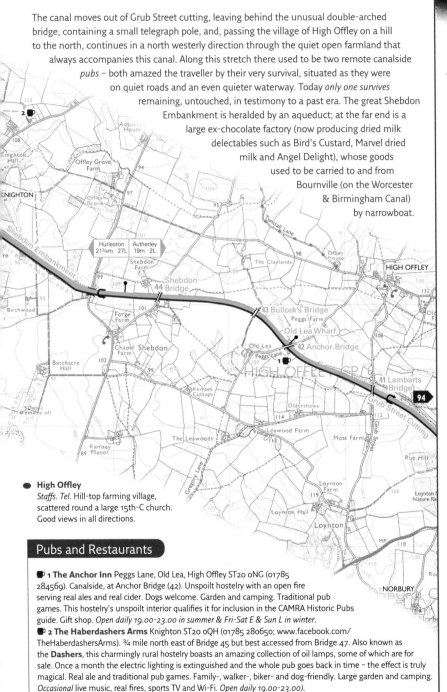

- ● **High Offley**
  Staffs. Tel. Hill-top farming village, scattered round a large 15th-C church. Good views in all directions.

Pubs and Restaurants

● **1 The Anchor Inn** Peggs Lane, Old Lea, High Offley ST20 0NG (01785 284569). Canalside, at Anchor Bridge (42). Unspoilt hostelry with an open fire serving real ales and real cider. Dogs welcome. Garden and camping. Traditional pub games. This hostelry's unspoilt interior qualifies it for inclusion in the CAMRA Historic Pubs guide. Gift shop. *Open daily 19.00-23.00 in summer & Fri-Sat E & Sun L in winter.*

● **2 The Haberdashers Arms** Knighton ST20 0QH (01785 280650; www.facebook.com/TheHaberdashersArms). ¾ mile north east of Bridge 45 but best accessed from Bridge 47. Also known as the **Dashers**, this charmingly rural hostelry boasts an amazing collection of oil lamps, some of which are for sale. Once a month the electric lighting is extinguished and the whole pub goes back in time – the effect is truly magical. Real ale and traditional pub games. Family-, walker-, biker- and dog-friendly. Large garden and camping. *Occasional* live music, real fires, sports TV and Wi-Fi. *Open daily 19.00-23.00).*

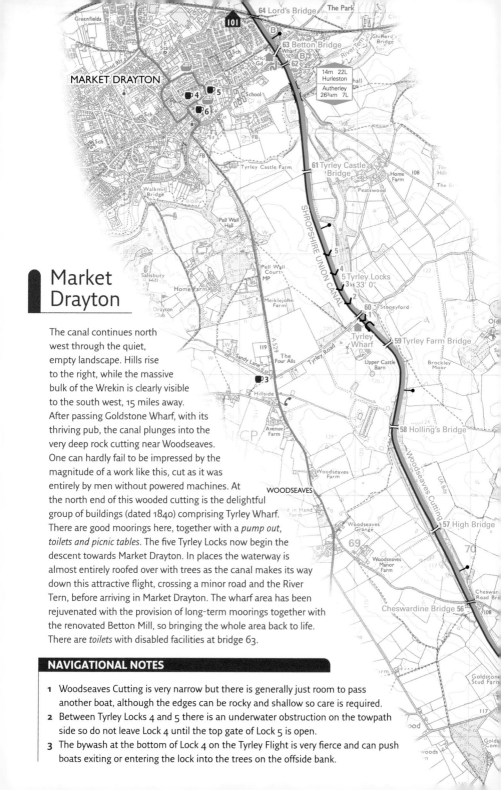

Market Drayton

The canal continues north west through the quiet, empty landscape. Hills rise to the right, while the massive bulk of the Wrekin is clearly visible to the south west, 15 miles away. After passing Goldstone Wharf, with its thriving pub, the canal plunges into the very deep rock cutting near Woodseaves. One can hardly fail to be impressed by the magnitude of a work like this, cut as it was entirely by men without powered machines. At the north end of this wooded cutting is the delightful group of buildings (dated 1840) comprising Tyrley Wharf. There are good moorings here, together with a *pump out, toilets and picnic tables*. The five Tyrley Locks now begin the descent towards Market Drayton. In places the waterway is almost entirely roofed over with trees as the canal makes its way down this attractive flight, crossing a minor road and the River Tern, before arriving in Market Drayton. The wharf area has been rejuvenated with the provision of long-term moorings together with the renovated Betton Mill, so bringing the whole area back to life. There are *toilets* with disabled facilities at bridge 63.

NAVIGATIONAL NOTES

1   Woodseaves Cutting is very narrow but there is generally just room to pass another boat, although the edges can be rocky and shallow so care is required.

2   Between Tyrley Locks 4 and 5 there is an underwater obstruction on the towpath side so do not leave Lock 4 until the top gate of Lock 5 is open.

3   The bywash at the bottom of Lock 4 on the Tyrley Flight is very fierce and can push boats exiting or entering the lock into the trees on the offside bank.

- **Market Drayton**

Shropshire. PO, tel, stores, banks, chemist, baker, butcher, off-licence, hardware, delicatessen, fish & chips, takeaways, laundrette, library, garage. On the west bank of the canal, the market centre for the surrounding district, is an attractive town with some splendid old buildings. It received its charter in the 13th C but was destroyed by fire in 1651. However, picturesque black and white timber framing was again used for the rebuilding, the best of which is the Tudor House Hotel in the market square and the adjacent Sandbrook Vaults (1653) in Shropshire Street. The parish church of St Mary is large and well-sited overlooking the Tern valley and dates from the 12th C. The ivy-clad Corbet Arms Hotel is a fine centre-piece to the main square. The town now claims to be the home of gingerbread – there are two bakeries, one producing the original Billingtons recipe which was sold at a weekly market in the Buttercross. The link may be somewhat tenuous, but is based on the town's connection with Clive of India who was known to have returned from the east with a plentiful selection of spices, one of which could well have been ginger. There is a useful cycle shop in the town: Brenin Bikes 79 Cheshire St, Market Drayton TF9 1PN (01630 656614; www.breninbikes.co.uk). **Swimming Centre** Newtown, Market Drayton TF9 1JT (0345 000 7004; www.shropshireleisurecentres.com/Market_Drayton). Swimming pool offering a variety of activity programmes: indoor and outdoor pools. *Open daily* – times and activities vary from holiday to term-time so telephone for details.

Pubs and Restaurants

1 The Red Lion High Street, Cheswardine TF9 2RS (01630 661234; www.facebook.com/theredlioncheswardine). A village local serving real ale and in excess of 130 malt whiskies. Dog- and family-friendly, garden. Real fires and traditional pub games. *Open Mon-Fri E; Sat 12.00-23.00 & Sun L and E.*

2 The Wharf Tavern Goldstone Wharf, Cheswardine, Market Drayton TF9 2LP (01630 661226; www.wharfcaravanpark.co.uk). Canalside, at bridge 55. Once a coal wharf and warehouse, now a popular canal venue. Real ale, together with meals *L and E* (book for restaurant meals *at weekends*). Garden with children's play area. Real fires and Wi-Fi. Mooring and caravan park. *Open Mon-Thu L and E & Fri-Sun 12.00-23.00 (Sun 22.30).*

3 The Four Alls Inn Newport Road, Woodseaves, Market Drayton TF9 2AG (01630 652995). Large roadside pub with food available *all day until 21.00.* Family-friendly with outside seating. Ten minutes walk west from Bridge 60, this hostelry has a somewhat thought-provoking pub sign! Real fires. *Open daily 11.00-23.00.*

4 The Hippodrome Queen Street, Market Drayton TF9 1PS (01630 650820; www.jdwetherspoon.com/pubs/all-pubs/england/shropshire/the-hippodrome-market-drayton). Based in the town's first purpose-built cinema – opened in 1927 and closed 40 years later – this hostelry serves real ales, real cider and food *daily 008.00-23.00.* Family-friendly, patio. Newspapers, real fires and Wi-Fi. *Open daily 08.00-00.00 (Sun 23.00).*

5 The Red Lion Inn Great Hales Street, Market Drayton, Shropshire TF9 1JP (01630 652602; www.joulesbrewery.co.uk/our-taphouses/our-pub-list/red-lion-market-drayton). This former coaching inn, built in 1623, shares a site with the Joules Brewery. The 'Mouse Room' is oak panelled with exquisite carvings and a view into the brewery itself. Appetising food is available *Mon-Fri L and E & Sat-Sun 12.00-21.00 (Sun 20.00).* Meat for the pork dishes is from the Joules herd, which is fed on the spent brewers grains. Real fires, newspapers and Wi-Fi. Garden and family room. *Open daily 11.00-23.00 (Fri-Sat 00.00).*

6 The Salopian Star 21 Stafford Street, Market Drayton TF9 1HX (01630 652530). This town-centre, black and white, timber-framed pub is a little gem, both inside and out. *Open daily 12.00-23.00 (Fri-Sun 09.00)* and serving excellent real ale. Dog friendly with traditional pub Games. Real fires, newspapers and outside seating. Wi-Fi.

Also try: **7 The Fox & Hounds** High Street, Cheswardine TF9 2RS (01630 661244; www.joulesbrewery.co.uk/our-taphouses/our-pub-list/fox-and-hounds).

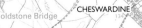

Adderley

The navigation leaves Market Drayton passing new housing development on the offside, somewhat softened by the orderly and colourful line of moored boats. Soon the canal regains its peaceful isolation, passing through a pleasant wooded cutting (which is alleged by the superstitious to shelter a vociferous ghost) before arriving at the five Adderley Locks: the middle of the three main groups of locks between Autherley and Nantwich.

● **Adderley**
Shropshire. PO box, tel. A rather under-populated village, bisected by the now-closed railway and flanked by the large Shavington and Adderley Parks. The unusual church, set by itself, was rebuilt of red sandstone in 1801 in neo-classical style. In 1958 a large portion of the church was closed to reduce maintenance costs, including the tower dated 1712, the transepts and the chancel. As a result the much smaller interior is better suited to contemporary needs and feels more like a large formal drawing room than a church. The Village Club welcomes visitors and is *open Mon-Fri 20.00-23.00.*

Boatyards

Ⓑ**Talbot Wharf** Newcastle Road, Market Drayton TF9 1HN (01630 652641; www.talbotwharf.co.uk). Gas, overnight mooring, long-term mooring, winter storage, slipway, crane, boat and engine sales, chandlery, maps, gifts, solid fuel. *Open Mon-Sat 09.30-17.00 (Sat 13.00).*

CANOEING AND PADDLEBOARDING

Since the beginning of the new decade paddling, in all its forms, has really taken off on the inland waterways – until recently the almost exclusive domain of the diesel-powered boat. Full integration may still be a little way off but the fundamental needs of all owners and their craft are remarkably similar, and include mutual respect, safety, support (including everything from boatyards to sustenance) and, above all, courtesy.

There are plenty of ready-made paddling opportunities detailed in these pages but for those who want to make their own way, listed below are a few useful pointers:

1 To avoid the repetition of 'out and back' trips, a waterway 'ring' or a linear expedition has many attractions. Typically, a hire boater may well feel the same way and in a week might undertake, say, the Cheshire Ring, the Warwickshire Ring or the Black Country Ring. General guidance is available at www.canalrivertrust.org.uk/enjoy-the-waterways/boating where you will also find details of specific 'ring' cruises.
2 Under the **Pubs and Restaurants** headings you will find details of both Bed & Breakfast and camping listed alongside the availability of food and drink. There is also mention of fixed 'pods' and cottages under both this heading and, occasionally, under **Boatyards**. The latter may not yet be totally aware of the nascent demand for somewhere safe for paddlers to leave their craft, on completion of a one-way trip but a polite phone call and the offer of payment is more than likely to procure secure storage and, probably, use of their facilities.
3 All Canal & River Trust licence holders are entitled to a Watermate key (often, for reasons of history, referred to as a BW key) which gives them access to basic facilities such as toilets, showers, laundry and water. This will be useful for paddlers that are on camping trips and can be obtained from www.canalrivertrust.org.uk/enjoy-the-waterways/boating/go-boating/boat-services-and-directory/where-to-buy-keys-cards-and-more or from internet sites such as eBay. You may also need to buy smart cards to operate some of these facilities which can be obtained through the same website.
4 To keep abreast of extreme weather events and stoppages that may affect navigation, real-time information can be delivered to your smartphone by registering for those waterways that you are interested in at www.canalrivertrust.org.uk/media/original/39685-getting-your-smartphone-to-tell-you-about-stoppages-on-your-canal-or-river.pdf. This will include the closure (and re-opening) of flood locks.

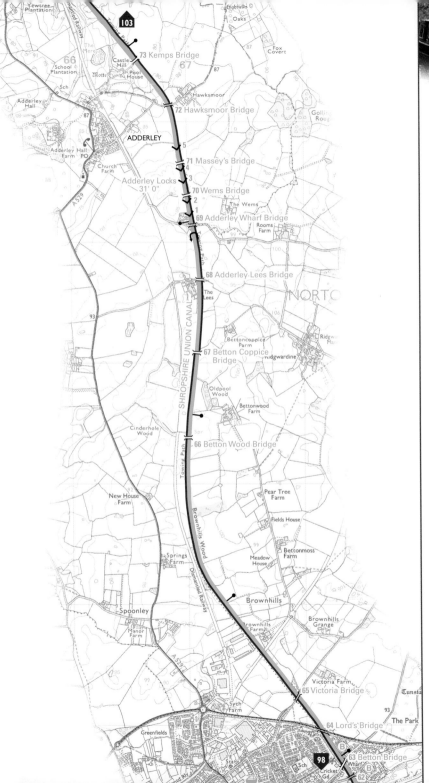

103

73 Kemps Bridge

66

72 Hawksmoor Bridge

Hawksmoor

67

Fox Covert

Golli Roug

ADDERLEY

71 Massey's Bridge

Adderley Locks
31' 0"

70 Wems Bridge

The Wems

69 Adderley Wharf Bridge

Rooms Farm

NORTO

68 Adderley Lees Bridge

The Lees

Bettoncoppice Farm

Ridgw Ma

67 Betton Coppice Bridge

Ridgwardine

Oldpool Wood

SHROPSHIRE UNION CANAL

Bettonwood Farm

66 Betton Wood Bridge

Pear Tree Farm

New House Farm

Fields House

Bettonmoss Farm

Springs Farm

Meadow House

Brownhills

Spoonley

Brownhills Grange

Manor Farm

Brownhills Farm

Victoria Farm

65 Victoria Bridge

Tunsta

The Park

64 Lord's Bridge

Greenfields

Sych Farm

98

63 Betton Bridge

Audlem

Adderley Locks are shortly followed by the 15 locks in the Audlem flight, lowering the canal by over 90ft to the dairylands of southern Cheshire. The locks are close together, well maintained, and provide over two hours' energetic navigating. There is an attractive cottage at the top lock, the wharf has a *craft shop*, and there are *two pubs* near bridge 78, along with a *general store*. The bottom of the locks is marked by a restored canal stable (base of the Day-Star Theatre Company (01270 811330; www.day-star-theatre.co.uk) and just to the north a minor aqueduct over the infant River Weaver. The canal flows northwards through an undisturbed stretch of pastoral land. Cows graze either side, clearly intent on maintaining Cheshire's reputation as a prime dairy county. It is chilling to reflect that in 1968 hardly a single beast was left alive for miles around here after the ravages of foot and mouth disease. Fortunately this area fared somewhat better in the 2001 outbreak. There is an attractive *picnic area* with *barbecue facilities* at Coole Pilate, just north of bridge 83.

Pubs and Restaurants

◗✕ 1 The Shroppie Fly The Wharf, Audlem CW3 0DX (01270 748898; www.facebook.com/TheShroppie). This converted warehouse, once owned by the Liverpool & Birmingham Canal Company, dispenses ale from a bar built from an old wooden BCN 'Joey' (or day boat) complete with cratch. Real ale and food served *Mon-Fri L and E & Sat-Sun 12.00-20.00*. Dog- and child-friendly, outside seating. Sports TV and Wi-Fi. *Open Wed-Mon, 12.00-23.00 (Sun 22.30).*

◗✕ 2 The Bridge Inn 12 Shropshire Street, Audlem CW3 0DX (01270 812928; www.facebook.com/phoenixpub.co.uk). Extended canalside pub and restaurant serving real ales and food *daily 12.00-20.30 (Sun 18.30)*. Dog- and family-friendly, canalside patio and conservatory. *Occasional* live music, newspapers, real fires, sports TV and Wi-Fi. *Open 12.00-00.00 (Sun 23.00).*

◗ 3 The White Lion Audlem Road, Hankelow CW3 0JA (01270 432606; www.whitelionhankelow.com). Run by a collective of 34 local investors, this true community pub serves real ale and food *Wed-Sat L and E & Sun 12.00-18.00*. Dog- and family-friendly. *Sun E* live music. Real fires. B&B. *Open Mon-Sat 10.00-23.00 (Mon-Tue 12.00) & Sun 12.00-22.00.*

✕ 4 The Old Priest House Coffee Shop Stafford Street, Audlem CW3 0AA (01270 811749). Opposite the church. 'The front of house resembles a Dickensian sweet shop while the façade belies the fact that there's a fine selection of wholesome hot foods available including an all day breakfast 'to die for'. A more than apt review that, however, fails to mention the delicious lunches, snacks, teas, friendly staff, excellent coffee and teacakes. *Open Wed-Sun 10.00-15.00.*

Tyrley Locks and Wharf

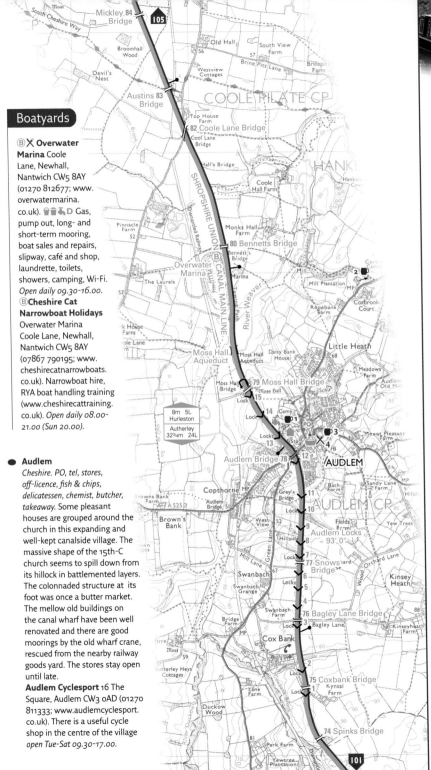

Boatyards

ⓑ ✕ **Overwater Marina** Coole Lane, Newhall, Nantwich CW5 8AY (01270 812677; www. overwatermarina. co.uk). 🚿🛁🔧D Gas, pump out, long- and short-term mooring, boat sales and repairs, slipway, café and shop, laundrette, toilets, showers, camping, Wi-Fi. *Open daily 09.30-16.00.*

ⓑ **Cheshire Cat Narrowboat Holidays** Overwater Marina Coole Lane, Newhall, Nantwich CW5 8AY (07867 790195; www. cheshirecatnarrowboats. co.uk). Narrowboat hire, RYA boat handling training (www.cheshirecattraining. co.uk). *Open daily 08.00-21.00 (Sun 20.00).*

● **Audlem**
Cheshire. PO, tel, stores, off-licence, fish & chips, delicatessen, chemist, butcher, takeaway. Some pleasant houses are grouped around the church in this expanding and well-kept canalside village. The massive shape of the 15th-C church seems to spill down from its hillock in battlemented layers. The colonnaded structure at its foot was once a butter market. The mellow old buildings on the canal wharf have been well renovated and there are good moorings by the old wharf crane, rescued from the nearby railway goods yard. The stores stay open until late.
Audlem Cyclesport 16 The Square, Audlem CW3 0AD (01270 811333; www.audlemcyclesport. co.uk). There is a useful cycle shop in the centre of the village *open Tue-Sat 09.30-17.00.*

Nantwich

Hack Green Locks briefly interrupt the navigation. The railway which once accompanied the canal has long since closed, although the line crossing from Shrewsbury to Nantwich and Crewe is still open. Swinging round Dorfold Park on a long embankment, the canal crosses the Nantwich–Chester road on a fine cast iron aqueduct and soon reaches an oblique canal junction at Nantwich Basin: this is where Telford's narrow Birmingham & Liverpool Junction Canal joins the older Chester Canal. The wide bridgehole at the next and all subsequent bridges reveals the difference in gauge of the two canals. The Chester Canal's width is complemented by its sweeping course, as it curves gracefully round the hillside towards Hurleston Junction. There is a sculpture trail along the towpath between bridges 91 and 92 to celebrate the restoration of the Nantwich embankment. At bridge 92 a *picnic site* has been created beside the largest of the sculptures.

NAVIGATIONAL NOTES

If you are heading southwards and wish to take on water at bridge 92, slow down well in advance. The water point is immediately south of the bridge where there are also *showers, toilets and rubbish disposal.*

Dorfold Hall ¼ mile south west of Nantwich Basin, CW5 8LD (01270 625245; www.dorfold.com). Built by Ralph Wilbraham in 1616, this beautiful Grade I listed Jacobean house is approached along an avenue of trees. The panelled rooms contain fine furnishings and family portraits. *Open Apr–Oct, Tue and B Hol Mon 13.00–17.00.* The house itself can only be visited during one of the guided tours *which take place on the hour.* Charge.

● **Nantwich**
Cheshire. All services. Prosperous since Roman times because of its salt springs, Nantwich was the country's main salt-mining centre until the 19th C. The town was devastated by fire in 1583 but rebuilt in fine Tudor style. Two especially interesting buildings on the road into town from the basin are the Cheshire Cat Inn and a tiny cottage built in 1502 and restored in 1971. On Beam Street are the Tollemache Almshouses, built in 1638 by Sir Edmund Wright who became Lord Mayor of London in 1641.
Church of St Mary Church Lane, Nantwich CW5 5RQ (01270 625268). Focal point of the town centre, it is a large and magnificent red sandstone Grade I listed church which stands behind its former graveyard, now an open green. It dates from the 14th C, though it was greatly restored in 1885. It has an unusual octagonal tower and the vaulted chancel contains 20 ornate 14th-C choir stalls with canopies. Fine collection of kneelers. *Open Mon–Sat 09.30–16.00 & Sun 07.45–12.30 and 17.45–19.00.* Donations.
Hack Green Secret Nuclear Bunker French Lane, Hack Green, Nantwich CW5 8AQ (01270 629219; www.hackgreen.co.uk). Described as: 'A unique and exciting day out discovering the secret world of Nuclear Government', this highly unusual attraction,

beside bridge 85, would have become home to the select few in the event of a nuclear strike. Too sinister for some; for others the chance to see the underground paraphernalia required to support existence in the face of nuclear holocaust. *Open daily Apr–Aug & Sep–Mar Wed–Sun 10.00–16.00.* Charge.
Nantwich Museum Pillory Street, Nantwich CW5 5BQ (01270 627104; www.nantwichmuseum.org.uk). An insight into the life and times of an historic market town. Roman and medieval treasures and a cheese-making display. Details on the Civil War Battle of Nantwich. *Open all year, Tue–Sat 10.30–16.30.* Free.
Players Theatre 17 Love Lane, Nantwich CW5 5BH (01270 624556; www.nantwichplayers.com). Regular productions *throughout the year.*
Tourist Information Centre The Civic Hall, Market Street, Nantwich CW5 5DG (01270 628633/303150; www.visitcheshire.com/visitor-information/visitor-information-centres). *Open Mon–Fri 09.00–16.30.*

● **Acton**
Cheshire. Tel. A small village with a large church of red stone and an old pub with a mounting block outside.

● **Nantwich Basin**
Chester Road CW5 8LB. A busy canal basin, once the terminus of the isolated Chester Canal from Nantwich to Ellesmere Port. When the B & LJ Canal was first authorised in 1826, Telford intended to bring it from Hack Green across Dorfold Park and straight into Nantwich Basin; but the owner of the park refused to allow it and forced the company to build the long embankment right round the park and the iron aqueduct over the main road. This proved a difficult and costly diversion since, as at Shelmore, the embankment repeatedly collapsed. Today the old canalside cheese warehouses are still in existence and there is a boatyard and a hire base here.

Boatyards

ⓑ✕ **Nantwich Canal Centre** Basin End, Nantwich
CW5 8LB (01270 625122; www.nantwichcanalcentre.com).
🛒🚿⛽D Gas, day-craft hire, overnight and long-term
mooring, winter storage, crane pad, boat building and
repairs, dry dock, wet dock, boat fitting out, engine
sales and Repairs, sign writing, chandlery, books,
maps and gifts, groceries, café, solid fuel, laundrette,
showers, toilets. *Emergency call out. Open Mon-Sat
09.00-17.00.*

Pubs and Restaurants

🍺✕ **1 The Crown Hotel** 24 High Street,
Nantwich CW5 5AS (01270 625283; www.
crownhotelnantwich.com). Real ales and food (with
Italian leanings) are available *daily 12.00-21.30 (Sun
20.30)* in this Grade II listed building dating from 1583.
Dog- and child-friendly, garden. *Regular* live music,
newspapers, real fires, sports TV and Wi-Fi. B&B. *Open
Mon-Sat 11.00-23.30 (Fri-Sat 00.00) & Sun 11.00-23.00.*

🍺✕ **2 The Black Lion** 29 Welsh Row, Nantwich CW5 5ED
(01270 628711; www.blacklionnantwich.co.uk). Cosy, timber-
framed pub of great character dispensing an excellent selection
of real ales and *summer* cider. Food available L and E Thu-Sun
(not Thu L and Sun E). Covered patio, dogs welcome. *Occasional*
live music. Newspapers, real fires and Wi-Fi. *Open Mon-Thu 17.00-
23.00 & Fri-Sun 12.00-23.00 (Sun 20.00).*

🍺 **3 The Vine Inn** 42 Hospital Street, Nantwich CW5 5RP (01270
619055; www.vineinnnantwich.co.uk). Real ale and real cider
served in in an old pub which seems to dive below street level. Food
available *daily 12.00-20.00 (Sun 18.00)*. Dog- and child-friendly,
garden. *Occasional* live music, newspapers, real fires, sports TV and
Wi-Fi. *Open 12.00-00.00 (Fri-Sat 00.30).*

🍺 **4 Wilbraham Arms** 58 Welsh Row, Nantwich CW5 5EJ (01270
620458). In yet another turn around, this pub has reverted to a
traditional hostelry, serving real ale and good honest cheer!
Thankfully, the elegant frontage, dating from 1695, has suffered
little in this re-invention! Dogs welcome. *Open Sun-Mon 12.00-
22.00 & Tue-Sat 12.00-23.00 (Fri-Sat 00.00).*

🍺 **5 The Oddfellows Arms** 97 Welsh Row, Nantwich
CW5 5ET (0270 260831; www.facebook.com/oddiesnantwich).
Small,, heavily-beamed, single-room pub serving an excellent
selection of real ales, together with food *Tue-Sat 12.00-18.00
& Sun 11.00-16.00*. Large garden, dog- and child-friendly.
Karaoke *Mon & Fri*; quiz *Wed*. Real fires and Wi-Fi. *Open
daily 12.00-22.00.*

WALKING AND CYCLING

Cyclists will find the going difficult between Bridges
89 and 91, which effectively spoils an otherwise
excellent off-road link between the Midlands and the
Mersey.
Nantwich Riverside Loop Walk is a circular 3-mile waymarked walk from Nantwich Riverside Park (CW5
5ED) and explores the River Weaver and the canal.
Visit www.discovercheshire.co.uk or telephone 01606
271817 for further details. More information and
further suggestions for walking/cycling can be found
at www.discovercheshire.co.uk or from Cheshire East
Council www.cheshireeast.gov.uk/prow.

105

Barbridge Junction

At Hurleston Junction the Llangollen Canal branches off up four narrow locks on its way to North Wales (*see* page 40). Meanwhile the main line of the Shropshire Union soon reaches Barbridge where there is a junction with the Middlewich Branch which, in 2018, suffered a serious breach at the River Wheelock Aqueduct, just outside Middlewich itself. This branch connects the Shropshire Union system to the Trent & Mersey Canal. The canal moves almost westwards now alongside a busy main road at a level slightly below the wheels of the passing juggernauts. The Middlewich

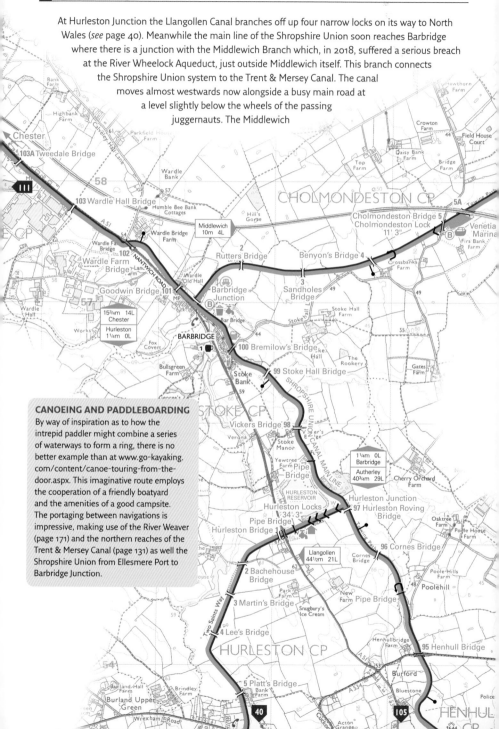

CANOEING AND PADDLEBOARDING
By way of inspiration as to how the intrepid paddler might combine a series of waterways to form a ring, there is no better example than at www.go-kayaking. com/content/canoe-touring-from-the-door.aspx. This imaginative route employs the cooperation of a friendly boatyard and the amenities of a good campsite. The portaging between navigations is impressive, making use of the River Weaver (page 171) and the northern reaches of the Trent & Mersey Canal (page 131) as well the Shropshire Union from Ellesmere Port to Barbridge Junction.

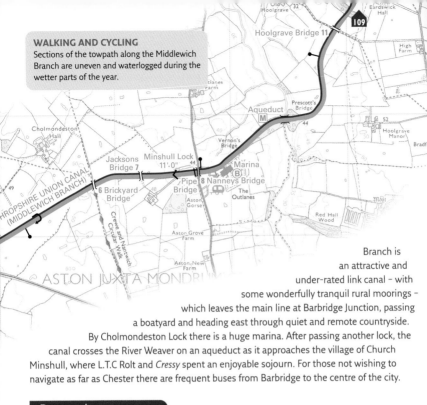

WALKING AND CYCLING
Sections of the towpath along the Middlewich Branch are uneven and waterlogged during the wetter parts of the year.

Branch is an attractive and under-rated link canal – with some wonderfully tranquil rural moorings – which leaves the main line at Barbridge Junction, passing a boatyard and heading east through quiet and remote countryside. By Cholmondeston Lock there is a huge marina. After passing another lock, the canal crosses the River Weaver on an aqueduct as it approaches the village of Church Minshull, where L.T.C Rolt and *Cressy* spent an enjoyable sojourn. For those not wishing to navigate as far as Chester there are frequent buses from Barbridge to the centre of the city.

Boatyards

ⓑ**Midway Boats, Barbridge Marina** Wardle, Nantwich CW5 6BE (01270 528682/ 528482; www.midwayboats.co.uk). Gas, short- and long-term mooring, slipway, boat sales and repairs, day boat and short-term hire, part and complete refits, engine sales and repairs, outboard specialist, chandlery, books and maps, boat building, upholstery, toilet.
ⓑ**Venetian Marina** Cholmondeston Lock, Nantwich CW5 6DB (01270 528251; www.venetianmarina.co.uk). short- and

long-term mooring, slipway, dry dock, boat and engine repairs, toilets, showers. *Open daily 09.00-18.00 (17.00 in winter).*
ⓑ**Venetian Hire Boats** Cholmondeston Lock, Nantwich CW5 6DB (01270 528122; www.venetianhireboats.co.uk). D Pump out, gas, narrowboat hire, chandlery, groceries, chandlery, gifts, café. *Open Tue-Sat 09.00-17.00 & Sun 10.00-16.00.*
ⓑ ✗ **Aqueduct Marina** The Outlanes, Church Minshull, Nantwich CW5 6DX (01270 525041; www.aqueductmarina.co.uk). D Pump out, long- and short-term mooring, winter storage, engine sales and repairs, repainting, blacking, gas, slipway, repairs, brokerage, laundrette, café *(open daily 09.30-16.00 – Fri-Sat 16.30)* chandlery, caravanning and camping. *Open daily 08.00-17.00 (Sun 09.00).*

Pubs and Restaurants

ⓟ✗ **1 The Barbridge Inn** Old Chester Road, Barbridge CW5 6AY (01270 528327; www.thebarbridgeinn.co.uk). Real ale. Food available *Mon-Fri 12.00-21.30 & Sat-Sun 11.00-22.00 (Sun 20.30).* Dog- and family-friendly, garden. Newspapers and Wi-Fi. *Open Mon-Fri 11.30-23.00 & Sat-Sun 12.00-22.30.*

Middlewich

This is a quiet stretch of canal passing through rich farmland interspersed with woods. There are superb views to the west over the River Weaver and Winsford Top Flash. At bridge 22A the West Coast Main Line makes a noisy crossing. The canal then descends through two locks to Middlewich, where it joins the Trent & Mersey. This last few yards of the Middlewich Branch used to belong to the Trent & Mersey, and the bridge over the entrance to the branch is grandiosely inscribed 'Wardle Canal 1829'. In 2018 there was a serious breach beside the Wheelock Aqueduct, the towpath washing away as the canal emptied its contents into the river.

Boatyards

ⓑ**Andersen Boats** Wych House, St Anne's Road, Middlewich CW10 9BQ (01606 833668/07771 693981; www.andersenboats.com). Pump out, gas, narrowboat hire, books and maps. *Useful DIY shop nearby. Boatyard open daily 09.00-19.00.*

ⓑ**Middlewich Wharf** Canal Terrace, Middlewich CW10 9BD (0330 043 0547; www.middlewichwharf.co.uk) D Pump out, gas, coal, narrowboat hire, boat painting, joinery, mechanical work, brokerage, chandlery, mooring, café. *Open Mar-Nov, Thu-Tue 09.00-17.30 & Dec-Feb, Mon-Fri 10.00-16.30.*

See also **Boatyards** *on page 162.*

● **Church Minshull**
Cheshire. PO box, tel. An old and mellow village embracing the infant River Weaver. The notable 18th-C church in the centre of the village is the subject of a preservation order – it is certainly the core of this most attractive place. Midway between bridges 14 and 15 there is a gateway in the hedge providing good access to the village.

● **Middlewich**
Cheshire. PO, tel, stores, chemist, butcher, baker, off-licence, fish & chips, takeaways, library, garage. A town that since Roman times has been dedicated to salt extraction. Most of the salt produced here goes to various chemical industries. Subsidence from salt extraction has prevented redevelopment for many years, but a big renewal scheme is now in progress. The canalside area is a haven of peace below the busy streets.
St Michael's Church High Town, Middlewich CW10 9AN (01606 738005). A handsome medieval church which was a place of refuge for the Royalists during the Civil War. It has a fine interior with richly carved woodwork.

CANOEING AND PADDLEBOARDING
The Middlewich Branch of the Shropshire Union Canal makes an attractive paddle in its own right but there is a dearth of public transport for a one-way voyage. However, the Trent & Mersey Canal, from Wheelock north to Middlewich, makes for an interesting and varied trip and, with a couple of boatyards at Middlewich as likely places to leave your craft, it should not be too difficult to organise a one-way trip. The return journey to pick up your car can be undertaken on a 37 or 37W bus which operates an *hourly daytime* service.

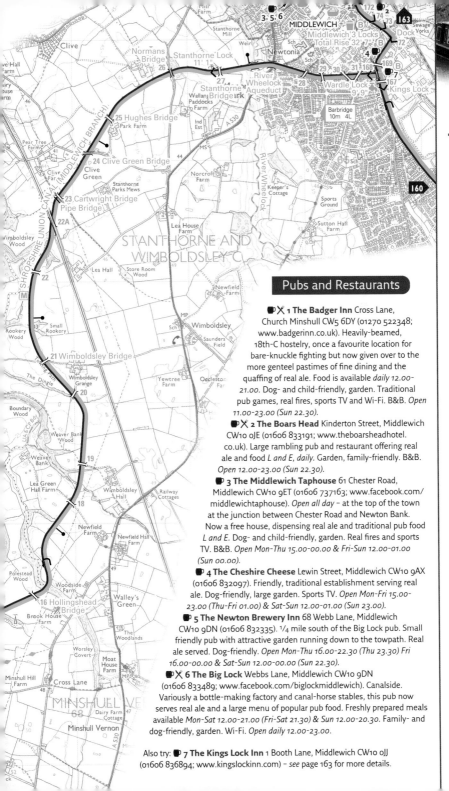

Pubs and Restaurants

🍺✕ **1 The Badger Inn** Cross Lane, Church Minshull CW5 6DY (01270 522348; www.badgerinn.co.uk). Heavily-beamed, 18th-C hostelry, once a favourite location for bare-knuckle fighting but now given over to the more genteel pastimes of fine dining and the quaffing of real ale. Food is available *daily 12.00-21.00*. Dog- and child-friendly, garden. Traditional pub games, real fires, sports TV and Wi-Fi. B&B. *Open 11.00-23.00 (Sun 22.30)*.

🍺✕ **2 The Boars Head** Kinderton Street, Middlewich CW10 0JE (01606 833191; www.theboarsheadhotel.co.uk). Large rambling pub and restaurant offering real ale and food *L and E, daily*. Garden, family-friendly. B&B. *Open 12.00-23.00 (Sun 22.30)*.

🍺 **3 The Middlewich Taphouse** 61 Chester Road, Middlewich CW10 9ET (01606 737163; www.facebook.com/middlewichtaphouse). *Open all day* – at the top of the town at the junction between Chester Road and Newton Bank. Now a free house, dispensing real ale and traditional pub food *L and E*. Dog- and child-friendly, garden. Real fires and sports TV. B&B. *Open Mon-Thu 15.00-00.00 & Fri-Sun 12.00-01.00 (Sun 00.00)*.

🍺 **4 The Cheshire Cheese** Lewin Street, Middlewich CW10 9AX (01606 832097). Friendly, traditional establishment serving real ale. Dog-friendly, large garden. Sports TV. *Open Mon-Fri 15.00-23.00 (Thu-Fri 01.00) & Sat-Sun 12.00-01.00 (Sun 23.00)*.

🍺 **5 The Newton Brewery Inn** 68 Webb Lane, Middlewich CW10 9DN (01606 832335). ¼ mile south of the Big Lock pub. Small friendly pub with attractive garden running down to the towpath. Real ale served. Dog-friendly. *Open Mon-Thu 16.00-22.30 (Thu 23.30) Fri 16.00-00.00 & Sat-Sun 12.00-00.00 (Sun 22.30)*.

🍺✕ **6 The Big Lock** Webbs Lane, Middlewich CW10 9DN (01606 833489; www.facebook.com/biglockmiddlewich). Canalside. Variously a bottle-making factory and canal-horse stables, this pub now serves real ale and a large menu of popular pub food. Freshly prepared meals available *Mon-Sat 12.00-21.00 (Fri-Sat 21.30) & Sun 12.00-20.30*. Family- and dog-friendly, garden. Wi-Fi. *Open daily 12.00-23.00*.

Also try: 🍺 **7 The Kings Lock Inn** 1 Booth Lane, Middlewich CW10 0JJ (01606 836894; www.kingslockinn.com) – *see page 163 for more details.*

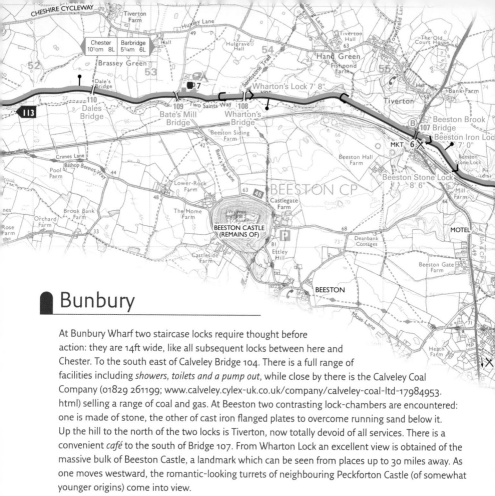

Bunbury

At Bunbury Wharf two staircase locks require thought before action: they are 14ft wide, like all subsequent locks between here and Chester. To the south east of Calveley Bridge 104. There is a full range of facilities including *showers, toilets and a pump out*, while close by there is the Calveley Coal Company (01829 261199; www.calveley.cylex-uk.co.uk/company/calveley-coal-ltd-17984953.html) selling a range of coal and gas. At Beeston two contrasting lock-chambers are encountered: one is made of stone, the other of cast iron flanged plates to overcome running sand below it. Up the hill to the north of the two locks is Tiverton, now totally devoid of all services. There is a convenient *café* to the south of Bridge 107. From Wharton Lock an excellent view is obtained of the massive bulk of Beeston Castle, a landmark which can be seen from places up to 30 miles away. As one moves westward, the romantic-looking turrets of neighbouring Peckforton Castle (of somewhat younger origins) come into view.

Boatyards

Ⓑ**Chas Hardern** Beeston Castle Wharf, Tiverton, nr Tarporley CW6 9NH (01829 732595; www.chashardern.co.uk). 🛢D Pump out, gas, coal, narrowboat hire, books, maps and gifts, Gas Safe registered. *24hr emergency call out. Open daily 09.00-17.00.*

Ⓑ**Anglo Welsh** Bunbury Lock Cottage, Bowe's Gate Road, Bunbury, Tarporley CW6 9QB (01829 260957; www.anglowelsh.co.uk/locations/bases/bunbury). 🛢🛢🔧D Pump out, gas, narrowboat hire, day-hire craft, overnight mooring, long-term mooring, books, maps and gifts, solid fuel, telephone, toilet. *24hr emergency call out. Open daily 08.30-17.00.*

● **Calveley**
Cheshire. Tel.
● **Bunbury**
Cheshire. PO, stores, fish & chips (closed Sun-Mon) off-licence. 1 Mile south west of Bunbury Locks. The church is an outstanding building: supremely light, airy and spacious, it stands as a fine monument to workmanship of the 14th and 15th C.
Bunbury Mill Bowe's Gate Road Mill Lane, Bowesgate Road, Bunbury, Tarporley CW6 9PP (01829 733244; www.bunburymill.com). Up the hill from Bunbury Wharf, towards the village. Fully

restored watermill, working until 1960 when it was destroyed by a massive flood. *Open Apr-Oct, Sun & B Hol Mon 13.00-17.00* and for pre-booked parties. Charge.
Beeston Castle Chapel Lane, Beeston CW6 9TX (01829 260464; www.english-heritage.org.uk/daysout/properties/beeston-castle-and-woodland-park). The impressive ruins of a 14th-C castle built by the Earl of Chester in 1337. Situated on top of a steep hill dominating the surrounding countryside, it was in an ideal, almost unassailable position. *Open Apr-Sep daily 10.00-17.00. Winter opening times vary* so telephone or visit the website for details. Charge.

Peckforton Castle Stone House Lane, Peckforton CW6 9TN (01829 260930; www.peckfortoncastle.co.uk). Built in the 1840s, overlooking the Cheshire plain. Open for special events, *see* website.

> ### WALKING AND CYCLING
> Between bridge 107 and the city of Chester, the Cheshire Cycleway runs close to the canal and can be used either instead of, or in conjunction with, a waterside route.

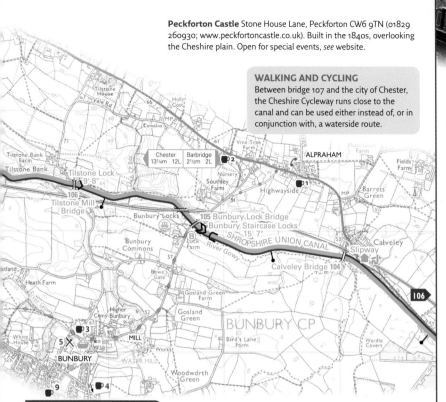

Pubs and Restaurants

🍺 **1 The Tollemache Arms** Chester Rd, Alpraham, Cheshire CW6 9JE (01829 261716; www.tollemachearmsalpraham.co.uk). 16th-C coaching inn serving real ales and food *daily 12.00-21.00 (Sun 20.00)*. Also breakfast *07.30-11.00*. Family-friendly, garden. *Occasional* live music, real fires and Wi-Fi. B&B. *Open daily 08.00-23.00.*

🍺 **2 The Travellers Rest** Chester Road, Alpraham CW6 9JA (01829 260523). This wee gem of a pub has been in the hands of the same family for more than 110 years and in that time the interior has not been greatly changed so the emphasis is still on good beer, good company and good conversation. Real ale and traditional pub games. Outside seating, dogs welcome. *Open Mon-Fri 18.30-23.00 & Sat-Sun L and E.*

🍺✕ **3 The Dysart Arms** Bowes Gate Road, Bunbury CW6 9PH (01829 260183; www.dysartarms-bunbury.co.uk). By the church. Once a farmhouse with stone-flagged floors, it now serves real ale. Large range of food available daily *12.00-21.30 (Sun 21.00)*. Dog-friendly, garden. Real fires and Wi-Fi. *Open Mon-Sat 11.30-23.00 & Sun 12.00-22.30.*

🍺 **4 The Nags Head** Vicarage Lane, Bunbury CW6 9PB (01829 260027). In centre of the village, a 300-year-old building featuring attractively decorated façade with a horse's head picked out in a central plaster frieze, and an inglenook fireplace. Real

ale and food available *Mon-Sat L and E & Sun 12.00-21.00*. Garden, dog- and child-friendly, and sports TV. *Open daily 10.00-00.00.*

✕ **5 Tilly's Coffee Shop** Bunbury Lane, Bunbury CW6 9QS (01829 261591; www.tillysbunbury.com). Warm, friendly staff make everyone entering this community hub feel immediately welcome. Breakfasts, light lunches, snacks, tea, coffee and cakes, high teas and sandwiches are all homemade and very appetising. Children of all ages welcome. Takeaway service. *Open Tue-Fri 08.30-16.30 & Sat and Mon 09.00-16.00.*

✕ **6 The Lockgate Coffee House** Whitchurch Road, Beeston, Tarporley CW6 9NJ (01829 730592; www.lockgatecoffee.co.uk). Friendly establishment serving teas, coffee, sandwiches, soup, a varied breakfast menu, light meals, afternoon tea, cakes and pastries and milkshakes. *Open daily 09.00-16.00.*

🍺✕ **7 The Shady Oak** 8 Bate's Mill Lane, Brassey Green CW6 9UE (01829 730581; www.shady-oak.com). Friendly canalside pub serving real ale and home-cooked food *daily 12.00-20.30*. Dog- and child-friendly, garden. Real fires and Wi-Fi. Camping. *Open daily 12.00-23.00 (Sun 22.30).*

Also try: ✕🍷 **8 Panama Hatty's** Whitchurch Road, Spurstow, Tarporley CW6 9TD (01829 260068; www.facebook.com/PanamaHattys) and 🍺 **9 The Yew Tree Inn** Long Lane, Spurstow, Tarporley CW6 9RD (01829 304384; www.theyewtreeinnbunbury.co.uk).

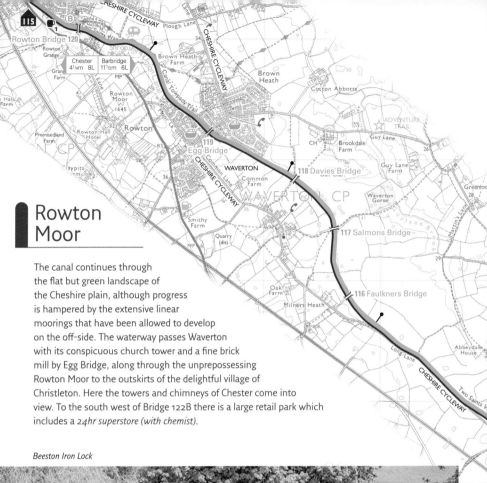

Chester	Barbridge
4¼m 8L	11½m 6L

Rowton
Grange

Grang
Farm

Rowton
Moor
1645

Rowton
Hall
Hotel

Rowton

Promisedland
Farm

se Hall
Farm

Claypits

Smithy
Farm

Quarry
(dis)

119
Egg Bridge

Common Lane

WAVERTON

Common
Farm

CHESHIRE CYCLEWAY

Oak
Farm

Milners Heath

Plough Lane

Brown Heath
Farm

CHESHIRE CYCLEWAY

Canal Towpath Trail

Brown
Heath

Cotton Abbotts

CH

Brookdale
Farm

Guy Lane

WAVERTON CP

118 Davies Bridge

Waverton
Gorse

117 Salmons Bridge

116 Faulkners Bridge

ADVENTURE
TRAIL

Guy Lane
Farm

Greenloons

Long Lane

Abbeydale
House

CHESHIRE CYCLEWAY

Two Saints Wa

Dismantled Railway

Rowton
Moor

The canal continues through
the flat but green landscape of
the Cheshire plain, although progress
is hampered by the extensive linear
moorings that have been allowed to develop
on the off-side. The waterway passes Waverton
with its conspicuous church tower and a fine brick
mill by Egg Bridge, along through the unprepossessing
Rowton Moor to the outskirts of the delightful village of
Christleton. Here the towers and chimneys of Chester come into
view. To the south west of Bridge 122B there is a large retail park which
includes a *24hr superstore (with chemist)*.

Beeston Iron Lock

● **Waverton**
Cheshire. Post office, stores, off-licence, takeaway.
Dormitory village for Chester and Merseyside.
Battle of Rowton Moor It was here,
3 miles from Chester, that one of the last major
battles of the Civil War took place in 1645. The
Parliamentarians completely routed the Royalists
who, still under fierce attack, retreated to
Chester. It is said that King Charles I watched the
defeat from the walls of Chester, but it is more
probable that he saw only the final stages under
the walls of the city. Charles fled, leaving 800
prisoners and 600 dead and wounded.
The Crocky Trail Guy Lane, Waverton, Chester
CH3 7PH (01244 336084; www.crockytrail.co.uk).
Within easy walking distance north of Bridge 118.
Mile-long adventure trail for children, with slides,
rope swings, climbs and a chain bridge. Café.
Open daily 10.00–17.00. Charge.

Boatyards

Ⓑ**The Workshop** The Moorings, Rowton
Bridge, Christleton, Chester CH3 7BD (01244
332633/07778 810187). Overnight mooring,
long-term mooring, winter storage, slipway,
engine sales and repairs (including outboards).
Emergency call out.
Ⓑ**Crow's Nest Boat Services** CW11 3PT.
Beside Crow's Nest bridge 113. (01829
772592/07870 472632). Engine repairs and
maintenance, electrics and gas, gear box repairs,
Gas Safe registered, boat safety examinations.
24hr emergency call out.
Ⓑ ✗♀ **Tattenhall Marina** Newton Lane,
Tattenhall CH3 9NE (01829 771742;
www.tattenhall-marina.co.uk). 🛢️🛒🔧 D Gas,
pump out, solid fuel, long- and short-term
mooring, boat repairs, slipway, boat sales,
winter storage, laundrette, shop, licensed café,
toilets, showers, Wi-Fi.

Pubs and Restaurants

🍺 **1 The Cheshire Cat** Whitchurch Road,
Christleton, Chester CH3 6AE (01244 332200;
www.innkeeperslodge.com/hotel/the-cheshire-
cat-christleton-chester). Large and imposing
canalside hotel and restaurant, reputedly sitting
astride the site of the 1645 Civil War battle,
serving real ales and food *daily 12.00–21.00.*
Garden, dog-friendly. Real fires. B&B. *Open
12.00–23.00 (Sun 22.30).*

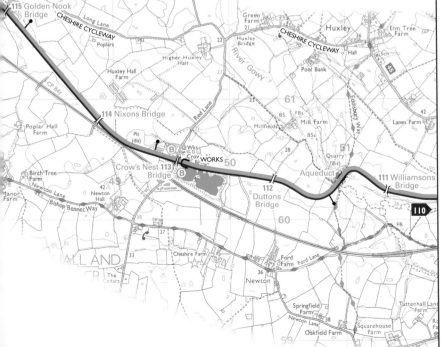

Chester

Leaving Christleton, the waterway soon begins the descent into the ancient city of Chester through five locks; none of these have top gate paddles, and they all take rather long to fill. The canal goes straight through the middle of the town. Passing the site of an old lead works, and a great variety of bridges, the navigation approaches the old city and suddenly curves round into a very steep rock cutting. Soon the Northgate Locks (a staircase) are reached: at the bottom is a sharp right turn to Tower Wharf. The area is much improved with a new development of warehouse-style apartments. On leaving North Gate Staircase Locks, boaters' facilities are found in two locations: near the visitor *moorings* and the Graving Dock and at the Graving Lock where there is 🚻♿, *a pump out and a toilet.* At bridge 126 the towpath changes sides, opposite Taylor's Boatyard and to the western corner of Tower Wharf there is a *CRT service block* with a further *toilet and a shower* (🚿 *not permitted here*). Here the line of the original Chester Canal once led straight down, via a further two locks (long since abandoned), into the River Dee. At the head of the present arm leading down to the Dee there is the site of an historic boatyard and Chester city centre is easily accessed from the canal at Bridge 123E. There is a useful *selection of shops, including a laundrette, butcher, takeaways, together with three pubs* to the north east of bridge 126.

Boatyards

ⓑ **Taylor's Boatyard Ltd** Taylor's Boatyard, Upper Cambrian Road, Chester CH1 4FB (01244 379922, 07552 127409; www. happyboatman.co.uk). ♿ Gas, coal, overnight and long-term mooring, dry dock, slipway, DIY facilities, hull blacking, winter storage, boat and engine repairs, boat fitting out, boat and engine sales, BSS examinations, hull surveys, Gas Safe registered, CRT pump out cards and Watermate keys. *Open Mon-Fri 10.00-16.00.*

● **Christleton**
Cheshire. stores, off-licence. ¼ mile east of Bridge 122. A very pleasant village near the canal, well worth visiting. The stores are *open daily 07.00-21.00.*

● **Chester**
Cheshire. All services. There is a wealth of things to see in this Roman city. It is in fact an excellent town to see on foot, because of the amazing survival of almost all the old city wall. This provides Chester with its best and rarest feature – one can walk right round the city on this superb footpath, over the old city gates and past the defensive turrets, including King Charles' Tower above the canal. Other splendid features are the race course – the Roodee – (just outside the city wall and therefore well inside the modern town) where Chester Races are held each year in *May and Jul–Sep* (it can easily be overlooked for free from the road that runs above and beside it), the superb old cathedral, the bold new theatre, the Rows (unique double-tier medieval shopping streets), and the immense number of old and fascinating buildings throughout the town.

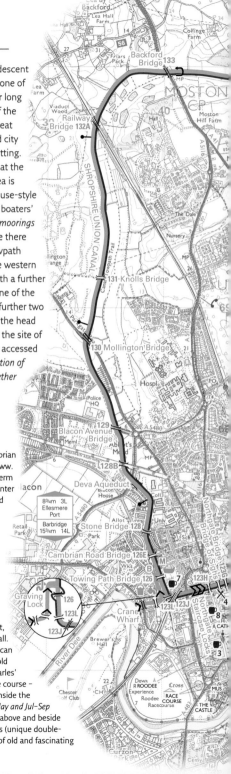

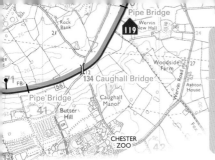

BOAT TRIPS

A range of luncheon and dinner cruises from the **Mill Hotel** Milton Street, Chester CH1 3NF (01244 350035; www.millhotel.com). *Two-hour cruises for up to 45 people, most days,* in both directions along the canal. **Chester Boat** Souters Lane, Chester CH1 1SZ (01244 325394; www.chesterboat.co.uk). On the River Dee, just off City Walls. A range of river trips introducing the canal boater to Chester's historic river. *Open throughout the year.* Telephone or visit website for further details.

Abbey Square Outside the cathedral, opposite the Victorian town hall, the square is entered through a massive gateway built in 1377.

Chester Cathedral St Werburgh Street, Chester CH1 2DY (01244 324756; www.chestercathedral.com). A magnificent building of dark-red stone on the site of a 10th-C minster. In 1092 the Earl of Chester and St Anselm founded a Benedictine abbey which was dissolved in 1540, but in the following year it was made a cathedral and the seat of a bishop. In 1742 Handel gave his first public performance of the *Messiah* in the cathedral and a copy of his marked score is on display. Café and gift shop. *Open daily 09.30-18.00 (Sun 17.00).*

Church of St John the Baptist St John's Street, Chester. Impressive 12th-C church that was built on the site of an earlier Saxon church. Licensed restaurant and shop. Charge.

Chester Castle Grosvenor Road, Chester (01244 327617). The original timber structure, c.1069, was replaced by stone walls and towers by Henry III. Unfortunately, in 1789 the defensive walls were removed to make way for the incongruous Thomas Harrison group of buildings, which include the Grand Entrance and Assize Courts. The main part of the castle is occupied by troops of the Cheshire Regiment.

Chester Market Forum Shopping Centre, Chester CH1 2HH (01244 973040; www.chester.market). There has been a traditional market in the city since the 14thC and today's undercover shopping

experience features up to 100 stalls selling fresh produce. *Open Mon-Sat 08.00-17.00 (Fri-Sat 22.00).*

Cheshire Military Museum The Castle, Chester CH1 2DN (01244 327617; www.cheshiremilitarymuseum. co.uk). Situated inside the tower of the castle. Experience 300 years of history amidst this inter-active display. *Open Thu-Sun 11.00-16.00.* Charge.

City Sightseeing Chester 55 Station Rd, Chester CH1 3DR (01244 347452; www.city-sightseeing.com/en/89/chester). *One hour* tour of the city by open top bus. Hop on-hop off tickets are valid for *24 or 48 hours.* Charge.

Dewa Roman Discovery Centre Pierpoint Lane, off Bridge Street, Chester CH1 1NL (01244 343407; www.devaromancentre.co.uk). Reconstruction of Roman Chester together with its sights, sounds and smells. Shop. *Open Mon-Sat 10.00-18.00 & Sun 09.00-17.00.* Charge.

Grosvenor Museum 27 Grosvenor Street, Chester CH1 2DD (01244 972197; www.grosvenormuseum. westcheshiremuseums.co.uk). Award-winning museum that introduces Chester's past, in particular the Roman fortress of Deva and its inhabitants. *Open Tue-Sat 10.30-17.00 & Sun 13.00-16.00.* Free.

Grosvenor Park Miniature Railway Grosvenor Park, Chester CH1 1QQ (07961 099572; www.facebook.com/gpmrshop). One of Chester's premier children's (9-90 years old) attractions laid out in Grosvenor Park amidst ducks, moorhens and geese. Steam and diesel hauled trains. *Open Apr-Sep, Wed and Fri 10.00-16.00 & Sat-Sun 10.00-17.00; Oct-Mar, Sat-Sun 10.00-16.00.* Charge.

Guided Walks are offered *daily at 10.30 and 14.00* by Chester Tours (www.chestertours.org.uk) starting from the Tourist Information Centre (*see over*). Charge.

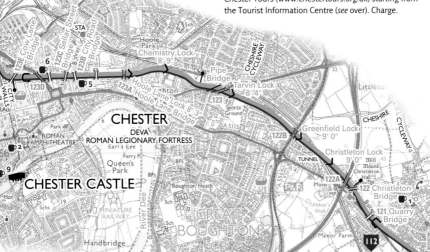

Tourist Information Centre The Town Hall, Northgate Street, Chester CH1 2HJ (01244 405340; www.visitcheshire.com/visitor-information/visitor-information-centres). *Open Mon-Sat 09.00-17.00 & Sun 10.00-16.00.* Guided walking tours start from here (*see* page 115).
Travel Contact Traveline on (0871 200 22 33; www.traveline.info) or visit www.merseytravel.gov.uk. for regular departures to Liverpool and The Wirral.

● **Northgate Locks**
Hewn out of solid rock, these three staircase locks lower the canal by 33ft, an impressive feat of engineering and a suitable complement to the deep rock cutting nearby.

● **The Dee Branch**
This branch into the tidal River Dee runs through three wide locks from the boatyard near Tower Wharf. At the time of going to press CRT and the Environment Agency have plans in hand to put these locks back into *regular* use. The Chester One City 15-year plan was unveiled in 2011 and includes a strategy to develop the Chester water space, which will include the canal, the tidal river and the non-tidal 12-mile stretch above the weir, which has a great deal to recommend it as an extremely attractive stretch of cruising water.

NAVIGATIONAL NOTES

Ellesmere Port Bottom Lock Entry into the Manchester Ship Canal from the Shropshire Union is restricted by a swing bridge over the first lock (adjacent to the Holiday Inn) which is not under the control of CRT. Boaters wishing to enter the canal must first contact Cheshire West and Chester Council (0300 123 7028) to make arrangements for the bridge to be swung. They require *eight hours notice* and will make a charge for weekend operation. Any difficulties in obtaining assistance should be referred to CRT at Northwich (0303 040 4040; enquiries.westmidlands@canalrivertrust.org.uk).

Manchester Ship Canal Harbour Master, Queen Elizabeth II Dock, Eastham, Wirral (0151 327 1461; www.shipcanal.co.uk). The ship canal currently carries 2,500 vessel movements each year, and this number is increasing. A great deal of it is hazardous, petro-chemical traffic and therefore a no smoking regime is enforced. The canal company is happy to allow pleasure boat use on the understanding that certain conditions are adhered to. It is not a navigation for the novice boater and should be viewed as a transit corridor for the experienced boat owner (not hire boater) to access the River Weaver, the River Mersey, the Shropshire Union Canal or the cruising waterways above Pomona Lock.

1 The boat must be carrying at least £3 million third party insurance cover.
2 The boat is subject to an annual Certificate of Seaworthiness carried out by an MSC approved surveyor (listed in the Pleasure Craft Transit Notes).
3 The appropriate fee is paid by cheque, currently set at £29 Ellesmere Port to Weston Marsh Lock and £143 Ellesmere Port to Manchester. Transit through Pomona Lock is £25 each way.
4 The boater must contact the harbourmaster at least 48 hours in advance of passage to obtain copies of:
   a) Pleasure Craft Transit Notes (or visit www.waterways.org.uk and search on 'Manchester Ship Canal').
   b) Bylaws. At this juncture the boater can discuss appropriate times of arrival and departure to coincide with scheduled shipping movements.
5 At all times the boater is required to act in a responsible manner and be aware that this is a daytime transit route only, with no lay-by facilities. One should familiarise oneself with the geography of the canal before setting out. A schematic map of the canal is appended to the Pleasure Craft Transit Notes.
6 VHF radio equipment is desirable (the Manchester Ship Canal Company call and operate on channel 14 in the canal and channel 7 on the River Mersey) and if not available a mobile phone should be considered essential.
7 There is further useful information, compiled by the local IWA Region, at www.waterways.org.uk/waterways/discover-the-waterways/manchester-ship-canal.

Weston Marsh Lock For access to the River Weaver, through Weston Marsh Lock, you must give *48 hours prior notice* to the Northwich office (0303 040 4040). Please note these locks are only operated *during office hours Mon-Fri*. All necessary paperwork MUST be in place for the Manchester Ship Canal prior to passage. During the summer season (*from approximately mid-March to end of October*) Weston Marsh Lock is also available for passage once in any *weekend period* subject to *prior notice* being given to the Northwich office *before 16:30pm on the previous Thu*. The passage is based on a first come first served basis and will normally mean the lock is available for a *4-hour period*. VHF channel for the River Weaver is 74.

WALKING AND CYCLING

Between Chester and Ellesmere Port the towpath is in excellent condition with a hard surface throughout and for the most part is used by National Cycle Network 56.

Bicycles can be hired from Victoria Lodge Guest House 64 Hoole Road, Chester CH2 3NL (01244 351305; www.chestercyclehire.com).

Chester Port has been recognised as the first inland Heritage Harbour, following a submission by the Inland Waterways Association. 'Heritage Harbours' is an initiative by the Maritime Heritage Trust and the National Historic Ships Shipshape Network, with support from European Maritime Heritage. It highlights historic ports that played an important role in the maritime and industrial history of the UK. For walking opportunities visit www.chesterheritagefestival.co.uk/a-heritage-port.

Pubs and Restaurants (pages 114–115)

◗✗ 1 Ring O'Bells Village Road, Christleton, Chester CH3 7AS (01244 335422; www.ringobellschester.co.uk). Large extended pub with a conservatory extension serving real ale and food *daily 12.00-21.00 (Sun 19.00)*. Outside seating and play area, dog- and child-friendly. Newspapers and Wi-Fi. Camping. *Open 11.30-23.00 (Sun 21.00)*.

There are many pubs in Chester including:

◗ 2 The Albion Park Park Street, Chester CH1 1RN. (01244 340345; www.albioninnchester.co.uk). City-centre pub of great character – a genuine living memorial to the memory of World War I and the last Victorian corner pub in Chester. Real ales. Food *L and E (not Wed & Sun)*. Dog-friendly, no children. Real fires. B&B. *Open L and E Mon-Tue & Thu-Sat*.

◗ 3 Ye Olde Custom House Inn 65-67 Watergate Street, Chester CH1 2LB (01244 324435; www.facebook.com/yeoldecustomhouse). Comfortable, 17th-C city pub, not far from the racecourse, serving real ale along with food *all day, every day*. Outside seating, live music and traditional pub games. *Open daily 12.00-23.00*.

◗ 4 Alexander's Live 2 Rufus Court, Chester CH1 2JW (01244 401402; www.alexanderslive.com). Situated in a picturesque courtyard, this establishment is a continental-style café by day and a jazz, blues and comedy venue by night. Real ales, fine wines, snacks and meals are available *Thu-Sun 13.00-18.00 (Sun 17.00)* together with pre-show meals *Thu-Sat at 19.00*. Children welcome *during the day*. In the evening you can reserve a table with a meal or just turn up at the door. Outside seating. Wi-Fi. *Open Mon-Sat 11.00-00.00 & Sun 12.00-22.30*. Admission fee.

◗ 5 The Old Harkers Arms 1 Russell Street, Chester CH3 5AL (01244 344525; www.brunningandprice.co.uk/harkers). Atmospheric converted canalside warehouse serving real ales and food *Mon-Fri 12.00-21.30 & Sat-Sun 12.00-19.00. (Brunch 10.30-12.00)*.

Canalside tables, dog-friendly. Wi-Fi. *Open Mon-Sat 10.30-23.00 & Sun12.00-22.30*.

◗✗ 6 The Mill Hotel Milton Street, Chester CH1 3NF (01244 350035; www.millhotel.com). Interesting and ever-changing range of guest real ales and real cider. There are several restaurants serving a range of food *daily 12.00-21.30*. Children welcome *until 21.00*. Jazz Mon. Newspapers, sports TV and Wi-Fi. B&B. *Open daily 10.00-00.00*.

◗✗ 7 Telford's Warehouse Tower Wharf, Raymond Street, Chester CH1 4EZ (01244 390090; www.telfordswarehousechester.com). Regular music venue, host to a varied range of bands, catering for most tastes and serving a selection of home-made bar meals *daily L and E & Sun 12.00-21.00*, together with real ales and real cider. Dog-friendly, Canalside seating, dog- and family-friendly. Wi-Fi. *Open Mon-Thu 12.00-23.00 (Wed-Thu 00.30) & Fri-Sun 12.00-01.00*.

◗✗ 8 The Pied Bull 57 Northgate Street, Chester CH1 2HQ (01244 325829; www.piedbull.co.uk). Reputed to be the oldest licensed house in Chester (and describing itself as a city centre inn with the warm feeling of a country pub), this haunted, oak-beamed, 11th-C hostelry serves real ales from its own microbrewery, together with a first-class range of homemade food *daily 11.00-21.00 (Sun 20.00)*. Real Cider. Quiz Thu. Dog- and child-friendly *(until 21.30)* & courtyard seating. Newspapers and Wi-Fi. B&B. *Open daily 11.00-23.00 (Fri-Sat 00.00)*.

◗✗ 9 The Bear & Billet 94 Lower Bridge Street, Chester CH1 1RU (01244 311886; www.markettowntaverns.co.uk/pub-and-bar-finder/north-west/bear-billet). Dating from 1664, this fine example of a timber-framed, black and white building (complete with resident ghosts) dispenses real ales and appetising homemade food *Tue-Sat 12.00-21.00 (Tue-Wed 20.00) & Sun 12.00-19.00)*. Real cider. Dog- and family-friendly, walled-garden. *Sun* folk music. Newspapers, real fires, sports TV and Wi-Fi. *Open Tue-Sun 12.00-23.00*.

117

Wirral

Sweeping northwards along the lock-free pound from Chester to the Mersey, the canal enters open country for the last time as it crosses the Wirral. The handsome stone railway viaduct over the navigation carries the Chester–Birkenhead line. The docks and basins of Ellesmere Port itself, where the Shropshire Union Canal meets the Manchester Ship Canal, are – or were – very extensive. Telford's famous warehouses in which the narrowboats and barges were loaded and discharged under cover were regrettably set alight by local hooligans and had to be demolished in the interests of safety. But now part of the old dock complex is the home of the Boat Museum, a large sub-aqua centre and the headquarters of the British Sub-Aqua Club. The sprawling museum site, making excellent use of the multitude of different buildings once part of the docks complex, plays host to a wide range of festive activity from boating jamborees to a variety of musical events. It has more than once been the venue for an excellent weekend of Cajun music and dance, the boats forming a strikingly colourful backdrop to non-stop revelling. Whatever one's interests, making the journey beyond Chester is always well worthwhile although weed can be a problem north of Bridge 134 *in summer*. There is still access for boats from the Shropshire Union through several wide locks down into the Manchester Ship Canal. But no pleasure boat may enter the ship canal without giving notice to the Ship Canal Company (*see* details on page 116). Those wishing to use it as a transit corridor to the River Weaver should also contact CRT on 0303 040 4040; enquiries.westmidlands@canalrivertrust.org.uk to arrange for the operation of Weston Marsh Lock *during duty hours only*. The North West Region of the Inland Waterways Association publishes an excellent guide to navigating the Ship Canal: visit www.waterways.org.uk/waterways/discover-the-waterways/manchester-ship-canal.

● **Stoak**
Cheshire. Tel. Also spelt Stoke, there is little of interest in this scattered village, except a pleasant country pub and a small, pretty church.
Chester Zoo Moston Road, Upton, Chester CH2 1EU (01244 380280; www.chesterzoo.org). ½ mile south of Caughall Bridge (134). Wide variety of animals, shown as much as possible without bars and fences, enhanced by attractive flower gardens and its own miniature canal. Largest elephant house in the world. *Open summer daily 10.00-17.00 (winter 16.00)*. Charge.

● **Ellesmere Port**
Cheshire. All services. An industrial town of little interest apart from its once fine Victorian railway station.
National Waterways Museum South Pier Road, Ellesmere Port CH65 4FW (0151 355 5017; www.canalrivertrust.org.uk/places-to-visit/national-waterways-museum). Established in the old Ellesmere Port basins. Exhibits, models and photos trace the development of the canal system from early times to its heyday in the 19th C. Vessels on display in the basin include a diverse and widely representative array of narrowboats, a tunnel tug, a weedcutter plus some larger vessels. Restored period cottages. An exciting and expanding venture in a splendid setting beside the ship canal, and not to be missed. Our canal heritage is still alive. Café *Open daily 10.00-16.00*. Charge. *See also* **Boatyards** page 119.

Tourist Information Centre Unit 22b, Cheshire Oaks Designer Outlet Ellesmere Port CH65 9JJ. (0115 348 5600; www.chestertourist.com/cheshireoaks.htm). *Opening hours vary so telephone for details.*

● **Wirral**
Cheshire. All services. A peninsula defined by the River Mersey on its east side and the River Dee along its west shore. Birkenhead is the focal town but it is the whole area that is now promoted rather than just a single habitation. The area's history dates back to the foundation of a Benedictine Priory created in 1150 and it was the monks who first established the ferry route across the Mersey. More recently shipbuilding became the dominant industry with the arrival of William Laird who, in 1825 set up his first shipyard here.
Birkenhead Market Claughton Road, Grange Precinct, Birkenhead CH41 2YH (0151 666 3194/5; www.birkenheadmarket.co.uk). Over 300 indoor and outdoor stalls to choose from. *Open Mon-Sat. 09.00-17.00.*
Birkenhead Park Visitor Centre Park Drive, Birkenhead CH41 4HY (0151 652 5197; www.birkenhead-park.org.uk). This elaborate park, designed by Joseph Paxton (of Crystal Palace fame) in 1847, was the first publicly funded civic park in the world and it went on to inspire the designs for Central Park in New York. Park *open daily 09.00-16.30*; playground *open 07.00-22.00.*

ELLESMERE PORT

Canal Court (Trading Estate)

NATIONAL WATERWAYS MUSEUM

Whitby Locks (paired) 14'11"

Chester 8¾m 3L

147A 9

147 Powell's Bridge

146A

146 Pickering's Bridge

145A

STA

145 Stanlow Bridge

144A

144 Bewley's Bridge

142 Weaver's Bridge

141A

LITTLE STANNEY CP

Cheshire Oaks Outlet Village

141 Stanney Mill Bridge

140A New Stanney Bridge

10

LITTLE STANNEY

140 Mason's Bridge

139 Meadow Lane Bridge

Stoak Grange

138 Dension's Bridge

3¼m 3L Ellesmere Port

Chester 5½m 0L

STOAK

STOAK CP

1

137 Stoak Bridge

136 Picton Lane Bridge

M56

135B

135A

15

WERVI

The Dungeon

Cheshire Way Croughton

135 Croughton Bridge

Croughton Cottage

Ashwood Ho

Chorlton Hall

Rock Bank

115

Pipe Bridge

Wervin New Hall

Boatyards

B National Waterways Museum South Pier Road, Ellesmere Port CH65 4FW (0151 355 5017; www.canalrivertrust.org.uk/places-to-visit/national-waterways-museum). Pump out, visitor moorings, Calor Gas, coal, wood. Boaters may use the museum's shop, café and toilets.

BOAT TRIPS

Arranged from the National Waterways Museum on *nb Centaur*. runs 30 min trips from the Waterways Museum, *daily throughout the summer, departing 13.00 and 14.00*. Telephone 0151 355 5017 for further details.

CANOEING AND PADDLEBOARDING

A useful insight into paddling opportunities for a family along this, the most northerly stretch of the waterway, can be found at www.getoutwiththekids.co.uk/water/canoeing-shropshire-union-canal. Canoe and paddleboard hire, covering Cheshire and North Wales, is available from Direct Kayaks at 07423 283050; www.wrexhamkayakhire.co.uk.

Pubs and Restaurants

1 The Bunbury Arms Little Stannley Lane, Stoak CH2 4HW (01244 951833; www.bunburyarms.co.uk). Real ales and food available *Mon-Fri L and E & Sat-Sun 12.00-20.30*. Garden, dog- and child-friendly. Real fires. *Open daily 12.00-22.00*.

2 The Wheatsheaf 43 Overpool Road, Ellesmere Port CH66 3LN (0151 356 7454; www.jdwetherspoon.com/pubs/all-pubs/england/cheshire/the-wheatsheaf-ellesmere-port). Close to Overpool railway station. Large, 1950s estate pub, serving real ale and food *daily 09.00-22.00*. Family-friendly and outdoor seating. Traditional pub games, library area, sports TV and Wi-Fi.*Open 09.00- 00.00 (Fri-Sat 01.00)*

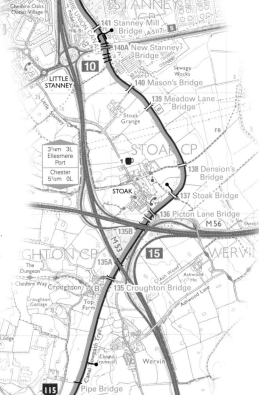

Blue Planet Aquarium Longlooms Road, Little Stanney, Ellesmere Port CH65 9LF (0151 357 8804; www.blueplanetaquarium.com). West of bridge 140A and M53 junction 10. New aquarium with two floors of interactive exhibits, themed restaurant, Caribbean reef, Amazon Jungle and Oil-Rig shop. An excellent all-weather attraction, but entry will cost a family of four more than £40. *Open daily 10.00–18.00 (closes at 17.00 Mon–Fri during term time)*.

Bromborough Pool Village Wirral (0151 649 6481; www.riverside.org.uk). Constructed in the shadow of its more famous neighbour – Port Sunlight – and today surrounded by modern factory complexes, this delightful village was the brainchild of the Prices family and was built to house their candle factory workers. It still retains its charm and tranquility and remains an historical example of Victorian philanthropy. Follow the Heritage Trail, visit the parish church or delve into the past via the Heritage Centre in the village hall. *There are no opening time restrictions on the village.* Trains from Ellesmere Port or Chester to Port Sunlight.

Charley's Ceramics 7b Craft Workshops, Ellesmere Port CH65 4FW (0151 538 7215/07594 675192; www.charleysceramics.co.uk). An opportunity for the whole family to paint a range ornaments ranging from plates to teapots. Painting, popcorn, coffee, ice cream and pancakes. *Opening times vary so telephone for details.* Charge.

Floral Pavilion Theatre Marine Promenade, New Brighton CH45 2JS (0151 666 0000; www.floralpavilion.com). A welcoming and upgraded theatre with a full and varied programme of entertainment throughout the year.

Lady Lever Art Gallery Lower Rd, Port Sunlight, Bebington, Wirral CH62 5EQ (0151 478 4136; www.liverpoolmuseums.org.uk/lady-lever-art-gallery). Assembled by William Hesketh Lever and dedicated to his wife, the gallery houses a collection of fine and decorative art treasures in a sumptuous Beaux-Arts building. Café. *Open Tue–Sun 10.00–18.00 & B Hol Mon.* Donations. Trains from Ellesmere Port or Chester to Bebington.

Mersey Ferries Pier Head, George Parade, Liverpool L3 1DP (0151 330 1003; www.merseyferries.co.uk). *50-min cruises daily* together with *regular cross-river ferry services.* Also cruises further afield including the Manchester Ship Canal (Apr–Oct). *Cruises Mon–Fri 10.00–15.00 & Sat–Sun 10.00–18.00.* Café and shop. Charge. Operates from ferry terminals at Woodside and Seacombe on Wirral and Pier Head, Liverpool. Also café and Playport at Seacombe – telephone for details. Charge.

Ness Botanic Gardens Neston Road, Neston CH64 4AY (0151 795 6300; www.liverpool.ac.uk/ness-gardens). Originating from the first seeds planted by Arthur Kilpin Bulley in 1898, a Liverpool cotton broker and founder of Bees Seeds Ltd. His insatiable appetite for rare and unusual species led him to sponsor early pioneer plant hunters on expeditions to the temperate regions of the Far East, in search of exotic species that could be cultivated in our climate. A striking location, set on the banks of the Dee, with views out over North Wales; in all 64 acres. The shop, tea room and plant sales are *open daily 10.00–17.00* and the gardens *10.00–dusk; last entry 17.00.* Charge.

Port Sunlight Museum & Garden Village, and the Lady Lever Art Gallery 23 King George's Drive, Port Sunlight Village, Wirral CH62 5DX (museum 0151 644 6466/07514 648571; www.portsunlightvillage.com). Picturesque style 19th-C model village built by the soap baron William Hesketh Lever for his Workers. Museum, Edwardian Worker's Cottage Experience, soap works and guided walking tours of the village. Tearoom and shop. Village *always open.* Other attractions *open Wed–Sun 10.00–16.30.* Charge. Online advanced booking for the whole Port Sunlight Experience encouraged.

Also **Gladstone Theatre** (0151 643 8757; www.gladstonetheatre.org.uk). Originally the men's dining hall, opened in 1891, today it is a venue for a variety of entertainment. Telephone for programme. Trains from Ellesmere Port or Chester to Port Sunlight for village and theatre.

Tam O'Shanter Urban Farm Boundary Road, Bidston CH43 7PD (0151 653 9332; www.tamoshanterfarm.org.uk). Small city farm on the edge of Bidston Hill. A safe place for children to visit, with a small but varied collection of farm animals. Café, picnic area, play area and nature trail. *Open daily 09.30–16.30.* Free but donations welcome.

Williamson Art Gallery and Museum Slatey Road, Birkenhead L43 4UE (0151 666 3537; www.williamsonartgallery.org). A permanent collection together with a wide range of changing exhibitions with particular relevance to the area. Café. *Open Wed–Fri 10.30–17.00 (Fri 21.00) & Sat 16.30. Closed B Hols.* Free.

Wirral Tourism & Marketing (0151 666 3188; www.visitwirral.com). Tourist information for the area.

Wirral Tramway 1 Taylor Street, Birkenhead CH41 1BG (0151 647 2128; www.visitwirral.com/things-to-do/wirral-tramway-and-wirral-transport-museum-p18340). Travel back in time on either a genuine Hong Kong Tram or the 1901 beautifully restored Birkenhead tram. Also trams and buses in various stages of restoration and the Baxter Collection of cars and motorcycles. *Open Sat–Sun; Wirral school holidays Wed–Sun & B Hols 13.00–16.30.* Charge. Other examples of the area's industrial heritage are the **Shore Road Pumping Station** (0151 650 1182) – *open as per Tramway and Transport Museum* - and the **Egerton Bridge**. (0151 666 4000). These are all visited as part of the Birkenhead Heritage Trail. Charge.

STAFFORDSHIRE & WORCESTERSHIRE CANAL: NORTH

MAXIMUM DIMENSIONS

Length: 72'
Beam: 7'
Headroom: 6' 0"

MANAGER

0303 040 4040
enquiries.westmidlands@canalrivertrust.org.uk

MILEAGE

AUTHERLEY JUNCTION to:
GREAT HAYWOOD JUNCTION: 20½ miles

Locks: 12

Canoeing and Paddleboarding: Category 1

Construction of this navigation was begun immediately after that of the Trent & Mersey, to effect the joining of the rivers Trent, Mersey and Severn. Engineered by James Brindley, the Staffordshire & Worcestershire was opened throughout in 1772, at a cost of rather over £100,000. It stretched 46 miles from Great Haywood on the Trent & Mersey to the River Severn, which it joined at Stourport. The canal was an immediate success. It was well placed to bring goods from the Potteries down to Gloucester, Bristol and the West Country; while the Birmingham Canal, which joined it half-way along at Aldersley Junction, fed manufactured goods northwards from the Black Country to the Potteries via Great Haywood. In 1815 the Worcester & Birmingham Canal opened, offering a more direct but heavily locked canal link between Birmingham and the Severn. The Staffordshire & Worcestershire answered this threat by gradually extending the opening times of the locks until, by 1830, they were open 24 hours a day. When the Birmingham & Liverpool Junction Canal was opened from Autherley to Nantwich in 1835, traffic bound for Merseyside from Birmingham naturally began to use this more direct, modern canal. The Staffordshire & Worcestershire lost a great deal of traffic over its length as most of the boats now passed along only the ½-mile stretch of the Staffordshire & Worcestershire Canal between Autherley and Aldersley Junctions. The company levied absurdly high tolls for this tiny length. The B & LJ Company therefore co-operated with the Birmingham Canal Company in 1836 to promote in Parliament a Bill for the Tettenhall & Autherley Canal and Aqueduct. This project was to be a canal flyover, going from the Birmingham Canal right over the profiteering Staffordshire & Worcestershire and locking down into the Birmingham & Liverpool Junction Canal. The Staffordshire & Worcestershire company had to give way, and reduced its tolls to an acceptable level. In spite of this set back, the Staffordshire & Worcestershire maintained a good profit, and high dividends were paid throughout the rest of the 19th C. From the 1860s onwards, railway competition began to bite, and the company's profits began to slip. Several modernisation schemes came to nothing, and the canal's trade declined. Now the canal is used almost exclusively by pleasure craft. It is covered in full in *the Severn, Avon & Birmingham Guide* of this series.

Autherley Junction

Autherley Junction is marked by a big white bridge on the towpath side. The stop lock just beyond marks the entrance to the Shropshire Union: there is a useful boatyard just to the north of it. Leaving Autherley, the Staffordshire & Worcestershire passes new housing before running through a very narrow cutting in rock, once known as 'Pendeford Rockin', after a local farm: there is only room for boats to pass in the designated places, so **a good lookout should be kept for oncoming craft**. After passing the motorway the navigation leaves behind the suburbs of Wolverhampton and enters pleasant farmland. The bridges need care: although the bridgeholes are reasonably wide, the actual arches are rather low.

● **Autherley Junction**
A busy canal junction with a full range of boating facilities close by.

● **Coven**
Staffs. PO, stores, chemist, *off-licence, takeaway, fish & chips.* The only true village on this section, Coven lies beyond a dual carriageway north west of Cross Green Bridge. There are a large number of shops, including a *laundrette.*

Boatyards

ⓑ**Napton Narrowboats** Autherley Junction, Oxley Moor Road, Wolverhampton WV9 5HW (01902 789942; www.napton-marina.co.uk/bases/autherley). 🛉🛠 D Pump out, gas, narrowboat hire, overnight mooring, short term mooring, slipway, limited chandlery, provisions, books and maps, boat repairs, solid fuel, gifts. *Emergency call out. Open daily 09.00-17.00.*

ⓑ**Oxley Marina** The Wharf, Oxley Moor Road, Wolverhampton WV10 6TZ (01902 789522; www.oxleymarina.co.uk). 🛉🛠 DE Pump out, gas, day boat hire, over night and long-term mooring, slipway, solid fuel, winter storage, lifting facility, DIY facilities, boat sales and repairs, engine sales and repairs, welding and fabrication, toilets, car parking, *emergency call out.* 🍺 3 Licensed bar *evenings and at weekends.* Snacks.

Pubs and Restaurants

🍺✗ 1 **The Harrowby Arms** Patshull Avenue, Fordhouses, Wolverhampton WV6 6RQ (01902 238555; www.facebook.com/thenewharrowby). An estate pub serving real ale and food *L and E.* Outside seating, children welcome. Traditional pub games. *Open daily 12.00-23.00.*

🍺✗ 2 **Fox Inn** Brewood Road, Cross Green, Wolverhampton WV10 7PW (01902 798786; www.vintageinn.co.uk/restaurants/midlands/thefoxandanchorcrossgreen). Large chain-pub, serving real ale and food throughout the day. Garden, dog- and child-friendly. Wi-Fi. *Open daily 11.30 -22.30.*

CANOEING AND PADDLEBOARDING
Apart from nudging the outskirts of Wolverhampton, the northern half of the Staffordshire & Worcestershire Canal is largely rural once through the M54 motorway bridge. Its exaggerated, meandering course tells the paddler that this is a contour canal, giving them the opportunity to enjoy features on the landscape from many, varying angles! There is the usual excellent overview at www.gopaddling.info/canals/staffordshire-and-worcestershire-canal and an active canoe club at Gailey. The club offers taster sessions *Sun 10.00-12.00 & Tue and Thu 18.00-20.00.* They can be contacted at Croft Lane, Gailey, Penkridge ST19 5PY (07790 216741; www.facebook.com/gaileycc).

91

125

69 Chillington Bridge

Park Lodge

Upper Cottages

8 Park Bridge

107

Brewood Park Farm

ROMAN ROAD (course of)

COVEN

941

Grange Farm

Slade Heath Bridge

72

57 Slade Heath Railway Bridges

SHROPSHIRE UNION CANAL

7 Hunting Bridge

117

River Penk

Lawn Farm

Lawn Lane

06

Three Hammers Golf Complex

FB

2

CROSS GREEN

71 Cross Green Bridge

Cross Green Farm

Three Hammer Farm

The Old Hattons

101

Coven Lawn

The Middle Hattons

6 Lower Hattons Bridge

Lower Pendeford Farm

05

104

Ash Coppice

Coven Lane

Monarch's Way

Shawhall Farm

102

70 Brinsford Bridge

Brinsford Farm

Cat and Kittens Lane

SHIRF

5 Upper Hattons Bridge

Island Pool

Sewage Works

STAFFORDSHIRE AND WORCESTERSHIRE CANAL

69 Coven Heath Bridge Pipe Bridge

COVEN HEATH

2

M54

Middle Lane

Clewley Coppice

Factory

M54 Motorway

A449

Works

Greenfield Golf C

Business Park

Cricket Ground

Works

P

Caravan Park

Pendeford Mill Nature Reserve

Solar Panels

113

Don Bay

4 Pendeford Bridge

Works

Upper Pendeford Farm

Forster Bridge 68

Marsh Lane Bridge 67

Fordhouses

Sch

OOK

P

B 3A

Turnover Bridge 3

Pendeford

Very Narrow Cutting

1

Academy

Sch

Bathurst Bridge 2

Sch

Autherley Junction

40¾m 29L Hurleston

Autherley Stop Lock

21m 12L Great Haywood

Aldersley Junction ½m 0L

Elston Hall

B

66 Blaydon Road Bridge

1 Junction Bridge

OXLEY

WOLVERHAMPTON

B

3

65 Oxley Moor Bridge

Pipe Bridge

Aqueducts

Railway Bridges

Blakeley Green

Pipe Bridge

Aldersley Junction Birmingham Main Line

see Books 2 & 3

Aldersley Bridge 64

ALDERSLEY

21

Staffs and Worcs

20

see Book 2

Claregate

Dunstall Park Bridge

Low Hill

Pol. Sta.

WALKING AND CYCLING
The towpath is generally in good condition for both walkers and cyclists.

Gailey Wharf

The considerable age of this canal is shown by its extremely twisting course, revealed after passing the railway bridge. There are few real centres of population along this stretch, which comprises largely former heathland. The canal widens just before bridge 74, where Brindley incorporated part of a medieval moat into the canal. Hatherton Junction marks the entrance of the former Hatherton Branch of the Staffordshire & Worcestershire Canal into the main line. This branch used to connect with the Birmingham Canal Navigations. It is closed above the derelict second lock, although the channel remains as a feeder for the Staffordshire & Worcestershire Canal. There is a campaign for its restoration. There is a *marina* at the junction. A little further along, a chemical works is encountered, astride the canal in what used to be woodlands. This was once called the 'Black Works', as lamp black was produced here. Gailey Wharf is about a mile further north: it is a small canal settlement that includes a *boatyard* and a large, round, toll keeper's watch-tower, containing a *canal shop* and there are *toilets* nearby. The picturesque Wharf Cottage opposite has been restored as a bijou residence. Half a mile west, along the busy A5, there is a useful *shop selling all manner of combustibles, from coal to kindling, and including gas.* The canal itself disappears under Watling Street and the descends rapidly through four locks into Penkridge. These locks are very attractive, and some are accompanied by little brick bridges. The M6 motorway, and the traffic noise, comes alongside for 1/2 mile, screening the reservoirs which feed the canal.

Pillaton Old Hall Penkridge, ST19 5RZ (01785 712200). South east of bridge 85. Only the gate house and stone-built chapel remain of this late 15th-C brick mansion built by the Littleton family, although there are still traces of the hall and courtyard. The chapel contains a 13th-C wooden carving of a saint. Visiting is by appointment only: telephone 01785 712200. The modest charge is donated to charity.

Gailey and Calf Heath Reservoirs 1/2 mile east of Gailey Wharf, either side of the M6. These are feeder reservoirs for the canal, though rarely drawn on. The public has access to them as nature reserves to study the wide variety of natural life, especially the long-established heronry which is thriving on an island in Gailey Lower Reservoir. In Gailey Upper, fishing is available to the public from the riparian owner. In Gailey Lower a limited number of angling tickets are available on a season ticket basis each year from CRT. There is club sailing on two of the reservoirs.

Boatyards

Ⓑ**Hatherton Marina** Kings Road, Calf Heath WV10 7DU (07476 372819; hathertonmarina.co.uk). Short- and long-term moorings, dry dock, boat building and repairs, engine sales and repairs, boat painting and electrical work, boat fitting out, boat sales, bottom blacking, showers, toilets. BSC Examiner.
Ⓑ**Otherton Boat Haven** Ltd Otherton Lane, Otherton, Penkridge ST19 5NX (01785 712515; 07581 459309; www.othertonboathaven.co.uk). 🛢🎁🔧D Pump out, gas, overnight and long-term mooring, boat and engine sales and repairs, toilets, coal.
Ⓑ**J D Boat Services** The Wharf, Gailey, Stafford ST19 5PR (01902 791811; www.jdboats.co.uk). D Pump out, gas, solid fuel, narrowboat hire, boat share, winter storage, DIY facilities, boat servicing and repairs, painting, wet dock, diesel heaters, boat and engine sales, boat building. Gifts, maps, guides, souvenirs, windlass's etc opposite in the Roundhouse. *Open Mon-Sat 10.30-16.00 (Sat 14.00).*
Ⓑ**ABC Boat Hire** At J D Boat Services (01905 610660; www.abcboathire.com). Narrowboat hire.

Pubs and Restaurants

🍺 **1 Cross Keys** Filance Lane, Penkridge ST19 5HJ (07810 080668; www.facebook.com/cross.keys.96). Once a lonely canal-side pub, it is now modernised and surrounded by a housing estate. Family-orientated, it serves real ale and food *daily 11.00-21.00.* Garden. Traditional pub games, real fires and sports TV. *Open 11.00-22.00 (Sat 23.00).*
🍺✕ **2 The Spread Eagle** Watling Street, Gailey ST19 5PN (01902 790212; www. spreadeaglepubgailey.co.uk). Imposing road house, with a massive garden and children's play area, serving real ale and food *all day (breakfast from 08.00).* *Daily* carvery, takeaway service and Wi-Fi. B&B. *Open 08.00-23.00 (Sun 22.30).*

84 Filance Bridge

126

Cross Keys 83A Bridge

BRIDGE

Bog Moor

Moor Hall Cottages

Pillaton Farm

PILLATON

Lyne Hill

Lynhill Bridge 83

Nursery

98

Depot

Otherton Lane

B

82 Otherton Bridge

OTHERTON

Otherton Farm

Lock

36 Otherton Lock Helipad 10' 3"

81 Otherton Lane Bridge

96

Mickleswood Lane

102

Rail Bridge

Aqueduct

Fullmoor Wood

BOAT TRIPS
Truman Enterprise Narrowboat Trust
Hatherton Marina, Queens Road, Calf Heath,
Near Cannock, WV10 7DT (01922 479926/07763
214524; www.truman-enterprise.org.uk).
nb Enterprise provides affordable residential
and day trips for youth and community groups.
Disabled access.

94

35 Rodbaston Lock 8' 6"

104

Galley Lea Farm

Galley Lea Lane

13¼m 11L
Great
Haywood

Autherley
Junction
7¾m 1L

34 Bogg's Lock 8' 6"

33 Brick Kiln Lock 8' 0"

97

Plough Farm

POTTERY

A5

2

102

91

GAILEY

Galley Farm

79 Gailey Bridge

B 32 Gailey Top Lock 8' 6"

WHARF

12

GAILEY LOWER RESERVOIR

106

GAILEY UPPER RESERVOIR

107

Croft Farm

Gravelly Way House

FB

78A Four Ashes Bridge

78 Gravelly Way Bridge

Gravelly Way

Quarry

Reservoir Plantation

CALF HEATH WOOD

CALF HEATH RESERVOIR

Watling Street Plantation

Vic

Woodlands Lane

Oak Lane

108

Heath Farm

CALF HEATH

Pipe Bridges

Woodside Farm

Vicarage Road

M6

Chemical Works

106

Straight Mile Farm

106

The Hollies

Works

Calf Heath Bridge 77

76

Marina

Lock

Hatherton Branch

B

Long Moll's Bridge

Aqueduct

FBs

Four Ashes

Sewage Works

Goldie Brook Bridge

Industrial Estate

Deepmore Farm

75 Deepmore Bridge

Standeford

Pool House

Latherford

Upper Latherford Farm

112

Aqueduct

Lower Latherford Farm

108

A449

123

73 Laches Bridge

Lower Laches Farm

74 Moat House Bridge

Aspley Farm

The Laches

Sch

Penkridge

The navigation now passes through Penkridge and is soon approached by the little River Penk: the two water courses share the valley for the next few miles. The Cross Keys at Filance Bridge (*see page 136*) was once an isolated canal pub – now it is surrounded by housing, which spreads along the canal in each direction. Apart from the noise of the motorway this is a pleasant valley: there are plenty of trees, a handful of locks and the large Teddesley Park alongside the canal. At Acton Trussell the M6 roars off to the north west and once again peace returns to the waterway. Teddesley Park Bridge was at one time quite ornamental, and became known as 'Fancy Bridge'. It is less so now. At Shutt Hill an iron post at the bottom of the lock is the only reminder of a small wharf which once existed here. The post was used to turn the boats into the dock.

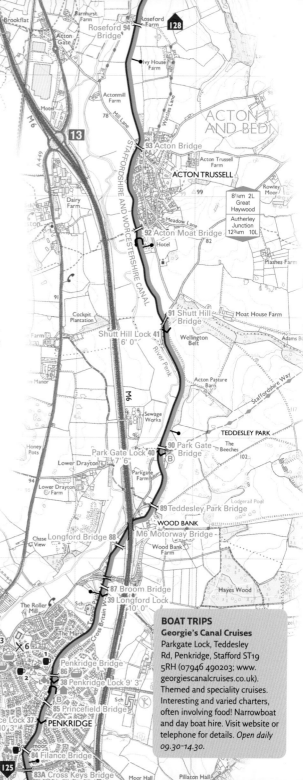

BOAT TRIPS

Georgie's Canal Cruises
Parkgate Lock, Teddesley Rd, Penkridge, Stafford ST19 5RH (07946 490203; www.georgiescanalcruises.co.uk). Themed and speciality cruises. Interesting and varied charters, often involving food! Narrowboat and day boat hire. Visit website or telephone for details. *Open daily 09.30-14.30.*

● **Penkridge**
Staffs. PO, stores, chemist, hardware, butcher, baker, takeaways, fish & chips, off-licence, garage, library, station. Above Penkridge Lock is a good place to tie up in this relatively old village. It is bisected by a trunk road, but luckily most of the village lies to the east of it. The church of St Michael is tall and sombre, and is well-kept. A harmonious mixture of styles, the earliest part dates from the 11th C, but the whole was restored in 1881. There is a fine Dutch 18th-C wrought iron screen brought from Cape Town, and the tower is believed to date from c.1500. There are fine monuments of the Littletons of Pillaton Hall (*see* page 124), dating from 1558 and later.

Teddesley Park On the east bank of the canal. The Hall, once the family seat of the Littletons, was used during World War II as a prisoner-of-war camp, but has since been demolished. Its extensive wooded estate still remains.

● **Acton Trussell**
Staffs. PO box, tel. A village overwhelmed by modern housing: much the best way to see it is from the canal. The church stands to the south, overlooking the navigation. The west tower dates from the 13th C, topped by a spire built in 1562.

Boatyards

Ⓑ **Bourne Boat Builders** Park Gate Lock, Teddesley Road, Penkridge ST19 5H (01785 714692; www.bourneboatbuilders.co.uk). Boat building and fitting out. Narrowboat and day boat hire – *see* Georgie's Canal Cruises on page 126.

CANOEING AND PADDLEBOARDING
C2C Outdoors offer a wide range of paddling opportunities on both canals and rivers, including trips along the northern section of the Staffordshire & Worcestershire Canal, using kayaks and open canoes. They can be contacted at 07730 405276; www.c2c-outdoors.co.uk/water-activities-2.

Pubs and Restaurants

🍺✕ **1 The Boat Inn** Cannock Road, Penkridge ST19 5DT (01785 715170; www.facebook.com/ TheBoatInnPenkridge). Mellow and friendly red-brick pub dating from 1779. Real ale. Food is available *Mon-Fri L and E & Sat-Sun 12.00-20.00 (Sun 19.00)*. Child- and dog-friendly, garden. Sports TV. *Open Mon 15.00-23.00; Tue-Sat 12.00-23.00 (Tue 17.00) & Sun 12.00-22.00.*

🍺 **2 The Star Inn** Market Place, Penkridge ST19 5DJ (01785 712513; thestarpenkridge.wixsite.com/ home). Fine old pub serving real ale and bar meals *Mon-Thu L and E & Fri-Sun L*. Patio, dogs and children (until 21.00) welcome. Real fires, sports TV and Wi-Fi. *Open Mon-Thu 16.30-22.00 (Wed 12.00) & Fri-Sun 12.00-22.00 (Sun 20.00).*

🍺 **3 White Hart** Stone Cross, Penkridge ST19 5AS (01785 380828; https://www.facebook.com/ The-White-Hart-Penkridge-109479930856679). This historic former coaching inn, visited by Mary, Queen of Scots, and Elizabeth I, has an impressive frontage, timber-framed with three gables. It serves real ale. Outside seating, dog-friendly.

Traditional pub games, real fires, sports TV and Wi-Fi. *Open 12.00-22.00.*

🍺✕ **4 The Bridge House** Stone Cross, Penkridge ST19 5AS (01785 714426; www.bridgehouse-hotel. co.uk). Rambling, timber-framed hostelry dispensing real ale and a varied restaurant menu *L and E (L served 12.00-18.00)*. Garden, family-friendly. Wi-fi. B&B. *Open Mon-Sat 07.30-23.00 (Mon 10.00) & Sun 10.00-22.00.*

🍺✕ **5 The Littleton Arms** St Michael's Square, Penkridge ST19 5AL (01785 716300; www. thelittletonarms.com). Hotel, bar and restaurant. Real ale and excellent food available *Mon-Fri L and E & Sat-Sun 12.00-21.00*. Garden, dog- and child-friendly *(until 21.00)*. *Open Mon 15.00-21.00 & Tue-Sun 11.00-23.00 (Sun 21.30).*

✕♀ **6 Flames** Mill Street, Penkridge ST19 5AY (01785 712955; www.bridgehouse-hotel.co.uk). Contemporary eastern cuisine. Takeaway service. *Open 17.00-23.00 (Fri-Sat 00.00).*

WALKING AND CYCLING
The Staffordshire Way crosses the canal at Bridge 90. This 90-mile path stretches from Mow Cop in the north (near the Macclesfield Canal) to Kinver Edge in the south, using the Caldon Canal towpath on the way. It connects with the Gritstone Trail, the Hereford & Worcester Way and the Heart of England Way. A guide book is available from local Tourist Information Centres.

Tixall

Continuing north along the shallow Penk valley, the canal soon reaches Radford Bridge, the nearest point to Stafford. It is about 1¹/₂ miles to the centre of town: there is a frequent bus service. A canal branch used to connect with the town via Baswich Lock and the River Sow. If you look carefully west of bridge 101 you can just about deduce where the connection was made – some remains of brickwork are the clue. A mile further north the canal bends around to the south east and follows the pretty valley of the River Sow, and at Milford crosses the river via an aqueduct – an early structure by James Brindley, carried heavily on low brick arches. Tixall Lock offers some interesting views in all directions: the castellated entrance to Shugborough Railway Tunnel at the foot of the thick woods of Cannock Chase and the distant outline of the remarkable Tixall Gatehouse. The canal now completes its journey to the Trent & Mersey Canal at Great Haywood. It is a length of waterway quite unlike any other. Proceeding along this very charming valley, the navigation enters Tixall Wide – an amazing and delightful stretch of water more resembling a lake than a canal, said to have been built in order not to compromise the view from Tixall House (alas, no more), and navigable to the edges. The Wide is noted for its kingfisher population. Woods across the valley conceal Shugborough Hall. The River Trent is met, on its way south from Stoke-on-Trent, and is crossed on an aqueduct. There is a wharf, and *fresh produce* (*see* page 189) can be purchased at the *farm shop* beside Bridge 75 on the Trent & Mersey, which

is entered through an elegantly arched bridge. The bridge is the subject of a very famous photograph taken by the canal historian Eric de Maré. Immediately before this bridge there is a useful *boatyard* which, amongst other services, provides *Elsan disposal* (charge).

Boatyards

Ⓑ**Stafford Boat Club** Off Maple Wood, Wildwood, Stafford ST17 4SG (01785 660725/07716 960049; staffordboatclub.co.uk). At Bridge 96. 🚿🛒 D Pump out, gas, solid fuel, overnight and short-term moorings, limited winter moorings, slipway, wet dock, laundry, print shop, use of clubhouse (bar *open every evening and 12.00-15.00 Sun*).

Ⓑ**Anglo Welsh** The Canal Wharf, Mill Lane, Great Haywood ST18 0RJ (01889 881711; www.anglowelsh.co.uk/locations/bases/great-haywood). 🚿🚿🛒D Pump out (not *Sat*), gas, narrowboat hire, day-hire craft, overnight and long-term mooring, coal, engine repairs, chandlery, toilets, books, maps and gifts, ice cream and soft drinks. *Open daily 08.30-17.00 (Sun 09.00).*

Ⓑ**Great Haywood Marina** The Marina Building, Canalside Farm, Mill Lane, Great Haywood ST18 0RQ (01889 883713/07771 685731; www.greathaywoodmarina.co.uk). 🚿🛒D Pump out, gas, short- and long-term mooring, boat sales and repairs, solid fuel, slipway, chandlery, laundrette, toilets, showers, Wi-Fi, CCTV. Farm shop adjacent.

WALKING AND CYCLING

There is a Nature Trail at Milford Common, and visitors to Shugborough Hall can enjoy excellent walks in the park. There are also a series of walks and rides available from Canalside Farm – *see page 130.*

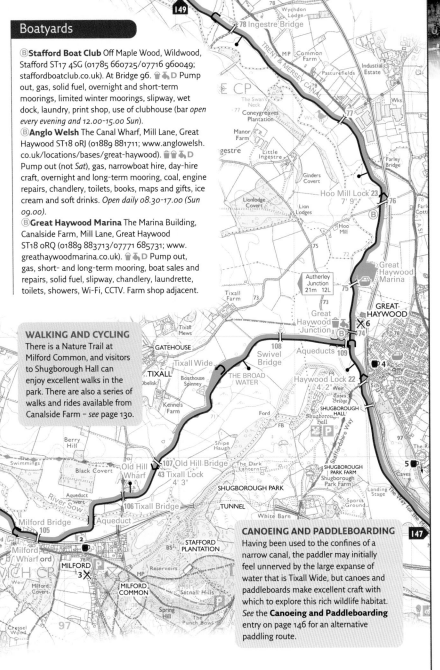

CANOEING AND PADDLEBOARDING

Having been used to the confines of a narrow canal, the paddler may initially feel unnerved by the large expanse of water that is Tixall Wide, but canoes and paddleboards make excellent craft with which to explore this rich wildlife habitat. *See* the **Canoeing and Paddleboarding** entry on page 146 for an alternative paddling route.

The Stafford Riverway Link will restore the old Sow Navigation, which once brought boats 1½ miles into the town from a junction with the Staffordshire & Worcestershire Canal before being closed in the 1920s. Planning permission was granted in 2020 for the basin, a junction with the

canal, a towpath bridge and 12 moorings. The moorings will provide income to continue the project in the future. Eventually it will connect with an aqueduct over the infant River Penk, locking down into the River Sow.

Canalside Farm Mill Lane, Great Haywood ST18 0RQ (01889 881747; www.canalsidefarm.co.uk). Immediately east of Bridge 75, beside the marina. Selling an excellent selection of local (within 30 miles) seasonal, fresh produce. Butcher, baker and delicatessen. PYO strawberries and raspberries. Bedding plants and ice creams. Shop *open daily 09.00–17.00* and cafe and the coffee hut *open 09.00–16.00.* Hot food served *until 15.00.*

- **Stafford**

Staffs. All services. This town is well worth visiting, since there is a remarkable wealth of fine old buildings. These include a handsome City Hall complex of ornamental Italianate buildings, c.1880. The robust-looking gaol is nearby; and the church of St Mary stands in very pleasing and spacious grounds. There are some pretty back alleys: Church Lane contains a splendid-looking eating house, and at the bottom of the lane a fruiterer's shop is in a thatched cottage built in 1610.

Tourist Information Centre Gatehouse Theatre, Eastgate Street, Stafford ST16 2LT (01785 619619; www.tourist.me.uk/staffordshire-tourist-information). *Open Mon-Fri 09.30–17.00 & Sat 09.00–16.00.*

- **The Stafford Branch**

Just west of bridge 101 there was once a lock taking a branch off the Staffordshire & Worcestershire to Stafford. One mile long, it was unusual in that it was not a canal but the canalised course of the River Sow.

- **Milford**

Staffs. PO box, tel, takeaway Best reached from Tixall Bridge (106). Milford Hall is hidden by trees.

- **Tixall**

Staffs. PO box, tel. Just to the east are the stables and the gatehouse of the long-vanished Tixall Hall. This massive square Elizabethan building dates from 1598 and is fully four storeys high. It stands alone in a field and is considered to be one of the most ambitious gatehouses in the country. The gatehouse is now available for holiday lets: telephone the Landmark Trust (01628 825925) for details.

- **Great Haywood**

Staffs. PO, stores, chemist. Centre of the Great Haywood and Shugborough Conservation Area, the village is attractive in parts, but it is closely connected in many ways to Shugborough Park, to which it is physically linked by the very old Essex Bridge, where the crystal clear waters of the River Sow join the Trent on its way down from Stoke.

Shugborough Hall *NT.* Milford, near Stafford ST17 0XB (01889 880160; www.nationaltrust.org.uk/ shugborough-estate). Walk west from Haywood Lock and through the park. The present house dates from 1693, but was substantially altered by James Stuart around 1760 and by Samuel Wyatt around the turn of the 18th C. It was at this time that the old village of Shugborough was bought up and demolished by the Anson family so that they should enjoy more privacy and space in their park. Family fortunes fluctuated greatly for the Ansons, the Earl of Lichfield's family; and crippling death duties in the 1960s brought about the transfer of the estate to the National Trust. The house has been restored at great expense and there are some magnificent rooms and many treasures inside.

Shugborough Park There are some remarkable sights in the large park which encircles the Hall. Thomas Anson, who inherited the estate in 1720, enlisted in 1744 the help of his famous brother, Admiral George Anson, to beautify and improve the house and the park. In 1762 he commissioned James Stuart, a neo-Grecian architect, to embellish the park. 'Athenian' Stuart set to with a will, and the spectacular results of his work can be seen scattered round the grounds. The stone monuments that he built have deservedly extravagant names such as the Tower of the Winds, the Lanthorn of Demosthenes and so on.

Park Farm at Shugborough (01889 880160; www.nationaltrust.org.uk/shugborough-estate/features/park-farm). Within Shugborough Park, and designed by Samuel Wyatt, this was a classic, innovative model farm in its time. Today the visitor can understand why through the excellent interpretation in the different exhibition spaces dotted around the courtyard. Heritage breeds, including longhorn cows, Southdown sheep and Tamworth pigs, can be seen grazing in the extensive pasture. Café. *Opening times* vary according to the season so visit the website for further details. Charge.

Pubs and Restaurants (pages 128–129)

⬤ 1 Radford Bank Inn Radford Bank, Stafford ST17 4PG (01785 242825). Canalside at bridge 98. Real ale. Food is served *daily 08.00–22.00* (including *weekday* breakfast *08.00–11.30*). Family-friendly, garden. Traditional pub games, sports TV and Wi-Fi. Quiz *Fri.* Takeaway service. *Open daily 08.00–23.00.*

⬤ 2 The Barley Mow 28 Main Road, Milford ST17 0UW (01785 665230; www.greeneking-pubs.co.uk/pubs/staffordshire/barley-mow). Predominantly aimed at the hungry, this pub also serves ales – food *09.00–22.00 daily* (including *weekday* breakfast *09.00–11.00*). Children's 'PlayZone' *open 11.00–20.00.* Garden and Wi-Fi. *Open 09.30–23.00 (Sun 22.30)*

✕ ⬤ 3 The Viceroy Indian Restaurant 8 Brocton Road, Milford ST17 0UH (01889 663239; www.viceroyrestaurant.co.uk). With its elegant, modern interior and warm welcome, this restaurant showcases its chef/proprietor's Indian and Bangladeshi culinary heritage. Food to savour is served *daily 17.30–23.00.* Takeaway service with online ordering.

Try also: **⬤✕ 4 The Clifford Arms** Main Road, Great Haywood ST18 0SR (01889 881321; www.cliffordarms.co.uk), **⬤ 5 The Red Lion** Main Road, Little Haywood ST18 0TS (01889 881314) and **✕ 6 Canalside Farm Café** Mill Lane, Great Haywood ST18 0RQ (01889 881747; www.canalsidefarm.co.uk).

TRENT & MERSEY CANAL

MAXIMUM DIMENSIONS

Derwent Mouth to Horninglow Basin, Burton upon Trent
Length: 72'
Beam: 14'
Headroom: 7'
Stenson lock is very tight for 14ft beam craft and Weston Lock is tight for boats of 72ft length.

Burton upon Trent to south end of Harecastle Tunnel
Length: 72'
Beam: 7'
Headroom: 6' 3"

Harecastle Tunnel
Length: 72'
Beam: 7'
Headroom: 5' 9"

North end of Harecastle Tunnel to Croxton Aqueduct
Length: 72'
Beam: 7'
Headroom: 7'

Croxton Aqueduct to Preston Brook Tunnel
Length: 72'
Beam: 8' 2"
Headroom: 6' 3"

MANAGERS:
0303 040 4040

Derwent Mouth to Stretton (Burton Upon Trent):
enquiries.eastmidlands@canalrivertrust.org.uk
Stretton (Burton Upon Trent) to Great Haywood:
enquiries.westmidlands@canalrivertrust.org.uk

MILEAGE

DERWENT MOUTH to:
Swarkestone Lock: 7 miles
Willington: 12¼ miles
Horninglow Wharf: 16½ miles
Barton Turn: 21¼ miles
Fradley, junction with Coventry Canal: 26¼ miles
Great Haywood, junction with Staffordshire & Worcestershire Canal: 39 miles
Stone: 48½ miles
Stoke Top Lock, junction with Caldon Canal: 58 miles
Harding's Wood, junction with Macclesfield Canal: 63¾ miles
King's Lock, Middlewich, junction with Middlewich Branch: 76¼ miles
Anderton Lift, for River Weaver: 86½ miles

PRESTON BROOK north end of tunnel and Bridgewater Canal: 93½ miles

Locks: 76

Canoeing and Paddleboarding: Category 1.
However, see Navigational Notes on page 141.

This early canal was originally conceived partly as a roundabout link between the ports of Liverpool and Hull, while passing through the busy area of the Potteries and mid-Cheshire, and terminating either in the River Weaver or in the Mersey. Its construction was promoted by Josiah Wedgwood (1730–95), the famous potter, aided by his friends Thomas Bentley and Erasmus Darwin. In 1766 the Trent & Mersey Canal Act was passed by Parliament, authorising the building of a navigation from the River Trent at Shardlow to Runcorn Gap, where it would join the proposed extension of the Bridgewater Canal from Manchester. The ageing James Brindley was appointed engineer for the canal. Construction began at once and in 1777 the Trent & Mersey Canal was opened. In the total 93 miles between Derwent Mouth and Preston Brook, the Trent & Mersey gained connection with no fewer than nine other canals or significant branches.

By the 1820s the slowly-sinking tunnel at Harecastle had become a serious bottle-neck, so Thomas Telford recommended building a second tunnel beside the old one. His recommendation was eventually accepted by the company and the new tunnel was completed in under three years, in 1827. Although the Trent & Mersey was taken over in 1845 by the new North Staffordshire Railway Company, the canal flourished until World War I. Look out for the handsome cast iron mileposts, which actually measure the mileage from Shardlow, not Derwent Mouth. There are 59 originals, from the Rougeley and Dixon foundry in Stone, and 34 replacements, bearing the mark of the Trent & Mersey Canal Society – T&MCS 1977.

Shardlow

The Trent & Mersey Canal begins at Derwent Mouth, some 2½ miles upstream of the point where the Soar Navigation enters the River Trent at a

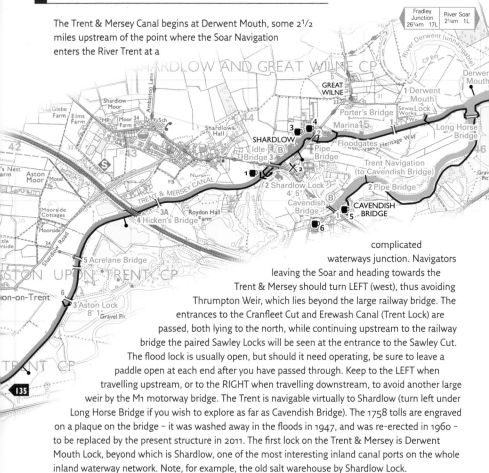

complicated waterways junction. Navigators leaving the Soar and heading towards the Trent & Mersey should turn LEFT (west), thus avoiding Thrumpton Weir, which lies beyond the large railway bridge. The entrances to the Cranfleet Cut and Erewash Canal (Trent Lock) are passed, both lying to the north, while continuing upstream to the railway bridge the paired Sawley Locks will be seen at the entrance to the Sawley Cut. The flood lock is usually open, but should it need operating, be sure to leave a paddle open at each end after you have passed through. Keep to the LEFT when travelling upstream, or to the RIGHT when travelling downstream, to avoid another large weir by the M1 motorway bridge. The Trent is navigable virtually to Shardlow (turn left under Long Horse Bridge if you wish to explore as far as Cavendish Bridge). The 1758 tolls are engraved on a plaque on the bridge – it was washed away in the floods in 1947, and was re-erected in 1960 – to be replaced by the present structure in 2011. The first lock on the Trent & Mersey is Derwent Mouth Lock, beyond which is Shardlow, one of the most interesting inland canal ports on the whole inland waterway network. Note, for example, the old salt warehouse by Shardlow Lock.

Boatyards

(B) **J.D Narrowboats Limited** Dobson Wharf, The Wharf, Shardlow DE72 2GJ (01332 792271/07952 378679; www.jdnarrowboats.com). 🛊🛊⚓ Gas, bespoke boat and shell builders, long and short-term mooring, crane, boat and engine sales, slipway, engine repairs, diesel fuel cleaning, wet dock, painting and blacking, solid fuel, toilets.

(B)✕ **Sawley Marina** Sawley, Long Eaton, NG10 3AE (0115 907 7400; www.aquavista.com/mooring-options/mooring-at-sawley-waterside-marina). 🛊🛊P D Pump out, gas, overnight and long-term mooring, winter storage, slipway, boat and engine sales, engine repairs, telephone, chandlery, solid fuel, toilets, showers, restaurant (*closed Mon*), laundrette. groceries.

(B)✕ **2 Shardlow Marina** London Road, Shardlow DE72 2GL (01332 792832; www.shardlowmarina.co.uk). On the River Trent. Facilities for moorers only. 🛊🛊⚓D Pump out, gas, long-term mooring, slipway, boat sales, chandlery, laundrette, toilets and showers, Wi-Fi. Caravan and camping site.

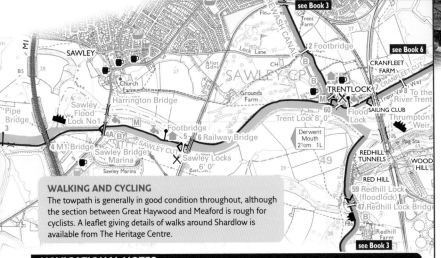

WALKING AND CYCLING
The towpath is generally in good condition throughout, although the section between Great Haywood and Meaford is rough for cyclists. A leaflet giving details of walks around Shardlow is available from The Heritage Centre.

NAVIGATIONAL NOTES

1 Those leaving the canal and heading towards the River Trent should not pass Shardlow floodgates if the warning light shows red.
2 The Derwent is not navigable north of Derwent Mouth and the Trent is not navigable beyond Shardlow Marina, Cavendish Bridge.
3 The entrance to Shardlow Marina can be difficult to spot and boaters should be aware of gravel banks in the area.

● **Sawley Cut**
In addition to a large marina and a well patronised CRT mooring site, the Derby Motor Boat Club has a base on the Sawley Cut. There are windlasses for sale at Sawley Lock, as well as the more conventional facilities, and CRT showers. It is beautifully tended, with lots of flowers and some jokey sculptures. Have a look at the flood level markers – they are astonishing! *PO and stores* in Aston-Upon-Trent ¾ mile west of Aston Lock.

● **Shardlow**
Derbs. Delicatessen, takeaway. Few canal travellers will want to pass through Shardlow without stopping. Everywhere there are living examples of large-scale canal architecture, as well as long-established necessities such as canal pubs. By the lock is the biggest and best of these buildings – the 18th-C Trent Mill, now the Clock Warehouse. Restored in 1979, it has a large central arch where boats once entered to unload.
Shardlow Heritage Centre London Road, Shardlow DE72 2GA (www.shardlowheritage.eclipse.co.uk). Adjacent to the Clock Warehouse. Exhibitions of local canal history and replica of a narrowboat back cabin. Plus a calendar of canal-centred events. *Open Easter–Oct, Sat, Sun and B Hols 12.00–17.00.* Modest entry charge.

Pubs and Restaurants

● 1 **The Clock Warehouse** 83 London Road, Shardlow DE72 2GL (01332 650556; www.clockwarehousepub.co.uk). Once the 'port's' transhipment warehouse and now dispensing real ale and food *daily 11.30–21.00 (Fri-Sat 21.30).* Outside seating, dog- and family-friendly. Traditional pub games and Wi-Fi. Camping nearby. *Open 11.30–23.00 (Sun 22.30).*

● 3 **The Navigation Inn** 143 London Road, Shardlow DE72 2HA (01332 792318; www.facebook.com/navigationinnshardlow). This friendly pub serves real ale and food *Mon-Fri E and Sat-Sun L and E.* Dog- and child-friendly, garden. Real fires and *monthly* live music. Camping nearby. *Open Mon-Fri 16.00–23.00 & Sat-Sun 12.00–23.00.*

●✕ 4 **The Malt Shovel** 49 The Wharf, Shardlow DE72 2HG (01332 792066; www.maltshovelshardlow.co.uk). By bridge 2. Friendly canalside pub, built in 1779 and serving real ale. Excellent food with home-made specials *L.* Outside seating and Wi-Fi. *Open daily 11.00–23.00 (Fri-Sat 00.00).*

●✕ 5 **The New Inn** 61 The Wharf, Shardlow DE72 2HG (01332 793330; www.thenewinnshardlow.co.uk). Next to the Malt Shovel. Real ale, and bar meals *Mon-Fri L and E & Sat-Sun 10.00-20.30 (Sun 18.00).* Children and dogs welcome. Garden and outside seating. Wi-Fi. *Open all day.*

● 6 **The Old Crown** Cavendish Bridge, Shardlow DE72 2HL (01332 792392). Friendly riverside pub. Real ale. Bar meals served *Sun and Fri L; Tue-Thu L and E & Sat 12.00-20.00.* Outside seating, dogs welcome. Traditional pub games, real fires and Wi-Fi. *Open Mon-Thu 11.00-23.00 (Mon 15.00) & Fri-Sun 11.00-00.00 (Sun 22.30).*

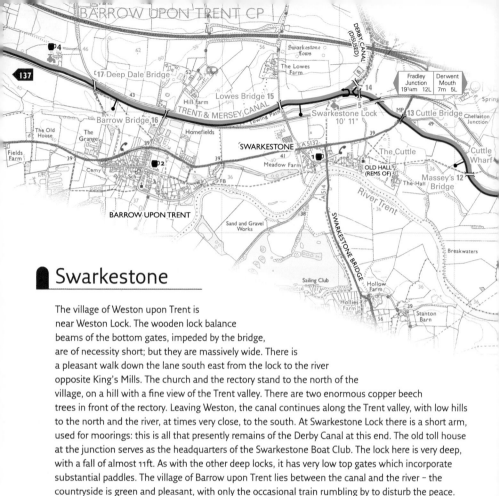

Swarkestone

The village of Weston upon Trent is
near Weston Lock. The wooden lock balance
beams of the bottom gates, impeded by the bridge,
are of necessity short; but they are massively wide. There is
a pleasant walk down the lane south east from the lock to the river
opposite King's Mills. The church and the rectory stand to the north of the
village, on a hill with a fine view of the Trent valley. There are two enormous copper beech
trees in front of the rectory. Leaving Weston, the canal continues along the Trent valley, with low hills
to the north and the river, at times very close, to the south. At Swarkestone Lock there is a short arm,
used for moorings: this is all that presently remains of the Derby Canal at this end. The old toll house
at the junction serves as the headquarters of the Swarkestone Boat Club. The lock here is very deep,
with a fall of almost 11ft. As with the other deep locks, it has very low top gates which incorporate
substantial paddles. The village of Barrow upon Trent lies between the canal and the river – the
countryside is green and pleasant, with only the occasional train rumbling by to disturb the peace.

- **Weston-on-Trent**
  Derbs. PO box. A scattered village that is in fact
  not very close to the Trent. The isolated church is
  splendidly situated beside woods on top of a hill,
  its sturdy tower crowned by a short 14th-C spire.
  Inside are fine aisle windows of the same period.
  The lock gardens make the approach from the canal
  particularly attractive.
- **Swarkestone**
  Derbs. PO box, tel. The main feature of Swarkestone
  is the 18th-C five-arch stone bridge over the main
  channel of the River Trent. An elevated causeway
  then carries the road on stone arches all the way
  across the Trent's flood plain to the village of Stanton
  by Bridge. It was at Swarkestone that Bonnie Prince
  Charlie, in the rising of 1745, gave up his attempt
  for the throne of England and returned to his defeat
  at Culloden. In a field nearby are the few remains
  of Sir Richard Harpur's Tudor mansion, which was

demolished before 1750. The Summer House,
a handsome, lonely building, overlooks a square
enclosure called the Cuttle. Jacobean in origin, it is
thought that it may have been the scene of bull-
baiting, although it seems more likely it was just a
'bowle alley'. Restored by the Landmark Trust, it is
available for holiday lets – telephone (01628 825925)
for details. The Harpurs moved to Calke following
the demolition of their mansion after the Civil War.
The pub in the village, and monuments in the
church, which is tucked away in the back lanes,
are a reminder of the family.
- **Barrow upon Trent**
  Derbs. PO box, tel. A small, quiet village set back
  from the canal. A lane from the church leads down
  to the River Trent. Opposite there is a 'pinfold',
  once an enclosure for stray animals. The surviving
  lodge house stands opposite a mellow terrace of old
  workmen's cottages.

CANOEING AND PADDLEBOARDING

The River Trent is navigable for powered craft as far west as Cavendish Bridge, just south of Shardlow. Beyond this point it becomes the territory of the canoeist and paddleboarder. As always www.gopaddling.info/rivers/river-trent provides a comprehensive overview and it can also be interrogated to provide a wealth of useful detail quite outside this guide to navigable waterways.

Trent Adventure offer 'canoe hire and adventures' on both the River Trent and on the Trent & Mersey Canal, from their base at Barrow Upon Trent. They accept 8 year-olds on the river and 6 year-olds on the canal. For further details contact Trent Adventure Poplars Farm, Derby DE73 7HJ (07876 751599; www.trentadventure.wixsite.com/mysite/adventures). Booking by email preferred: office@trentadventure.co.uk. Also, horsebox glamping.

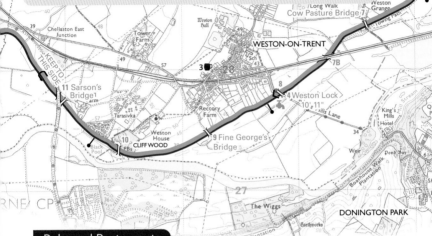

Pubs and Restaurants

1 The Crew & Harpur Arms Swarkestone Road, Swarkestone DE73 7JA (01332 700641; www.creweharpurpub.co.uk). By the river bridge. Real ale, and bar meals served *daily 12.00-22.00 (Sun 21.00)* – with breakfast *07.00-11.00* – in this handsome pub. Riverside seating and garden. Children welcome. B&B.

2 The Brookfield Brookfield, Barrow upon Trent D73 7HG (01332 700128; www.facebook.com/TheBrookfield). A friendly village pub, dispensing real ale and food *Mon-Sat 17.00-23.00*, that welcomes walkers, cyclists and boaters. Garden, dog- and child-friendly. Traditional pub games, sports TV and Wi-Fi. *Open Mon-Fri 16.00-00.00 & Sat-Sun 12.00-00.00.*

X 3 The Coopers Arms Weston Hall, The Green, Weston upon Trent DE72 2BJ (01332 690002; www.thecoopers-arms.co.uk). So dark was the basement area of Weston Hall, that the Cooper family used it to force rhubarb and chicory. Today, re-invented as a country pub, this establishment serves appetising food *daily L and E (not Sun E)*, together with a selection of real ales. Garden. Traditional pub games, newspapers, real fires and Wi-Fi. *Open Mon-Sat 11.30-23.30 & Sun 12.00-22.30.*

4 The Ragley Boat Stop Deepdale Lane, Sinfin Lane, Barrow upon Trent DE73 7FY (01332 703919; www.king-henrys-taverns.co.uk/our-pubs/the-ragley-boat-stop). Comfortable, contemporary pub clad with mock-Tudor timbering, dispensing real ale and food *daily 12.00-22.00*. Balcony and large canalside garden; family-friendly. Wi-Fi. *Open 11.30-23.00.*

A HOP, A SKIP, AND A JUMP TO DERBY

The Derby Canal, which left the Trent & Mersey at Swarkestone and joined the Erewash at Sandiacre, has long been disused. One condition of its building, and a constant drain on its profits, was the free carriage of 5000 tons of coal to Derby each year, for the use of the poor.

But one of the most unusual loads was transported on 19 April 1826, when 'a fine lama, a kangaroo, a ram with four horns, and a female goat with two young kids, remarkably handsome animals' arrived in Derby by canal 'as a present from Lord Byron to a Gentleman whose residence is in the neighbourhood, all of which had been picked up in the course of the voyage of the *Blonde* to the Sandwich Islands in the autumn of 1824'.

Willington

Just by bridge 18 is Arleston House, an attractive old building with ground-floor walls of stone and the upper tiers of brick. This is followed by Stenson Lock, the last of the wide locks until Middlewich – it has a massive fall of 12ft 4in, and is overlooked by a useful *coffee shop* – (07949 980884; www.stensonlock.co.uk) which is *open from 09.00 (Sun 10.00)* and serves an excellent breakfast. Stenson is a small farming centre and a popular mooring spot with a large marina. After passing through a railway bridge, the canal changes course and heads off in a

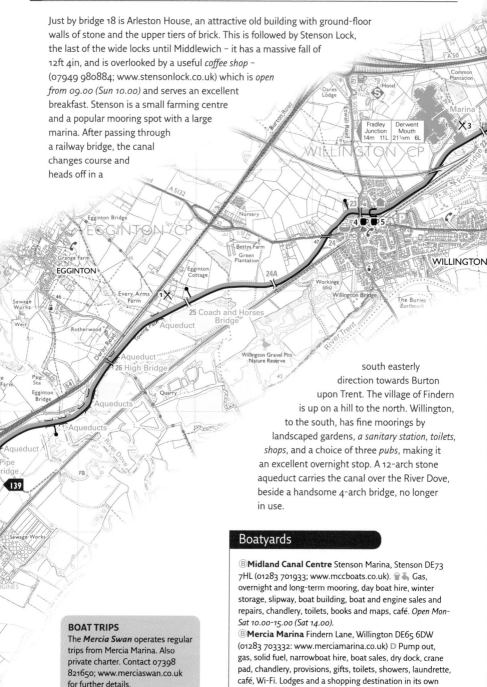

south easterly direction towards Burton upon Trent. The village of Findern is up on a hill to the north. Willington, to the south, has fine moorings by landscaped gardens, *a sanitary station*, *toilets*, *shops*, and a choice of three *pubs*, making it an excellent overnight stop. A 12-arch stone aqueduct carries the canal over the River Dove, beside a handsome 4-arch bridge, no longer in use.

BOAT TRIPS
The *Mercia Swan* operates regular trips from Mercia Marina. Also private charter. Contact 07398 821650; www.merciaswan.co.uk for further details.

Boatyards

Ⓑ**Midland Canal Centre** Stenson Marina, Stenson DE73 7HL (01283 701933; www.mccboats.co.uk). 🛒🛠 Gas, overnight and long-term mooring, day boat hire, winter storage, slipway, boat building, boat and engine sales and repairs, chandlery, toilets, books and maps, café. *Open Mon-Sat 10.00-15.00 (Sat 14.00).*

Ⓑ**Mercia Marina** Findern Lane, Willington DE65 6DW (01283 703332; www.merciamarina.co.uk) Ⓓ Pump out, gas, solid fuel, narrowboat hire, boat sales, dry dock, crane pad, chandlery, provisions, gifts, toilets, showers, laundrette, café, Wi-Fi. Lodges and a shopping destination in its own right. *Open daily 09.00-17.30.*

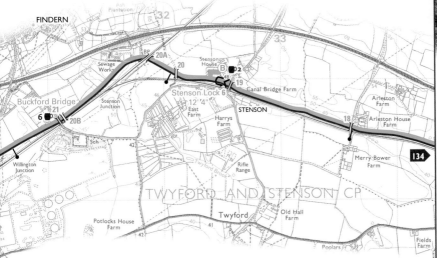

Repton

Derbs. PO. 1½ miles south east of Willington (over the River Trent) is Repton, one of the oldest towns in England, which was once the capital of Mercia. The crypt below St Wystan's Church was built in the 10th C. One of the finest examples of Saxon architecture in the country, this crypt was completely forgotten until the end of the 18th C when a man fell into it while digging a grave. Repton public school dates from 1557, and there is much of historical interest in the school and the town.

Willington

Derbs. PO, tel, stores, hardware, chemist, off-licence, fish & chips, takeaway, station. The railway bisects this busy little village on an embankment. There are three pubs, all close together. Shop *open daily 07.00-22.00.*

Findern

Derbs. PO, tel, stores. A small, quiet village where Jedekiah Strutt, the inventor of the ribbed stocking frame, served a 7-year apprenticeship with the local wheelwright. At one time the village green was no more than a waste patch used by cars as a short cut, and a parking place. When suggestions were made to turn it into a formal cross roads, the indignant Women's Institute galvanised the villagers into actually uprooting all traces of tarmac from the green and turfing the whole area properly.

Egginton

Derbs. A quiet village lying off the A38. The church, set apart from the village, is pleasingly irregular from the outside, with a large chancel and a squat tower.

Pubs and Restaurants

✕♀ **1 Anoki Indian Restaurant** Burton Road, Eggington DE65 6GZ (01283 704888; www. anokionline.co.uk). Well-regarded Indian restaurant and takeaway close to Bridge 25. *Open daily 17.30-23.00.* Children welcome.

🍺✕ **2 The Bubble Inn** The Marina, Derby Road, Stenson DE73 1HL (01283 703113). Alongside Stenson Lock and Marina, this modern pub in a converted barn, serves real ale and bar meals *daily L and E.* Garden, dog- and child-friendly. Wi-Fi. B&B. *Open 11.00-23.30 (Fri-Sat 00.00).*

✕ **3 Willow Tree Tearoom** Findern Lane, Willington DE65 6DW (01285 703700; www.facebook.com/WillowTeaRoom). *Open daily 08.30-16.30,* this tearoom serves a range of appetising food from breakfast through to lunches and afternoon tea, including toasties, salads, sandwiches, jacket potatoes cakes, coffee and teas.

🍺 **4 The Rising Sun** The Green, Willington DE65 6BP (01283 702116; www.facebook.com/risingsunwillington). Friendly village pub serving real ale and real cider. Outside seating, dog- and child-friendly. Live music *Fri.* Traditional pub games, sports TV and Wi-Fi. *Open daily 12.00-23.00.*

🍺 **5 The Dragon** 13 The Green, Willington DE65 6BP (01283 704795; www.thedragonatwillington.co.uk). Popular and welcoming pub, with plenty of low beams. Real ale and real ciders. Wide range of food available *Mon-Thu L and E & Fri-Sun 12.00-21.00 (Sun 20.00).* Outside seating, dog- and family-friendly. Live music *Fri-Sat.* Newspapers, real fires, sports TV and Wi-Fi. *Open daily 10.00-00.00.*

🍺✕ **6 Nadee** 130 Heath Lane, Findern DE65 6AR (01283 701333; www.nadee.co.uk). Adjacent to canal at bridge 21. Bar and Indian restaurant. Landscaped garden, including a 5-a-side football pitch. Children welcome. Marquee available for celebrations and parties. Mooring. *Open daily 16.00-22.00 (Sun 12.00).*

Burton upon Trent

Ice cream, cold drinks and a *burger van* are available between Bridges 28 and 29. *Fish & chips* can be obtained 100yds north of Horninglow Basin, which has some services and a butterfly garden. The canal then passes along one side of Burton upon Trent, without entering the town. Many of the old canalside buildings have been demolished, but the waterside has been nicely tidied up, making the passage very pleasant. The lovely aroma of brewing – malt and hops – often pervades the town, usually strongest to the west. Dallow Lock is the first of the narrow locks, an altogether easier job of work than the wider ones to the east. Shobnall Basin is now used by a boatyard, and visitor moorings nearby are available from which to explore the town. The A38 then joins the canal, depriving the navigator of any peace. On the hills to the north west is the well-wooded Sinai Park – the moated 15th-C house here, now a farm, used to be the summer home of the monks from Burton Abbey. There is a fine canalside pub at Bridge 34. The village of Branston can be accessed from here via a pedestrian route passing under the busy A38 dual carriageway. The canal enters the new National Forest at bridge 30 – indeed an intricately carved seat reminds us of this – and will leave it just beyond Alrewas. The Bass Millennium Woodland, to the west of Branston Lock, is part of this major project.

● **Burton upon Trent**
Staffs. All services. Known widely for its brewing industry, which originated here in the 13th C, when the monks at Burton Abbey discovered that an excellent beer could be brewed from the town's waters, because of their high gypsum content. At one time there were 31 breweries producing 3 million barrels of ale annually: alas, now only a few remain. The advent of the railways had an enormous effect on the street geography of Burton, for gradually a great network of railways took shape, connecting with each other and with the main line. These branches were mostly constructed at street level, and until recent years it was common for road traffic to be held up by endless goods trains chugging all over the town. Only the last vestiges of this system now remain. The east side of the town is bounded by the River Trent, on the other side of which are pleasant hills. The main shopping centre lies to the east of the railway station. **Marston's Brewery Visitor Centre** Shobnall Road, Burton upon Trent DE14 2BG (01283 507391; 507328; www.marstonsbrewery.co.uk/visit/book-a-tour). Tours of the brewery, including the unique and world-famous Burton Union system are available *Tue-Sat 10.00-16.00 (Sat 14.00).* At the end of the tour you can enjoy a drink of real ale in the Visitor Centre. *Please telephone or visit website to check availability and to book.*
The Brewhouse Union Street, Burton upon Trent DE14 1AA (01283 508100; www.brewhouse.co.uk). Live entertainment in a 230-seat theatre, plus a gallery and bistro bar. *Open Mon-Sat 09.00-20.00.*

Tourist Information Centre Customer Service Centre, Market Place, High Street, Burton upon Trent DE14 1AH (01283 508000; www.enjoyeaststaffs.co.uk). *Open Mon-Fri 09.00-17.00 & Sat 11.00-16.00.*
● **Shobnall Basin**
This is all that remains of the Bond End Canal, which gave the breweries the benefit of what was modern transport, before the coming of the railways.
● **Branston**
Staffs. PO, tel, stores, chemist, takeaway, fish & chips. This is apparently the place where the famous pickle originated.

WALKING AND CYCLING
Cycle Route 54 uses the towpath north of Burton upon Trent. It links Lichfield with Derby. Three walking trails around Burton upon Trent are available from the TIC. There are pleasant walks through Branston Water Park – telephone (01283) 508000 for more information.

Boatyards

Ⓑ**Jannel Cruisers** Shobnall Marina, Shobnall Road, Burton upon Trent DE14 2AU (01283 542718; www.jannel.co.uk). In Shobnall Basin. 🚿🛒D Pump out, gas, coal, overnight mooring, long-term mooring, winter storage, slipway, dry dock, chandlery, books and maps, boat-fitting, boat sales, engine repairs, surveyor, BSS inspections, toilets. ✗ **11 Café**.

Pubs and Restaurants

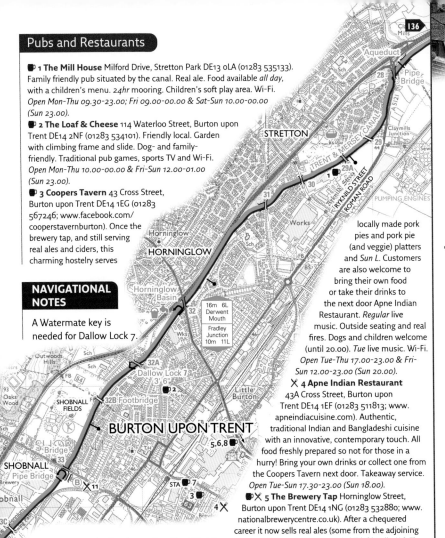

1 The Mill House Milford Drive, Stretton Park DE13 0LA (01283 535133). Family friendly pub situated by the canal. Real ale. Food available *all day*, with a children's menu. *24hr* mooring. Children's soft play area. Wi-Fi. *Open Mon-Thu 09.30-23.00; Fri 09.00-00.00 & Sat-Sun 10.00-00.00 (Sun 23.00).*

2 The Loaf & Cheese 114 Waterloo Street, Burton upon Trent DE14 2NF (01283 534101). Friendly local. Garden with climbing frame and slide. Dog- and family-friendly. Traditional pub games, sports TV and Wi-Fi. *Open Mon-Thu 10.00-00.00 & Fri-Sun 12.00-01.00 (Sun 23.00).*

3 Coopers Tavern 43 Cross Street, Burton upon Trent DE14 1EG (01283 567246; www.facebook.com/cooperstavernburton). Once the brewery tap, and still serving real ales and ciders, this charming hostelry serves

NAVIGATIONAL NOTES

A Watermate key is needed for Dallow Lock 7.

locally made pork pies and pork pie (and veggie) platters and *Sun L.* Customers are also welcome to bring their own food or take their drinks to the next door Apne Indian Restaurant. *Regular* live music. Outside seating and real fires. Dogs and children welcome (until 20.00). *Tue* live music. Wi-Fi. *Open Tue-Thu 17.00-23.00 & Fri-Sun 12.00-23.00 (Sun 20.00).*

✕ 4 Apne Indian Restaurant 43A Cross Street, Burton upon Trent DE14 1EF (01283 511813; www.apneindiacuisine.com). Authentic, traditional Indian and Bangladeshi cuisine with an innovative, contemporary touch. All fare freshly prepared so not for those in a hurry! Bring your own drinks or collect one from the Coopers Tavern next door. Takeaway service. *Open Tue-Sun 17.30-23.00 (Sun 18.00).*

✕ 5 The Brewery Tap Horninglow Street, Burton upon Trent DE14 1NG (01283 532880; www.nationalbrewerycentre.co.uk). After a chequered career it now sells real ales (some from the adjoining museum's micro-brewery) and food *Wed-Sun 12.00-21.00 (Sun 15.00).* Dog- and child-friendly. Wi-Fi. *Open Wed-Sun 12.00-23.00 (Sun 21.00).*

6 Burton Bridge Inn 24 Bridge Street, Burton upon Trent DE14 1SY (01283 536596; www.burtonbridgeinn.co.uk). The brewery tap for the eponymously named brewers, this traditional 17th-C pub serves real ales and real cider. Patio seating, dog-friendly. Traditional pub games, real fires and Wi-Fi. *Opens at 17.00 (Sat 16.00).*

7 The Devonshire Arms 86 Station St, Burton upon Trent DE14 1BT (01283 480022; www.facebook.com/devonshirearmsburton). Another excellent Burton Bridge Brewery establishment, offering a warm, friendly welcome, and serving a wide range of real ales and real cider. Patio, dogs and children welcome *(until 20.00).* Traditional pub games, real fires and Wi-Fi. *Open Mon-Thu 16.00-23.00 & Fri-Sun 12.00-23.00 (Sun 22.30).*

8 Lord Burton 154 High St, Town Centre, Burton upon Trent DE14 1JE (01283 517587; www.jdwetherspoon.co.uk/home/pubs/the-lord-burton). Once home to Woolworths, this busy pub now serves real ales, real cider and food *08.00-22.00.* Children welcome. Beer garden. Wi-Fi. *Open daily 08.00-00.00 (Fri-Sat 01.00).*

✕ 9 The Blacksmith's Arms Main Street, Branston DE14 3EY (01283 564332; www.blacksmithsarmsbranston.co.uk). Comfortable pub serving real ale and home-made food *daily 12.00-21.00 (Sun 20.00).* Traditional pub games, real fires, sports TV and Wi-Fi. *Open Mon-Thu 12.00-23.00 & Fri-Sun 11.30-00.00 (Sun 23.30).*

10 The Bridge Tatenhill Lane, Branston DE14 3EZ (01283 564177; www.thebridgeinnbranston.com). Real ale and good food (predominantly Italian) available *daily 12.00-21.00.* Outside seating, family-friendly. Real fires and Wi-Fi. *Open 12.00-23.00.*

Barton Turn

Beside Tatenhill Lock there is an attractive cottage; at the tail of the lock is yet another of the tiny narrow brick bridges that are such an engaging feature of this navigation. Note the very fine National Forest seat just north of the lock – there is another at Bagnall Lock, along with a 'living willow' sculpture. After passing flooded gravel pits and negotiating another tiny brick arch at bridge 36, the canal and the A38, the old Roman road, come very close together – thankfully the settlement of Barton Turn has been bypassed, leaving the main street (the old Roman road of Ryknild Street) wide and empty. It is with great relief that Wychnor Lock, with its diminutive crane and warehouse, is reached – here the A38 finally parts company with the canal, and some peace returns. To the west is the little 14th-C Wychnor church. Before Alrewas Lock the canal actually joins the River Trent – there is a large well-marked weir which should be given a wide berth. The canal then winds through the pretty village of Alrewas, passing the old church, several thatched cottages and a charming brick bridge.

● **Barton-under-Needwood**
Staffs. PO, tel, stores, chemist, off-licence, library.
Many years ago, when there were few roads and no canals in the Midlands, the only reasonable access to this village was by turning off the old Roman road, Ryknild Street: hence, probably, the name Barton Turn. The village is indeed worth turning off for, although unfortunately it is nearly a mile from the canal. A pleasant footpath from Barton Turn Lock leads quietly to the village, which is set on a slight hill. Its long main street has many attractive pubs. The church is battlemented and surrounded by a very tidy churchyard. Pleasantly uniform in style, it was built in the 16th C by John Taylor, Henry VIII's private secretary, on the site of his cottage birthplace. The former Royal Forest of Needwood is to the north of the village.
● **Wychnor**
Staffs. A tiny farming settlement around the church of St Leonards.
● **Alrewas**
Staffs. PO, tel, stores, garage, butcher, chemist, tearoom, fish & chips, takeaway, off-licence. Just far enough away from the A513, this is an attractive village whose rambling back lanes harbour some excellent timbered cottages. The canal's meandering passage through the village, passing well tended gardens and a bowling green, and the presence of the church and its pleasant churchyard creates a friendly and unruffled atmosphere. The River Trent touches the village, and once fed the old Cotton Mill (now converted into dwellings), and provides it with a fine background which is much appreciated by fishermen. The somewhat unusual name Alrewas, pronounced 'olrewus', is a corruption of the words Alder Wash – a reference to the many alder trees which once grew in the often-flooded Trent valley and gave rise to the basket weaving for which the village was once famous.
Alrewas Church Mill End Lane, Alrewas DE13 7BT. A spacious building of mainly 13th-C

and 14th-C construction, notable for the old leper window, which is now filled by modern stained glass.

Boatyards

Ⓑℙ✕ **3 Barton Turns** Barton Turn, Barton-under-Needwood DE13 8DZ (01283 711666; www.bartonmarina.co.uk). 🛉🛉🛢D Pump out, gas, overnight and long-term mooring, winter storage, slipway, boat sales and repairs, engine repairs, chandlery, toilets, showers, books, maps and gifts, laundrette, Wi-Fi. Also pub, restaurant and shops, including a deli and bakery/butcher. Fly and course fishing.
Ⓑ**Fradley Marina** Daisy Lane, Alrewas, Burton on Trent DE13 7EW (07941 167087; www.livethedreamnarrowboats.co.uk). D Gas, solid fuel, Long- and short-term moorings, boat building and fitting out, engineering and repairs, engine sales and repairs, painting and blacking, boat sales, slipway, dry dock, DIY facilities, holiday accommodation, toilets, showers, laundrette, Wi-Fi.
Boat Doctor (01332 771622). Advice and information only
Ⓑ**Wychnor Moorings** Wychnor, Burton upon Trent DE13 8BY (07778 668388). 🛉🛠 Gas, private mooring, coal.

NAVIGATIONAL NOTES

1 In *times of flood* great caution should be exercised along the stretch of the navigation immediately north west of Alrewas Lock where the canal shares its bed with the River Trent. Keep well over to the towpath side at all times.
2 Canoeists and paddleboarders should disembark well before this section and form a judgement from the towpath as to water conditions and their ability to navigate safely.

Pubs and Restaurants

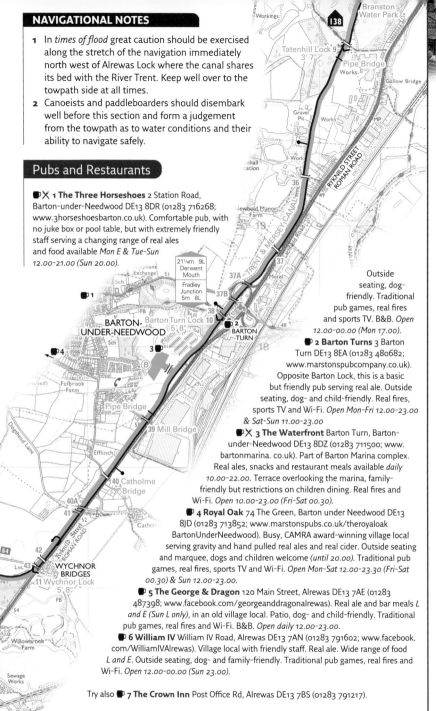

🍺✕ **1 The Three Horseshoes** 2 Station Road, Barton-under-Needwood DE13 8DR (01283 716268; www.3horseshoesbarton.co.uk). Comfortable pub, with no juke box or pool table, but with extremely friendly staff serving a changing range of real ales and food available *Mon E & Tue–Sun 12.00–21.00 (Sun 20.00).*

Outside seating, dog-friendly. Traditional pub games, real fires and sports TV. B&B. *Open 12.00–00.00 (Mon 17.00).*

🍺 **2 Barton Turns** 3 Barton Turn DE13 8EA (01283 480682; www.marstonspubcompany.co.uk). Opposite Barton Lock, this is a basic but friendly pub serving real ale. Outside seating, dog- and child-friendly. Real fires, sports TV and Wi-Fi. *Open Mon–Fri 12.00–23.00 & Sat–Sun 11.00–23.00*

🍺✕ **3 The Waterfront** Barton Turn, Barton-under-Needwood DE13 8DZ (01283 711500; www. bartonmarina. co.uk). Part of Barton Marina complex. Real ales, snacks and restaurant meals available *daily 10.00–22.00.* Terrace overlooking the marina, family-friendly but restrictions on children dining. Real fires and Wi-Fi. *Open 10.00–23.00 (Fri–Sat 00.30).*

🍺 **4 Royal Oak** 74 The Green, Barton under Needwood DE13 8JD (01283 713852; www.marstonspubs.co.uk/theroyaloak BartonUnderNeedwood). Busy, CAMRA award-winning village local serving gravity and hand pulled real ales and real cider. Outside seating and marquee, dogs and children welcome *(until 20.00).* Traditional pub games, real fires, sports TV and Wi-Fi. *Open Mon–Sat 12.00–23.30 (Fri–Sat 00.30) & Sun 12.00–23.00.*

🍺 **5 The George & Dragon** 120 Main Street, Alrewas DE13 7AE (01283 487398; www.facebook.com/georgeanddragonalrewas). Real ale and bar meals *L and E (Sun L only)*, in an old village local. Patio, dog- and child-friendly. Traditional pub games, real fires and Wi-Fi. B&B. *Open daily 12.00–23.00.*

🍺 **6 William IV** William IV Road, Alrewas DE13 7AN (01283 791602; www.facebook.com/WilliamIVAlrewas). Village local with friendly staff. Real ale. Wide range of food *L and E.* Outside seating, dog- and family-friendly. Traditional pub games, real fires and Wi-Fi. *Open 12.00–00.00 (Sun 23.00).*

Try also 🍺 **7 The Crown Inn** Post Office Rd, Alrewas DE13 7BS (01283 791217).

WALKING AND CYCLING
There is an excellent circular walk from Alrewas along the east side of the Trent, then along the A38 for a short while before turning back beside the canal at Wychnor Lock.

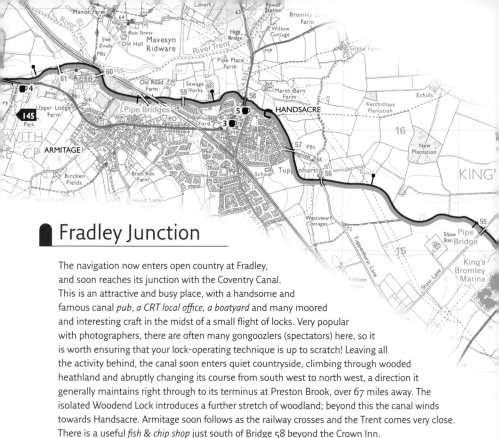

Fradley Junction

The navigation now enters open country at Fradley, and soon reaches its junction with the Coventry Canal. This is an attractive and busy place, with a handsome and famous canal *pub*, *a CRT local office, a boatyard* and many moored and interesting craft in the midst of a small flight of locks. Very popular with photographers, there are often many gongoozlers (spectators) here, so it is worth ensuring that your lock-operating technique is up to scratch! Leaving all the activity behind, the canal soon enters quiet countryside, climbing through wooded heathland and abruptly changing its course from south west to north west, a direction it generally maintains right through to its terminus at Preston Brook, over 67 miles away. The isolated Woodend Lock introduces a further stretch of woodland; beyond this the canal winds towards Handsacre. Armitage soon follows as the railway crosses and the Trent comes very close. There is a useful *fish & chip shop* just south of Bridge 58 beyond the Crown Inn.

NAVIGATIONAL NOTES

West of bridge 61 the canal is very narrow, due to the removal of Armitage Tunnel, and wide enough for one boat only. Check that the canal is clear before proceeding.

Boatyards

Ⓑ✕ **Fradley Marine Services** Fradley Junction, Alrewas, Burton-on-Trent DE13 7DN (01283 790332/07971 686516). 🛉🛒🅳 Pump out, gas, solid fuel, overnight and long-term mooring, DIY facilities, boat repairs, gift shop, chandlery, provisions, gallery of artists and crafters, tearoom. Can issue CRT boat licences.

Ⓑ**Bromley Wharf Narrowboats Ltd** Bromley Wharf, Riley Hill, Bromley Hayes, Nr Lichfield WS13 8HS (01543 419695/ 07815 577788; www.bromleywharf.co.uk).

🅳 Pump out, gas, solid fuel, covered dry dock, long- and short-term mooring, engineering services.

Ⓑ**King's Bromley Marina** Lichfield Road, Bromley Hayes WS13 8HT (01543 417209; www.castlemarinas.co.uk/marina/kings-bromley). 🛉🛉🛒🅳 Pump out, gas, solid fuel, overnight and long-term mooring, slipway, boat sales, chandlery, coal, toilets, showers, laundrette, Wi-Fi. *Open Mon-Sat 09.00-17.00 & Sun 10.00-16.00.*

● **Fradley Junction**
Staffs. PO box, tel. A long-established canal centre where the Coventry Canal joins the Trent & Mersey. Like all the best focal points on the waterways, it is concerned solely with the life of the canals, and has no relationship with local roads or even with the village of Fradley. The junction bristles with boats for, apart from it being an inevitable meeting place for canal craft, there is a boatyard, a Canal & River Trust information centre and café (01283 790236, guided tours), CRT moorings, a boat club, a popular pub and another café at the holiday park – all in the middle of a 5-lock flight.

- **Fradley**
Staffs. PO, tel, stores, chemist, butcher, fish and chips. A small village set to the east of the canal and now totally overwhelmed with factory and distribution units where a large airfield once stood. *Shop open daily 07.00-22.00.*

- **Armitage**
Staffs. PO, tel, stores, chemist, butcher, baker. A main road village, whose church is interesting: it was rebuilt in the 19th C in a Saxon/Norman style, which makes it rather dark. The organ is 200 years old and it is enormous: it came from Lichfield Cathedral and practically deafens the organist at Armitage.

> **WALKING AND CYCLING**
> You can complete a circular walk if you head off along the Coventry Canal to Fradley Bridge (90), walk through the village and on to Alrewas, returning along the Trent & Mersey. Fradley Pool Nature Reserve can be accessed from the towpath, and makes for a pleasant walk.

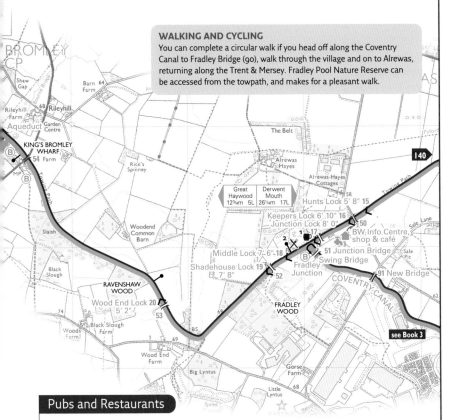

Pubs and Restaurants

🍺 **1 The Swan** Fradley Junction, Alrewas, Burton-on-Trent DE13 7DN (01283 790330; www. swaninnfradley.co.uk). Known as 'The Mucky Duck'. Canalside, it is the focus of the junction and justly famous: this is reputedly one of the most photographed pubs in the country! It is in a 200-year-old listed building, with a fine public bar warmed by a coal fire, a comfortable lounge, and a vaulted cellar room. Real ale, and bar meals are served *Mon-Sat 12.00-20.00 (Fri-Sat 21.00) & Sun 12.00-18.00*. Garden, dog- and child-friendly. Traditional pub games and Wi-Fi. *Open daily 12.00-23.00.*

✗ **2 Canalside Café Bistro** Fradley Junction, Alrewas DE13 7DN (01283 792919; www.facebook. com/canalsidecafefradley). Beside the Swan Inn. Attached to the adjacent swimming pool and caravan park, this café serves a range of hot and cold snacks, drinks and light meals. Breakfast. *Open 09.30-18.00 (Sun 09.00).*

🍺 **3 The Olde Peculiar** The Green, Handsacre WS15 4DP (01543 491891; www.theoldepeculiar.uk). Traditional English pub. Real ale, and food available *L and E (not Mon or Tue L)*. Garden, dog- and family-friendly. Wi-Fi. B&B. *Open daily L and E.*

🍺✗ **4 The Plum Pudding** Rugeley Road, Armitage WS15 4AZ (01543 490330; www. plumpudding. co.uk). Modern, award-winning restaurant serving real ale and meals *Mon-Fri L and E & Sat-Sun 12.00-21.30 (Sun 21.00)*. Garden. *Open 12.00-23.00.*

🍺 **5 The Crown Inn** 24 The Green, Handsacre WS15 4DT (01543 325568). Canalside pub serving real ale and food *Mon-Fri 12.00-18.00*. Traditional pub games, real fires, sports TV and Wi-Fi. *Open 12.00-23.00 (Thu-Sat 00.00).*

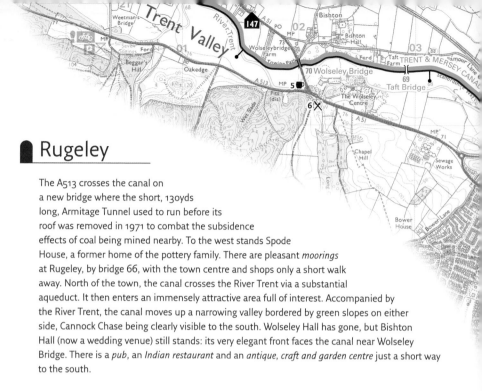

Rugeley

The A513 crosses the canal on
a new bridge where the short, 130yds
long, Armitage Tunnel used to run before its
roof was removed in 1971 to combat the subsidence
effects of coal being mined nearby. To the west stands Spode
House, a former home of the pottery family. There are pleasant *moorings*
at Rugeley, by bridge 66, with the town centre and shops only a short walk
away. North of the town, the canal crosses the River Trent via a substantial
aqueduct. It then enters an immensely attractive area full of interest. Accompanied by
the River Trent, the canal moves up a narrowing valley bordered by green slopes on either
side, Cannock Chase being clearly visible to the south. Wolseley Hall has gone, but Bishton
Hall (now a wedding venue) still stands: its very elegant front faces the canal near Wolseley
Bridge. There is a *pub*, an *Indian restaurant* and an *antique, craft and garden centre* just a short way
to the south.

- **Spode House** WS15 1PU Spode House and
Hawkesyard Priory stand side by side. The priory
was founded in 1897 by Josiah Spode's grandson
and his niece Helen Gulson when they lived
at Spode House. The Priory is now known as
Hawkesyard Hall, and is a restaurant and spa.
- **Rugeley**
Staffs. All services. A bustling and much
re-developed town, with many shops at the centre.
There are two churches by bridge 67; one is a 14th-
C ruin, the other is the parish church built in 1822
as a replacement.
- **Cannock Chase**
Covering an area of 26 square miles, and designated
as an Area of Outstanding Natural Beauty in 1949,
the Chase is all that remains of what was once
a Norman hunting ground known as the King's
Forest of Cannock. Large parts are recognised as
Sites of Special Scientific Interest, and exceptional
flora and fauna are abundant. This includes a herd
of fallow deer whose ancestors have grazed in this

region for centuries. An area of 4¾ square miles
forms a Country Park, one of the largest in Britain.
Near the Sherlock Valley an area was chosen in 1964
as the site of the Deutscher Soldatenfriedhof, and
was built by the German War Graves Commission.
It contains the graves of 2143 German servicemen
from World War I, and 2786 from World War II. It
is an intentionally sombre place. A small area is
devoted to the crews of German airships, shot down
over the UK in 1916 and 1917. There were two huge
army camps on the Chase during World War I, but
today little remains, apart from some anonymous
and overgrown concrete foundations.
Museum of Cannock Chase Valley Road,
Hednesford WS12 1TD (01543 877666;
www.museumofcannockchase.org). This site was
at one time the Valley Colliery. Local history and
interactive galleries. *Open Tue-Sat 11.00-16.00.* Free.

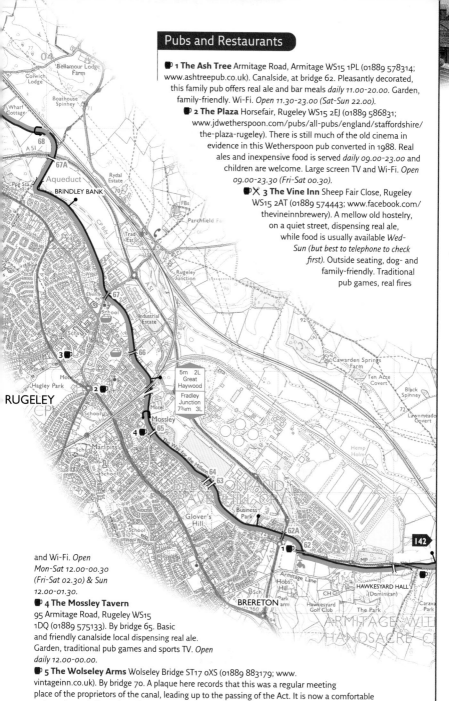

Pubs and Restaurants

1 The Ash Tree Armitage Road, Armitage WS15 1PL (01889 578314; www.ashtreepub.co.uk). Canalside, at bridge 62. Pleasantly decorated, this family pub offers real ale and bar meals *daily 11.00-20.00*. Garden, family-friendly. Wi-Fi. *Open 11.30-23.00 (Sat-Sun 22.00)*.

2 The Plaza Horsefair, Rugeley WS15 2EJ (01889 586831; www.jdwetherspoon.com/pubs/all-pubs/england/staffordshire/the-plaza-rugeley). There is still much of the old cinema in evidence in this Wetherspoon pub converted in 1988. Real ales and inexpensive food is served *daily 09.00-23.00* and children are welcome. Large screen TV and Wi-Fi. *Open 09.00-23.30 (Fri-Sat 00.30)*.

3 The Vine Inn Sheep Fair Close, Rugeley WS15 2AT (01889 574443; www.facebook.com/thevineinnbrewery). A mellow old hostelry, on a quiet street, dispensing real ale, while food is usually available *Wed-Sun (but best to telephone to check first)*. Outside seating, dog- and family-friendly. Traditional pub games, real fires

and Wi-Fi. *Open Mon-Sat 12.00-00.30 (Fri-Sat 02.30) & Sun 12.00-01.30*.

4 The Mossley Tavern 95 Armitage Road, Rugeley WS15 1DQ (01889 575133). By bridge 65. Basic and friendly canalside local dispensing real ale. Garden, traditional pub games and sports TV. *Open daily 12.00-00.00*.

5 The Wolseley Arms Wolseley Bridge ST17 0XS (01889 883179; www.vintageinn.co.uk). By bridge 70. A plaque here records that this was a regular meeting place of the proprietors of the canal, leading up to the passing of the Act. It is now a comfortable pub serving real ale, and meals *12.00-22.00 (Sun 21.30)*. Outside seating, dog- and child-friendly. Real fires. *Open 11.30-23.30 (Sun 22.30)*.

6 Shimla Palace Cromwell House, Wolseley Bridge ST17 0XS (01889 881325; www.shimlapalace.com). South of Wolseley Bridge (70). Friendly Indian restaurant and takeaway. Children welcome. *Open daily 17.30-23.00*.

145

Great Haywood

The pleasant surroundings continue as the canal passes Colwich. As the perimeter of Shugborough Park is reached the impressive façade of the Hall can be seen across the parkland. Haywood Lock and a line of moored craft announce the presence of Great Haywood and the junction with the Staffordshire & Worcestershire Canal (*see* page 157), which joins the Trent & Mersey under a graceful and much photographed towpath bridge: just the other side there is a useful *boatyard* which, amongst other services, provides *Elsan disposal* (charge). Beyond the junction the Trent valley becomes much broader and more open. There is another *boatyard* by Hoo Mill Lock.

● **Little Haywood**
Staffs. PO box. An elegant residential village, with a shop and two pubs.
● **Great Haywood**
Staffs. PO, stores. The Centre of the Great Haywood and Shugborough Conservation Area, the village is not particularly beautiful, but it is closely connected in many ways to Shugborough Park, to which it is physically linked by the very old Essex Bridge, where the crystal clear waters of the River Sow join the Trent on its way down from Stoke. Haywood Lock is beautifully situated between this packhorse bridge (which is an ancient monument) and the unusually decorative railway bridge that leads into Trent Lane. The lane consists of completely symmetrical and very handsome terraced cottages: they were built by the Ansons to house the people evicted from the former Shugborough village, the site of which is now occupied by the Arch of Hadrian within the park, built to celebrate Anson's circumnavigation of the globe in 1740–44. About 100yds south of Haywood Lock is an iron bridge over the canal. This bridge, which now leads nowhere, used to carry a private road from Shugborough Hall which crossed both the river and the canal on its way to the church just east of the railway. This was important to the Ansons, since the packhorse bridge just upstream is not wide enough for a horse and carriage, and so until the iron bridge was built the family had to *walk* the 300yds to church on Sunday mornings! There is a fresh fish shop behind the Clifford Arms *open Tue-Fri 09.30-16.30.*
Shugborough Hall *NT.* Milford, near Stafford ST17 0XB (01889 880160; www.nationaltrust.org.uk/shugborough-estate). Walk west from Haywood Lock and through the park. The present house dates from 1693, but was substantially altered by James Stuart around 1760 and by Samuel Wyatt around the turn of the 18th C. It was at this time that the old village of Shugborough was bought up and demolished by the Anson family so that they should enjoy more privacy

and space in their park. Family fortunes fluctuated greatly for the Ansons, the Earl of Lichfield's family; and crippling death duties in the 1960s brought about the transfer of the estate to the National Trust. The house has been restored at great expense and there are some magnificent rooms and many treasures inside.
Shugborough Park There are some remarkable sights in the large park which encircles the Hall. Thomas Anson, who inherited the estate in 1720, enlisted in 1744 the help of his famous brother, Admiral George Anson, to beautify and improve the house and the park. In 1762 he commissioned James Stuart, a neo-Grecian architect, to embellish the park. 'Athenian' Stuart set to with a will, and the spectacular results of his work can be seen scattered round the grounds. The stone monuments that he built have deservedly extravagant names such as the Tower of the Winds, the Lanthorn of Demosthenes and so on.
Park Farm at Shugborough (01889 880160; www.nationaltrust.org.uk/shugborough-estate/features/park-farm). Within Shugborough Park, and designed by Samuel Wyatt, this was a classic, innovative model farm in its time. Today the visitor can understand why through the excellent interpretation in the different exhibition spaces dotted around the courtyard. Heritage breeds, including longhorn cows, Southdown sheep and Tamworth pigs, can be seen grazing in the extensive pasture. Café. *Opening times* vary according to the season so visit the website for further details. Charge.
Canalside Farm Mill Lane, Great Haywood ST18 0RQ (01889 881747; www.canalsidefarm.co.uk). Immediately east of Bridge 74. Selling an excellent selection of local (within 30 miles) seasonal, fresh produce. Butcher, baker and delicatessen. PYO strawberries and raspberries. Bedding plants and ice creams. Café. *Open Apr-Oct, daily 09.00-18.00 & Nov-Mar, Tue-Sat 09.00-18.00 & Sun 10.00-17.00.*

CANOEING AND PADDLEBOARDING
This makes an interesting variation on straightforward paddling along inland waterways and, as such, should encourage the canoeist and paddleboarder to be creative in devising loops that do not necessarily rely totally upon recognised navigations: www.ruthonanadventure.com/2020/07/23/river-sow-canal-adventure.
See also **Canoeing and Paddleboarding** on pages 127 and 129.

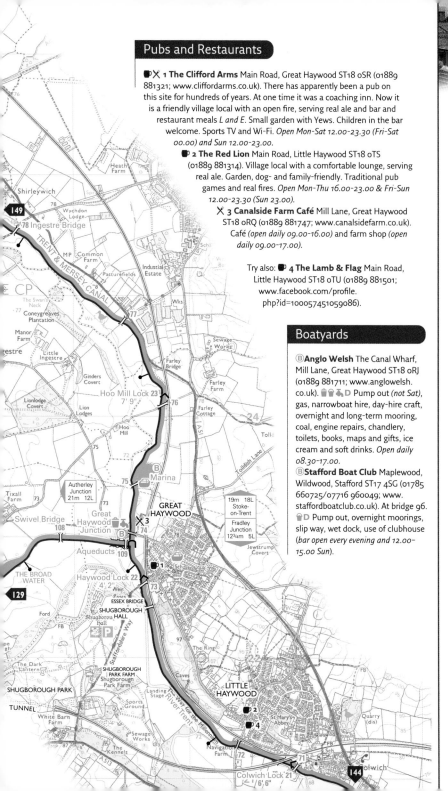

Pubs and Restaurants

🍺✕ **1 The Clifford Arms** Main Road, Great Haywood ST18 0SR (01889 881321; www.cliffordarms.co.uk). There has apparently been a pub on this site for hundreds of years. At one time it was a coaching inn. Now it is a friendly village local with an open fire, serving real ale and bar and restaurant meals *L and E*. Small garden with Yews. Children in the bar welcome. Sports TV and Wi-Fi. *Open Mon-Sat 12.00-23.30 (Fri-Sat 00.00) and Sun 12.00-23.00.*

🍺 **2 The Red Lion** Main Road, Little Haywood ST18 0TS (01889 881314). Village local with a comfortable lounge, serving real ale. Garden, dog- and family-friendly. Traditional pub games and real fires. *Open Mon-Thu 16.00-23.00 & Fri-Sun 12.00-23.30 (Sun 23.00).*

✕ **3 Canalside Farm Café** Mill Lane, Great Haywood ST18 0RQ (01889 881747; www.canalsidefarm.co.uk). Café *(open daily 09.00-16.00)* and farm shop *(open daily 09.00-17.00).*

Try also: 🍺 **4 The Lamb & Flag** Main Road, Little Haywood ST18 0TU (01889 881501; www.facebook.com/profile. php?id=100057451059086).

Boatyards

ⓑ**Anglo Welsh** The Canal Wharf, Mill Lane, Great Haywood ST18 0RJ (01889 881711; www.anglowelsh. co.uk). 🚿🚽🛒D Pump out *(not Sat)*, gas, narrowboat hire, day-hire craft, overnight and long-term mooring, coal, engine repairs, chandlery, toilets, books, maps and gifts, ice cream and soft drinks. *Open daily 08.30-17.00.*

ⓑ**Stafford Boat Club** Maplewood, Wildwood, Stafford ST17 4SG (01785 660725/07716 960049; www. staffordboatclub.co.uk). At bridge 96. 🛒D Pump out, overnight moorings, slip way, wet dock, use of clubhouse *(bar open every evening and 12.00-15.00 Sun).*

Weston upon Trent

The canal now leaves behind the excitement and interest of Great Haywood to continue its quiet north westerly passage through a broad valley towards Stone and Stoke-on-Trent. Hoo Mill Lock is a busy spot with many moored boats, and a useful *boatyard*. North of the lock a main road joins the hitherto quiet canal for a while. To the west is Ingestre Hall: beyond here the locks are broadly spaced and, although roads are never far away, the atmosphere is one of remoteness and peace. The village of Weston upon Trent is pretty, and there are pleasant pubs to visit.

Amerton Farm Stowe-by-Chartley, Near Weston ST18 0LA (01889 270294; www.amertonfarm. co.uk). Popular attraction featuring a playbarn, businesses and attractions, farmyard, licensed tearooms, narrow gauge railway (*see below*). *Open daily 09.30-17.00.* Charge.

Amerton Railway Stowe-by-Chartley, Near Weston ST18 0LA (01889 271337; www. amertonrailway.co.uk). ¾ mile east of Weston upon Trent, along A518. Steam and diesel hauled narrow gauge railway established and operated by a dedicated band of volunteers. A wide range of events take place throughout the year. *See* website for details and the timetable. *Open weekends 11.15-16.45.* Charge.

● **Weston upon Trent**
Staffs. PO box, tel. A pretty village of cottages and new houses, stretching away from St Andrew's church. There is a mobile *PO* in the village hall *Wed 13.00-16.00.*

Boatyards

Ⓑ**Great Haywood Marina** The Marina Building, Canalside Farm, Mill Lane, Great Haywood ST18 0RQ (01889 883713/07771 685 731; www. greathaywoodmarina.co.uk). 🛒♿D Pump out, gas, short- and long-term mooring, boat sales and repairs, solid fuel, slipway, chandlery, laundrette, toilets, showers, Wi-Fi, CCTV. Farm shop adjacent. *Open Mon-Sat 09.00-17.00 & Sun 10.00-16.00.*

The Old Joule's Brewery, Stone

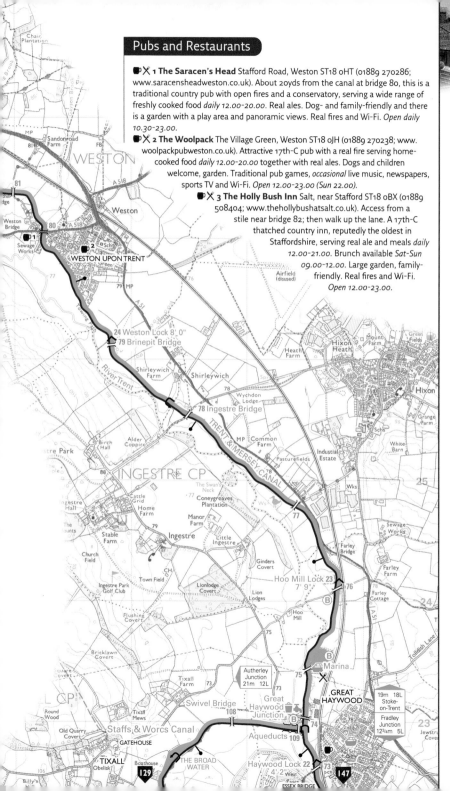

Pubs and Restaurants

🍴✗ **1 The Saracen's Head** Stafford Road, Weston ST18 0HT (01889 270286; www.saracensheadweston.co.uk). About 20yds from the canal at bridge 80, this is a traditional country pub with open fires and a conservatory, serving a wide range of freshly cooked food *daily 12.00-20.00*. Real ales. Dog- and family-friendly and there is a garden with a play area and panoramic views. Real fires and Wi-Fi. *Open daily 10.30-23.00*.

🍴✗ **2 The Woolpack** The Village Green, Weston ST18 0JH (01889 270238; www.woolpackpubweston.co.uk). Attractive 17th-C pub with a real fire serving home-cooked food *daily 12.00-20.00* together with real ales. Dogs and children welcome, garden. Traditional pub games, *occasional* live music, newspapers, sports TV and Wi-Fi. *Open 12.00-23.00 (Sun 22.00)*.

🍴✗ **3 The Holly Bush Inn** Salt, near Stafford ST18 0BX (01889 508404; www.thehollybushatsalt.co.uk). Access from a stile near bridge 82; then walk up the lane. A 17th-C thatched country inn, reputedly the oldest in Staffordshire, serving real ale and meals *daily 12.00-21.00*. Brunch available *Sat-Sun 09.00-12.00*. Large garden, family-friendly. Real fires and Wi-Fi. *Open 12.00-23.00*.

Stone

The wooded Sandon Park rises steeply on the north bank as the canal continues in a north westerly direction, passing through quiet meadows to the little village of Burston. The 100-year-old tower of Aston Church is prominent as the canal passes through the quiet water meadows of the Trent valley. Soon Stone is entered – note the sign on a narrowboat cabin at the bridge. Below the bottom lock is a good place *to moor* – a fine old canal *pub* by the lockside, *children's playground* and *shops* are close by to the north east. The locks are deeper than most on the narrow canals – their average rise is about 10ft. Just above the second lock there is a *boatyard* and three dry docks: there is another *boatyard* a few yards further on. Look out for the sculpture of 'Christina' by bridge 94. Lock 29 is accompanied by a little tunnel under the road for boat horses, and there are towline rollers at the bridge by lock 30. Stone quite justly calls itself 'a canal town.' Gas is available from Morrisons fuel station *Mon-Sat 06.00-22.00 & Sun 08.00-20.00.*

● **Sandon**
Staffs. Tel, stores. A small estate village clustered near the main gates to Sandon Park. The main road bisecting the place is enough to send any canal boatman scurrying back to the safety of the relative peace and quiet of Sandon Lock. There is a pub, however, opposite the park gates.

● **Burston**
Staffs. Tel. A hamlet apparently untouched by modern times, in spite of the proximity of three transport routes. Most of the village is set around the village pond. A surprisingly quiet place.

● **Stone**
Staffs. All services. A very busy and pleasant town with strong canal associations, and excellent boating and shopping facilities. The old priory church began to fall down in 1749, so in 1753 an Act of Parliament was obtained to enable the parishioners to rebuild it. The canalside is splendid, with dry docks, wharves and the impressive old Joules brewery buildings having a timeless air. There are always interesting craft to admire.

Pubs and Restaurants

●✕ **1 The Dog & Doublet Inn** Sandon ST18 0DJ (01889 508331; www.doganddoubletsandon.co.uk). Friendly pub, serving real ale and food *L and E*. Bar snacks available. Dog- and child-friendly, garden. *Occasional* live music, traditional pub games, real fires and Wi-Fi. Electric car charging points. B&B. *Open Wed-Sun 09.00-23.00 (Wed-Thu 11.30).*

●✕ **2 The Greyhound Inn** Burston ST18 0DR (01889 508263; www.greyhoundinn.info). Real ale and food available *Mon-Sat L and E & Sun 11.30-21.00.* Dog- and child-friendly, small garden. Traditional pub games, newspapers, real fires and Wi-Fi. Camping. *Open Mon-Fri L and E & Sat-Sun 11.30-23.00 (Sun 11.00).*

🍺✗ **3 The Three Crowns** Litchfield Road, Stone ST15 8QU (01785 819516; www.vintageinn.co.uk/restaurants/midlands/thethreecrownsstone). Old coaching inn serving real ale and food *daily 12.00-22.00 (Sun 21.30)*. Garden, dog- and family-friendly. Real fires and Wi-Fi. *Open 11.30-23.00 (Sun 22.30)*

🍺✗ **4 The Star Inn** 21 Stafford Street, Stone ST15 8QW (01785 813096; www.facebook.com/starinstone). Beside Star Lock 27. Traditional lockside pub, which apparently dates from the 14th C and is one of the oldest on the waterways, where none of the rooms are on the same level (it is noted in the *Guinness Book of Records* for this fact). Real ale and food served *daily 12.00-20.00*. Dog- and child-friendly, garden. Traditional pub games, real fires, sports TV and Wi-Fi. *Open daily 12.00-23.00*.

🍺 **5 The Royal Exchange** 26 Radford Street, Stone ST15 8DA (01785 812685; www.titanicbrewery.co.uk/our-pubs/the-royal-exchange). Lively one-roomed pub with *regular* music nights serving an excellent range of real ales together with food *Mon E and Sun 12.00-21.00*. Dog- and child-friendly (*until 21.00 – 19.30 Fri-Sat*) and outside drinking area. Traditional pub games (including children's games) newspapers, real fires and Wi-Fi.

Open Mon-Thu 16.00-23.00 & Fri-Sun 12.00-23.00 (Sun 21.00).

🍺 **6 The Swan Inn** 18 Stafford Street, Stone ST15 8QW (01785 815570; www.facebook.com/TheSwanInnStone). Built in 1771 as a warehouse for the Trent & Mersey Canal, the building was converted into a pub in the mid-19th C. Now serving a wide range of real ale and cider, this hostelry dispenses live music *Tue*. No children. Newspapers, real fires and Wi-Fi. *Open Mon 14.00-22.00; Tue-Fri 14.00-23.00 (Thu-Fri 00.00) & Sat-Sun 13.00-01.00 (Sun 22.00)*.

🍺 **7 The Poste of Stone** 1 Granville Square, Stone ST15 8AB (01785 827920; www.jdwetherspoon.com/pubs/all-pubs/england/staffordshire/the-poste-of-stone-stone). Once the town's post office, now dispensing real ales and food *daily 08.00-23.00*. Outside drinking area, children welcome *until 21.00*. Real fires, sports TV and Wi-Fi. *Open 08.00-00.00*.

🍺 **8 Crown Wharf** Crown Street, Stone ST15 8NQ (01785 550450; www.joulesbrewery.co.uk/our-taphouses/our-pub-list/crown-wharf-stone). Flagship Joule's Brewery tap, finally re-established in the town of the company's origin, serving real ales and food *12.00-21.00 (Sun 16.00)*. Outside seating, dog- and family-friendly. Live music *Fri & Sun*. Traditional pub games, newspapers, real fires and Wi-Fi. *Open daily 11.00-23.00 (Fri-Sat 00.30)*.

Boatyards

ⓑ**Canal Cruising Co** Ltd Crown Street, Stone ST15 8QN (01785 813982; www.canalcruising.co.uk). 🚲D Pump out, gas, narrowboat hire, boat and engine repairs, dry docks (including emergency dock), painting and hull blacking, telephone. *Open Mon-Sat 08.30-17.00*. Supermarket adjacent and 🛒 nearby.

ⓑ**Aston Marina** Lichfield Road, Stone ST15 8QU (01785 819702; www.astonmarina.co.uk). 🛒🚲D Gas, pump out, electricity, long- and short-term mooring, slipway, workshop, boat lift, winter storage, DIY facilities, solid fuel, laundry, showers, toilets, farm shop, Wi-Fi. Also ✗🍷 **9 No 26 Bar and Dining** open for breakfast, lunch, afternoon tea and dinner *daily 09.00 'til late*.

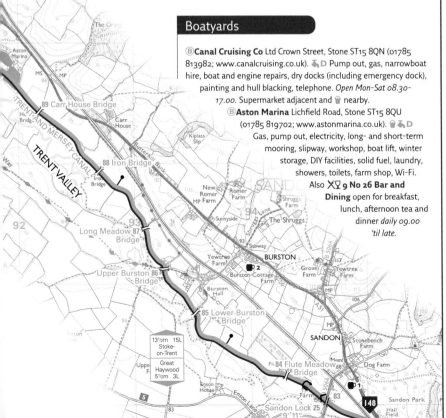

Barlaston

Stone Locks are soon followed by another flight of four, climbing up the valley to Meaford. The present Meaford Locks replaced an earlier staircase of three, the remains of which can be seen by lock 33. Here the railway line draws alongside, while the valley widens out and becomes flatter and less rural. The railway continues to flank the canal as it approaches the straggling village of Barlaston *(PO, stores, chemist, off-licence, butcher and station)*. Just before Trentham Lock, where there are good *moorings*, is the Wedgwood Pottery, set back from the canal. The factory is conveniently served by Wedgwood Halt, immediately east of Oldroad Bridge 104. Conveniently grouped either side of Hemheath Bridge 106 are a *PO, off-licence and garage* complete with a useful *shop*. A sign gives details of the nearby Newstead Wood and Hem Heath Nature Reserves, both refreshing open spaces before you tackle Stoke.

World of Wedgewood Wedgewood Drive, Barlaston, Stoke-on-Trent ST12 9ER (01782 282986; www.worldofwedgwood.com). The Wedgewood Group is the largest china and earthenware manufacturer in the world. It was started in 1759 in Burslem by the famous Josiah Wedgwood, the Father of English Potters, who came from a small pottery family. By 1766 he was sufficiently prosperous to build a large new house and factory which he called Etruria – a name suggested by his close friend Dr Erasmus Darwin – and to use the canal, of which he was a promoter, for transport. It was here that he produced his famous Jasper unglazed stoneware with white classical portraits on the surface. He revolutionised pottery-making with his many innovations and after his death in 1795 the company continued to expand.

In the 1930s the Wedgwoods decided to build a new factory because mining subsidence had made Etruria unsuitable. The Etruria factory has unfortunately since been demolished but the large new factory began production in 1940 in Barlaston and is still the centre of the industry, with six electric tunnel ovens which produce none of the industrial smoke that is commonly associated with the Potteries. The Wedgwood Museum at Barlaston has a vast range of exhibits of Wedgwood pottery. The works is only a few yards from the canal, accessible from bridge 104. Combine your visit to the museum with a trip to the nearby Wedgwood Visitor Centre and a factory tour (when available). The museum and visitor centre are *open Wed-Sun 10.00–17.00*. Charge. Self-guided tours. There are demonstrations, a shop, a museum, bistro and a restaurant. Parties of 12 people and over must book. A stop here should be on every canal traveller's itinerary.

CANOEING AND PADDLEBOARDING

Within easy reach of this northern stretch of the Trent & Mersey Canal, there are canoe clubs that make use of the local water space, at Derby – The Midland Canoe Club Darley Abbey, Derby DE22 1EB (www.midlandcanoeclub. com) – Burton upon Trent – Burton Canoe Club Newton Road Park, Newton Road, Burton upon Trent DE15 0TU (www.burtoncanoeclub.co.uk) – Stone – Stafford & Stone Canoe Club Westbridge Park, Stafford Road, Stone ST15 8QW (www.staffordandstonecc.co.uk) – and Trentham – Trentham Gardens Estate, Stoke-on-Trent ST12 9HR (www.trenthamcanoeclub.co.uk). There is also a canoe polo club based between Derby and the canal – Viking Canoe Polo Club Moor Lane, Allenton, Derby DE24 9HY (www.vikingcanoepolo.com) that welcomes beginners and competes successfully at all levels.

There is also the opportunity to experience Hawaiian canoeing at Trentham. The group meets regularly at Trentham Lake (access via the Monkey Forest entrance). They have two 6-seater outrigger canoes plus access to a twin hull craft when needed. In the course of most sessions everyone has the chance for couple of paddles on the water. They maintain that there is no special equipment needed – just enthusiasm! For further details contact 01785 814224; www.u3asites.org.uk/stone/page/112402.

Locally, Moorland Adventure provide a whole range of Canadian canoeing experiences, from introductory sessions on flat water through to river trips and canoe camping trips on moving water. For further details contact 07870 693816; www.moorlandadventure.co.uk/canoeing.

Rudyard Lake is one of Moorland Adventure's sites and the Rudyard Lake Trust has recently produced a mobile app for iOS or Android that acts as a guide to the lake and the nearby Moorlands. Called Rudyard Lake, the app uses GPS to show details of nearby attractions.

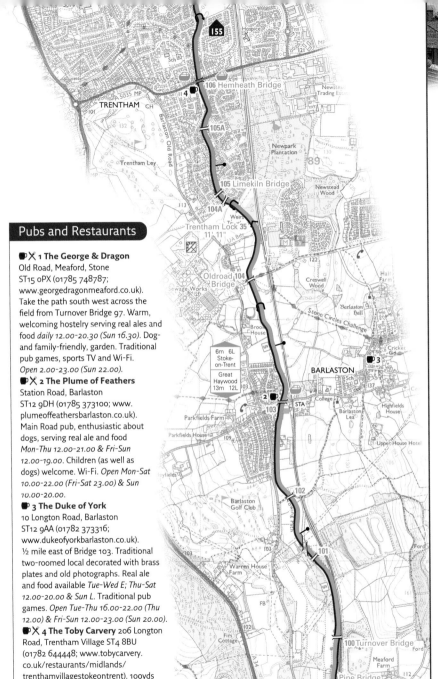

Pubs and Restaurants

⬤✕ 1 The George & Dragon
Old Road, Meaford, Stone
ST15 0PX (01785 748787;
www.georgedragonmeaford.co.uk).
Take the path south west across the
field from Turnover Bridge 97. Warm,
welcoming hostelry serving real ales and
food *daily 12.00–20.30 (Sun 16.30)*. Dog-
and family-friendly, garden. Traditional
pub games, sports TV and Wi-Fi.
Open 2.00–23.00 (Sun 22.00).

⬤✕ 2 The Plume of Feathers
Station Road, Barlaston
ST12 9DH (01785 373100; www.
plumeoffeathersbarlaston.co.uk).
Main Road pub, enthusiastic about
dogs, serving real ale and food
*Mon–Thu 12.00–21.00 & Fri–Sun
12.00–19.00*. Children (as well as
dogs) welcome. Wi-Fi. *Open Mon–Sat
10.00–22.00 (Fri–Sat 23.00) & Sun
10.00–20.00*.

⬤ 3 The Duke of York
10 Longton Road, Barlaston
ST12 9AA (01782 373316;
www.dukeofyorkbarlaston.co.uk).
½ mile east of Bridge 103. Traditional
two-roomed local decorated with brass
plates and old photographs. Real ale
and food available *Tue–Wed E; Thu–Sat
12.00–20.00 & Sun L*. Traditional pub
games. *Open Tue–Thu 16.00–22.00 (Thu
12.00) & Fri–Sun 12.00–23.00 (Sun 20.00)*.

⬤✕ 4 The Toby Carvery 206 Longton
Road, Trentham Village ST4 8BU
(01782 644448; www.tobycarvery.
co.uk/restaurants/midlands/
trenthamvillagestokeontrent). 100yds
west of Bridge 106. Real ale and a variety
of restaurant food and a carvery *daily
07.00–23.00* with a children's menu.
Patio and garden. Children welcome.
Traditional pub games and sports TV.
B&B. *Open daily 07.00–23.00*.

▌Stoke-on-Trent

This is a fascinating length of canal, not always (if ever) beautiful but all extremely interesting, passing right through the centre of Stoke-on-Trent, where all was once factories and warehouses – but which are now being rebuilt. Signs of the pottery industry still survive, its most remarkable manifestation being the bottle kilns – the brick furnaces shaped like gigantic bottles about 30ft high that still stand, cold and disused (but, happily, to be preserved), at the side of the canal. The Caldon Canal (*see* page 16) leaves the main line just above Stoke Top Lock. A statue of James Brindley, who built the Trent & Mersey Canal, stands near the junction. The Trent & Mersey then passes a *marina* and a *pub*, built for the National Garden Festival, before heading towards the south portal of the great Harecastle Tunnel. The Roundhouse, the very last remains of the original Wedgwood factory built in 1769, is easily missed – it stands beside bridge 117. Further along, by bridge 119, moor to visit the Royal Doulton shop.

● **Stoke-on-Trent**
Staffs. All services. The city was formed in 1910 from a federation of six towns (Burslem, Fenton, Hanley, Longton, Stoke and Tunstall) but became known as the Five Towns in the novels of Arnold Bennett. The thriving pottery industries are the source of the city's great prosperity. The town hall, in Glebe Street, is an imposing and formal 19th-C building. Opposite the town hall is the parish church of St Peter, which contains a commemorative plaque to Josiah Wedgwood. Festival Park has been built on the site of the old Shelton Steelworks, with a dry ski slope, Waterworld and a multi-screen cinema amongst other attractions.
Potteries Museum & Art Gallery Bethesda Street, Hanley ST1 3DW (01782 232323; www. stokemuseums.org.uk/pmag). Where the history of the area is brought to life. There is also a fine ceramics collection. Café and Wi-Fi. *Open Wed-Sat 10.00-17.00 & Sun 11.00-16.00.* Free.

Etruria Industrial Museum Lower Bedford Street, Etruria, Stoke-on-Trent ST4 7AF (07900 267711; www. etruriamuseum.org.uk). At the junction with the Trent & Mersey. This is a Grade II* Victorian steam-powered potter's miller's works, built in 1857 and which ground bone, flint and stone for the pottery industry, until closure in 1972. It has now been restored as part of an industrial complex incorporating a blacksmith's shop with working steam-powered machinery. Originally the raw materials and ground products were transported by canal, and present-day canal travellers will find plenty of moorings available. *Open approximately one weekend per month Spring-Autumn – visit the website or telephone for details.* Car park SatNav post code ST1 4RP.
Gladstone Pottery Museum Uttoxeter Road, Longton, Stoke-on-Trent ST3 1PQ (01782 237777; www.stokemuseums.org.uk/gpm). The last remaining Victorian pottery factory. Tearoom. *Open Apr-Oct, Wed-Sat 10.00-17.00 & Sun 11.00-16.00.* Charge.

Pubs and Restaurants

There are many pubs to choose from in Stoke-on-Trent. These are examples within reach of moorings at Etruria and Festival Park:

🍺 **1 The Holy Inadequate** 67 Etruria Old Road, Etruria ST1 5PE (07771 358238; www.facebook. com/TheHolyInadequate). ¼ mile west of Bridge 117. Multiple award-winning hostelry dispensing an excellent range of real ales (and ciders) and good cheer, together with bar snacks. Also an extensive range of bottled beers from British microbreweries. Dogs welcome. Real fires and outdoor drinking area. Wi-Fi. *Open 16.00-00.00 (Sat-Sun 12.00).*
🍺 **2 The Unicorn Inn** 40 Piccadilly, Hanley, Stoke-on-Trent ST1 1EG (www.facebook.com/unicorninn). Theatre-goers watering hole, complete with resident ghost, this traditional pub serves real ales. Interval drinks can be pre-ordered. Sports TV and Wi-Fi. *Open Mon-Sat 12.00-22.00 (Fri-Sat 23.00) & Sun 12.00-21.00.*
🍺 **3 The Albion** 2 Old Hall Street, Hanley, Stoke-on-Trent ST1 1QT (01782 287087; www.marstons.co.uk).

Bustling, traditional, one-roomed pub serving real ale and food *daily 12.00-20.00 (Sun 15.00).* Family-friendly and traditional pub games. *Open Mon-Sat 11.00-23.00 & Sun 12.00-22.00.*
🍺 **4 The Wheatsheaf Hotel** Sheaf Street, Shelton ST1 4LW (01782 212384). ¼ mile east of Locks 1 & 2. Old film memorabilia line the walls of this community local which serves real ale and offers B&B. Traditional pub games and sports TV. *Open daily 11.00-23.00.*
🍺 **5 The Gin Rummy** 41 Piccadilly, Hanley, Stoke-on-Trent ST1 1EN (01782 768075; www.theginrummy. co.uk). Small craft beer pub serving a good range of bottled beers in the 'Cultural Quarter' of Hanley. Wi-Fi. *Open Fri-Sat 13.00-22.00 (Sat 12.00) & Sun 12.00-19.00.*
🍺✕ **6 The Toby Carvery** Marina Way, Festival Park, Etruria ST1 5PA (01782 260199; www.tobycarvery. co.uk/restaurants/midlands/festivalparkstokeontrent). Canalside at Stoke Marina. Large lounge, a carvery restaurant. Real ale, and meals *daily 08.00-22.00.* Children welcome, outside seating. Traditional pub games. Moorings. *Open daily 08.00-23.00.*

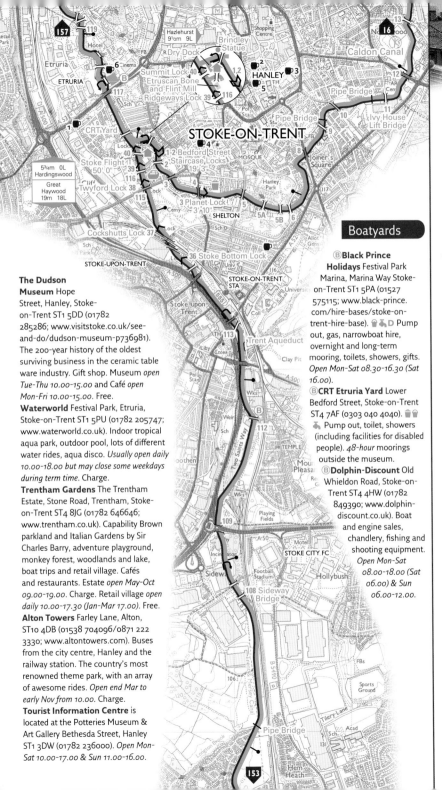

Boatyards

ⓑ**Black Prince Holidays** Festival Park Marina, Marina Way Stoke-on-Trent ST1 5PA (01527 575115; www.black-prince. com/hire-bases/stoke-on-trent-hire-base). 🏠🔧D Pump out, gas, narrowboat hire, overnight and long-term mooring, toilets, showers, gifts. *Open Mon-Sat 08.30-16.30 (Sat 16.00).*

ⓑ**CRT Etruria Yard** Lower Bedford Street, Stoke-on-Trent ST4 7AF (0303 040 4040). 🏠🏠 🔧 Pump out, toilet, showers (including facilities for disabled people). *48-hour* moorings outside the museum.

ⓑ**Dolphin-Discount** Old Whieldon Road, Stoke-on-Trent ST4 4HW (01782 849390; www.dolphin-discount.co.uk). Boat and engine sales, chandlery, fishing and shooting equipment. *Open Mon-Sat 08.00-18.00 (Sat 06.00) & Sun 06.00-12.00.*

The Dudson Museum Hope Street, Hanley, Stoke-on-Trent ST1 5DD (01782 285286; www.visitstoke.co.uk/see-and-do/dudson-museum-p736981). The 200-year history of the oldest surviving business in the ceramic table ware industry. Gift shop. Museum *open Tue-Thu 10.00-15.00* and Café *open Mon-Fri 10.00-15.00.* Free.

Waterworld Festival Park, Etruria, Stoke-on-Trent ST1 5PU (01782 205747; www.waterworld.co.uk). Indoor tropical aqua park, outdoor pool, lots of different water rides, aqua disco. *Usually open daily 10.00-18.00 but may close some weekdays during term time.* Charge.

Trentham Gardens The Trentham Estate, Stone Road, Trentham, Stoke-on-Trent ST4 8JG (01782 646646; www.trentham.co.uk). Capability Brown parkland and Italian Gardens by Sir Charles Barry, adventure playground, monkey forest, woodlands and lake, boat trips and retail village. Cafés and restaurants. Estate *open May-Oct 09.00-19.00.* Charge. Retail village *open daily 10.00-17.30 (Jan-Mar 17.00).* Free.

Alton Towers Farley Lane, Alton, ST10 4DB (01538 704096/0871 222 3330; www.altontowers.com). Buses from the city centre, Hanley and the railway station. The country's most renowned theme park, with an array of awesome rides. *Open end Mar to early Nov from 10.00.* Charge.

Tourist Information Centre is located at the Potteries Museum & Art Gallery Bethesda Street, Hanley ST1 3DW (01782 236000). *Open Mon-Sat 10.00-17.00 & Sun 11.00-16.00.*

Harecastle Tunnel

The canal swings past what was the junction with the old Burslem Arm (hopefully to be restored) which headed north for about a ¼ of a mile just before bridge 123, and continues through the flattened remains of an industrial area, before reaching the weathered and evocative red-brick and slate buildings of the Middleport Pottery, with kilns, cranes and cobbles right beside the canal. A large *boatyard*, with boats moored almost across the width of the canal then follows. Burslem lies to the east of the canal here and offers a selection of *takeaways, fish & chips and a chemist* within easy reach of the waterway. Before long the navigation passes the open expanse of Westport Park Lake, popular with fishermen and a useful *mooring* beside the Visitor Centre (01782 826983) and finally abandons its very twisting course to make a beeline for Harecastle Hill and the famous 2926yd tunnel. There were once two tunnels here: only one is now navigable. Beyond lies Kidsgrove and Hardings Wood Junction.

● The Three Harecastle Tunnels

There are altogether three parallel tunnels through Harecastle Hill. The first, built by James Brindley, was completed in 1777, after 11 years' work. To build a 9ft-wide tunnel 1¾ miles long represented engineering on a scale quite unknown to the world at that time, and the world was duly impressed. Since there was no towpath in the tunnel the boats – which were of course all towed from the bank by horses at that time – had to be legged through by men lying on the boat's cabin roof and propelling the boat by walking along the tunnel roof. The towing horse would, in the meantime, have to be walked over the top of the hill. This very slow means of propulsion, combined with the great length of the narrow tunnel and the large amount of traffic on the navigation, made Harecastle a major bottleneck for canal boats. So in 1822 the Trent & Mersey Canal Company called in Thomas Telford, who recommended that a second tunnel be constructed alongside the first one. This was done: the new tunnel was completed in 1827, with a towpath (now removed), after only three years' work. Each tunnel then became one-way until in the 20th C Brindley's bore had sunk so much from mining subsidence that it had to be abandoned. Its entrance can still be seen to the west of the newer tunnel mouth. An electric tug was introduced in 1914 to speed up traffic through Telford's tunnel; this service was continued until 1954. The third tunnel through Harecastle Hill was built years after the other two, and carried the Stoke-Kidsgrove railway line. It runs 40ft above the canal tunnels and is slightly shorter. This tunnel was closed in the 1960s: the railway line now goes round the hill and through a much shorter tunnel. Thus two out of the three Harecastle tunnels are disused.

CANOEING AND PADDLEBOARDING

For most of its length, the Trent & Mersey Canal has pretty much followed the course of the River Trent, crossing it on two occasions: once on the level and once on an aqueduct. At Great Haywood the river is also crossed by the Staffordshire & Worcestershire Canal close to its junction with the Trent & Mersey Canal. Whilst something of a dull navigation from the point of view of the canoeist and paddleboarder once east of Shardlow, the Trent provides many opportunities to plan a paddle that merges the best of both waterways when heading west from here. Both navigations are used by Inland Inspiration Paddlesports Tuition (07761 060551; https://inlandinspirationpaddlesports.business.site) for a wide range of courses covering everything from improving technique through to water safety.

Further afield, and just as likely to be linked with a visit to the Caldon Canal (*see* page 15 for the full coverage and page 155 for details of its junction with the Trent & Mersey Canal) there are two excellent paddling opportunities in the form of the Rivers Dove and Churnet, the latter providing some mild white water excitement as well as paralleling the Caldon Canal itself for part of its length.

Canoeists and paddleboarders should note that Harecastle Tunnel (*see* above) – over 1½ miles in length – cannot be used by unpowered craft, so a portage is required for the long distance paddler: *see* **Walking and Cycling** on the adjoining page for the route.

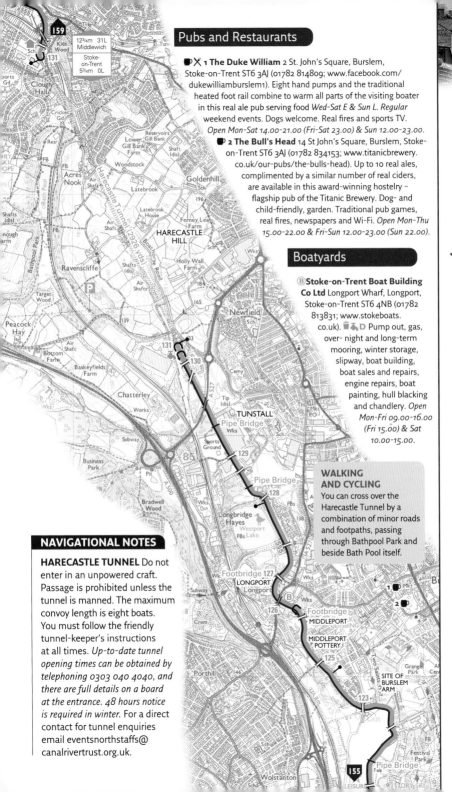

Pubs and Restaurants

1 The Duke William 2 St. John's Square, Burslem, Stoke-on-Trent ST6 3AJ (01782 814809; www.facebook.com/dukewilliamburslem1). Eight hand pumps and the traditional heated foot rail combine to warm all parts of the visiting boater in this real ale pub serving food *Wed-Sat E & Sun L. Regular weekend events.* Dogs welcome. Real fires and sports TV. *Open Mon-Sat 14.00-21.00 (Fri-Sat 23.00) & Sun 12.00-23.00.*

2 The Bull's Head 14 St John's Square, Burslem, Stoke-on-Trent ST6 3AJ (01782 834153; www.titanicbrewery.co.uk/our-pubs/the-bulls-head). Up to 10 real ales, complimented by a similar number of real ciders, are available in this award-winning hostelry – flagship pub of the Titanic Brewery. Dog- and child-friendly, garden. Traditional pub games, real fires, newspapers and Wi-Fi. *Open Mon-Thu 15.00-22.00 & Fri-Sun 12.00-23.00 (Sun 22.00).*

Boatyards

Ⓑ **Stoke-on-Trent Boat Building Co Ltd** Longport Wharf, Longport, Stoke-on-Trent ST6 4NB (01782 813831; www.stokeboats.co.uk). Pump out, gas, over- night and long-term mooring, winter storage, slipway, boat building, boat sales and repairs, engine repairs, boat painting, hull blacking and chandlery. *Open Mon-Fri 09.00-16.00 (Fri 15.00) & Sat 10.00-15.00.*

WALKING AND CYCLING

You can cross over the Harecastle Tunnel by a combination of minor roads and footpaths, passing through Bathpool Park and beside Bath Pool itself.

NAVIGATIONAL NOTES

HARECASTLE TUNNEL Do not enter in an unpowered craft. Passage is prohibited unless the tunnel is manned. The maximum convoy length is eight boats. You must follow the friendly tunnel-keeper's instructions at all times. *Up-to-date tunnel opening times can be obtained by telephoning 0303 040 4040, and there are full details on a board at the entrance. 48 hours notice is required in winter. For a direct contact for tunnel enquiries email eventsnorthstaffs@canalrivertrust.org.uk.*

Harding's Wood Junction

At the north end of Harecastle Tunnel (2926yds long) the navigation passes Kidsgrove station and a coal yard; there is also a *shower* in the facilities block beside the north tunnel portal. Beyond is Harding's Wood and the junction with the Macclesfield Canal, which crosses the T & M on Poole Aqueduct. There are *showers, laundry facilities and toilets* at the CRT yard at Red Bull. The canal continues to fall through a heavily locked stretch sometimes called 'heartbreak hill' but known to the old boatmen as the 'Cheshire Locks'. Two minor aqueducts are encountered, and most of the locks are narrow pairs – the chambers side by side.

Pubs and Restaurants

1 The Blue Bell 25 Hardingswood, Kidsgrove ST7 1EG (01782 774052; www.bluebellinnkidsgrove. com). Canalside, at Hardings Wood Junction. Friendly, quiet, one-bar local, winnner of many CAMRA awards. Real ale, plus a range of specialist bottled beers, including many from Belgium, plus real cider and perry. No juke box, pool table or gaming machines. Note the trapdoor in the lounge ceiling. Food is available *Tue-Sun 16.00-21.00*. Garden, dog- and child-friendly. Wi-Fi. *Open Tue-Fri 16.00-23.00 (Fri 00.00) & Sat-Sun 12.00-00.00 (Sun 23.00)*.

✕ 2 The Red Bull Hotel Congleton Road South, Church Lawton ST7 3AJ (01782 782600; www. robinsonsbrewery.com/redbullchurchlawton) By Lock 43. Popular pub close to Hardings Wood Junction, serving real ale and substantial bar meals *12.00-20.30 (Sun 19.30)*. Family-friendly, garden. *Occasional* live music. Moorings. *Open daily 12.00-23.00 (Sun 22.30)*.

3 The Broughton Arms Sandbach Road, Rode Heath ST7 3RU (01270 883203; www. broughtonarmspub.co.uk). Canalside at Rode Heath. Friendly family pub, with comfortable bars and canalside seating. Range of real ale. Food available in bar and dining area *L and E*. Children welcome away from the bar. Wi-Fi. Dog-friendly, waterside garden. *Open daily 12.00-23.00 (Fri-Sat 00.00)*.

4 The Royal Oak 41 Sandbach Road, Rode Heath ST7 3RW (01270 875670). Spacious, roadside pub, close to the navigation serving a selection of real ales and food *L and E*. Dog- and child-friendly, garden. Sports TV and Wi-Fi. *Open daily 11.30-23.00 (Sun 11.00)*.

Northern entrance to Harecastle Tunnel

- **Kidsgrove**
  Staffs. All services. Originally an iron and coal producing
  town, Kidsgrove was much helped by the completion of the
  Trent & Mersey Canal. James Brindley is buried here.
- **Rode Heath**
  Cheshire. PO, tel, stores, off-licence, takeaway. A useful
  shopping area right by bridge 140.
  Rode Heath Rise ST7 3QD Once the site of a salt works,
  it has now been landscaped and restored as a wildflower
  meadow. Telephone (01260 297237/01625 383777) for
  further information.

NAVIGATIONAL NOTES

HARECASTLE TUNNEL Do not enter in an unpowered craft. With the complete removal of
the towpath, headroom is no longer the problem it once was. A one-way system operates,
so follow the instructions of the tunnel keepers. *For updated tunnel opening times, telephone
0303 040 4040.*

Boatyards

Ⓑ**David Smithson** Liverpool Road, Kidsgrove ST7 1EA (01782
787887; www.davidsmithson.co.uk/index.html). Near Bridge
132. **D** Gas, solid fuel, caravan fittings which can be used
as chandlery. Also bicycles and bicycle spares for sale.
Moorings at Kinnersley Wharf.

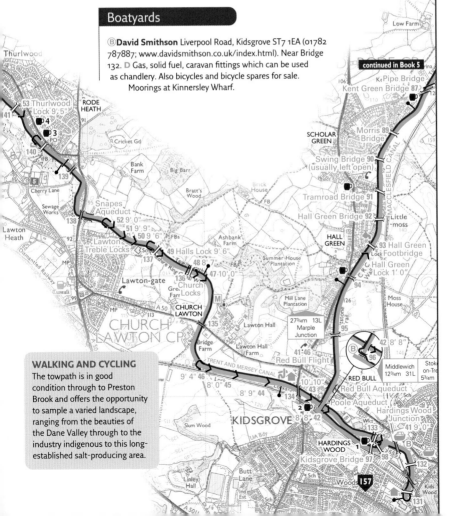

WALKING AND CYCLING
The towpath is in good
condition through to Preston
Brook and offers the opportunity
to sample a varied landscape,
ranging from the beauties of
the Dane Valley through to the
industry indigenous to this long-
established salt-producing area.

continued in Book 5

Wheelock

The canal now descends the Wheelock flight of eight locks, which are the last paired locks one sees when travelling northwards. The countryside continues to be quiet and unspoilt but unspectacular. The pair of locks half-way down the flight is situated in the little settlement of Malkin's Bank, overlooked by terraced houses. The boatman's co-op used to be here, in the small terrace of cottages. The adjoining boatyard now specialises in the restoration of traditional working boats. At the bottom of the flight is the village of Wheelock (*toilets* and *shower*); west of here the navigation curls round the side of a hill before entering the very long-established salt-producing area that is based on Middlewich. The 'wild' brine pumping and rock-salt mining that has gone on hereabouts has resulted in severe local subsidence; the effect on the canal has been to necessitate the constant raising of the banks as lengths of the canal bed sink. This of course means that the affected lengths tend to be much deeper than ordinary canals. Non-swimmers beware of falling overboard. The navigation now begins to lose the rural character it has enjoyed since Kidsgrove. Falling through yet more locks, the canal is joined by a busy main road (useful for *fish & chips*, west of Kings Lock; and *Chinese takeaway*, west of bridge 166) which accompanies it into an increasingly flat and industrialised landscape, past several salt works and into Middlewich, where a branch of the Shropshire Union leads off westwards towards that canal at Barbridge. The first 100yds or so of this branch is the Wardle Canal, claimed to be the shortest canal in the country.

- **Wheelock**
  Cheshire. Tel, stores, off-licence, fish & chips, takeaway. Busy little main road village on the canal.
- **Sandbach**
  Cheshire. PO, tel, stores, garage, chemist, takeaways, bank, fish & chips, station (distant). 1½ miles north of Wheelock. An old market town that has maintained its charm despite the steady growth of its salt and chemical industries. After walking from the canal you can refresh yourself with a pint of real ale from any of the seven pubs visible from the seat in the market place. From the canal, the railway station is best accessed from Elton Moss Bridge 160.
  Ancient Crosses In the cobbled market place on a massive base stand two superb Saxon crosses, believed to commemorate the conversion of the area to Christianity in the 7th C. They suffered severely in the 17th C when the Puritans broke them up and scattered the fragments for miles. After years of searching for the parts, George Ormerod succeeded in re-erecting the crosses in 1816, with new stone replacing the missing fragments.
  St Mary's Church High Street, Sandbach CW11 1AN. A large, 16th-C church with a handsome battlemented tower. The most interesting features of the interior are the 17th-C carved roof and the fine chancel screen.
  The Old Hall Hotel High Street, Sandback CW11 1AL. An outstanding example of Elizabethan half-timbered architecture, which was formerly the home of the lord of the manor, but is now used as an hotel.

Boatyards

Ⓑ**Malkins Bank Canal Services** 35 Betchton Road, Malkins Bank, Sandbach CW11 4XN (01270 764595). ⚓ Long-term mooring, boat building and historic boat restoration, boat repairs, will help with breakdowns where possible.

Ⓑ**The Northwich Boat Company** Kings Lock Boatyard, Booth Lane, Middlewich CW10 0JJ (01270 760160/07970 151996; www.thenorthwichboat.com). D Pump out, gas, boat repairs, boat building and fitting out, new and used boat sales, boatshare sales and management. Open Mon-Fri 09.00-17.00; Sat 10.00-16.00 & Sun 11.00-15.00.

Pubs and Restaurants

1 Barchetta Restaurant 464a Crewe Road, Wheelock CW11 3RL (01270 314183; www.barchettarestaurant.com). Established in a canalside mill building, this independent, family-run restaurant uses fresh local ingredients to create authentic Italian and Mediterranean dishes. *Open Mon-Sat 16.30-21.30 (Fri-Sat 12.00) & Sun 12.00-20.00.*

2 The Cheshire Cheese 466-468 Crewe Road, Wheelock CW11 3RL (01270 346600; www.cheshirecheesewheelock.co.uk). Heavily-beamed, canalside pub serving real ale and a range of meals and snacks *daily 12.00-20.00*. Family-friendly, garden. Quiz *Tue*. Traditional pub games, Wi-Fi and sports TV. *Open daily 12.00-23.30 (Fri-Sat 00.30).*

3 The Shampaan 504 Crewe Road, Wheelock CW11 3RL (01270 753528/753511; www.shampaan.com). Authentic South Asian cuisine to eat in or takeaway. Children welcome. *Open daily 17.00-23.00.*

4 The Market Tavern 8 The Square, Sandbach CW11 1AT (01270 762099; www.themarkettavern-sandbach.co.uk). Opposite the crosses. Lively, old, traditional town pub, dating from 1680, dispensing a good selection of real ales. Large beer garden. Children welcome. Folk club *Tue* and live bands *Sat. Open 12.00-00.30 (Fri-Sat 02.30).*

5 The Lower Chequer Inn Crown Bank, Sandbach CW11 1DB (01270 750214; www.facebook.com/TheLowerChequer). Delightful 16th-C, timber-framed hostelry serving an excellent range of real ale. Food available *Fri E; Sat L and E & Sun L.* Dog-friendly, patio. Real fires, sports TV and Wi-Fi. *Open daily 12.00-23.00 (Sat 01.00).*

6 The Old Hall High Street, Sandbach CW11 1AL (01270 758170; www.brunningandprice.co.uk/oldhall). Microbreweries are well represented in this stunning, Grade 1 listed, timber-framed building recently completely restored to a very high standard, displaying it's wood panelling and Tudor fireplace to perfection. Family-friendly and garden – dogs on a leash welcome. Food available *Mon-Fri 10.00-21.30 (Fri 22.00) & Sat-Sun 09.00-22.00 (Sun 21.00).* Newspapers, real fires, traditional pub games and Wi-Fi. *Open daily 11.00-23.00 (Sun 22.30).*

7 The Fox Inn London Road, Elworth CW11 3BF (01270 761641; www.thefoxinnsandbach.com). Welcoming, multi-roomed, Grade II listed pub serving real ale and food *daily 12.00-20.00 (Sun 18.00).* Garden, dog- and family-friendly. Traditional pub games, newspapers, sports TV and Wi-Fi. *Open Mon-Sat 12.00-23.30 (Fri-Sat 00.30) & Sun 12.00-23.00.*

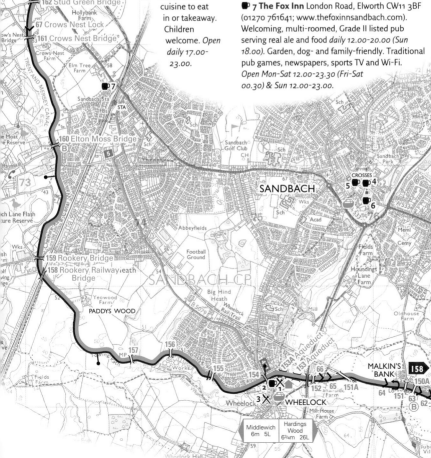

Middlewich

The Trent & Mersey skirts the centre of the town, passing lots of moored narrowboats and through three consecutive narrow locks, arriving at a wide (14ft) lock (which has suffered from subsidence) with a pub beside it. This used to represent the beginning of a wide, almost lock-free navigation right through to Preston Brook, Manchester and Wigan (very convenient for the salt industry when it shipped most of its goods by boat), but Croxton Aqueduct had to be replaced many years ago, and is now a steel structure only 8ft 2in wide. The aqueduct crosses the River Dane, which flows alongside the navigation as both water courses leave industrial Middlewich and move out into fine open country. Initially, this is a stretch of canal as beautiful as any in the country. Often overhung by trees, the navigation winds along the side of a hill as it follows the delightful valley of the River Dane. There are pleasant moorings with *picnic tables and barbecue facilities*, created by the Broken Cross Boating Club in old clay pits, just north of bridge 176, on the off-side. The parkland on the other side of the valley encompasses Bostock Hall, a Georgian house rebuilt in 1775 to a design thought to have been by Samuel Wyatt: it has now been converted into apartments. At Whatcroft Hall (privately owned), the canal circles around to the east, passing under a railway bridge before heading for the industrial outskirts of Northwich and shedding its beauty and solitude once again.

NAVIGATIONAL NOTES

There are several privately owned wide 'lagoons' caused by subsidence along this section of the Trent & Mersey, in some of which repose the hulks of abandoned barges and narrowboats, lately being salvaged. Navigators should be wary of straying off the main line, since the off-side canal bank is often submerged and invisible just below the water level.

Boatyards

Ⓑ**Kings Lock Chandlery** Booth Lane, Middlewich CW10 0JJ (01606 737564; www.kingslock.co.uk). Ⓓ Gas, overnight mooring, long-term mooring, slipway, engine sales and repairs, boat repairs, Webasto dealer, chandlery (including mail order), books, maps, gifts, solid fuel, Vetus dealer. *Open Mon-Fri 09.00-17.00 (Fri 16.00).*

Ⓑ**Kings Lock Boat Yard Services** Booth Lane, Middlewich CW10 0JJ (01606 610610; www.kingslock.com). Slipway, engine servicing, painting, hull blacking, shot blasting, fuel polishing. *Open Mon-Fri 09.00-17.00.*

See also **Boatyards** on page 108.

See also **Boatyards** on page 108.

> **CANOEING AND PADDLEBOARDING**
> *See* **Canoeing and Paddleboarding** on page 108.

See **Canoeing and Paddleboarding** on page 108.

Pubs and Restaurants

🍺✕ **1 The Kings Lock Inn** 1 Booth Lane, Middlewich CW10 0JJ (01606 836894; www.kingslockinn.com). Traditional, canalside hostelry, that once provided facilities and stabling for boating families. This so-called 'stack pub' – being built on two levels – today sells real ale, real cider and serves food *Mon–Sat 12.00-20.30 (Fri-Sat 21.00) & Sun 12.00-18.00*. Dog- and family-friendly, garden. *Monthly live music, real fires and Wi-Fi. Open Tue-Sun 12.00-23.00.*

🍺✕ **2 The Boars Head** Kinderton Street, Middlewich CW10 0JE (01606 833191; www.theboarsheadhotel.co.uk). Large rambling pub and restaurant offering real ale and food *L and E, daily*. Garden, family-friendly. B&B. *Open 12.00-23.00 (Sun 22.30)*

🍺 **3 The Middlewich Taphouse** 61 Chester Road, Middlewich CW10 9ET (01606 737163; www.facebook.com/middlewichtaphouse). *Open all day* – at the top of the town at the junction between Chester Road and Newton Bank. Now a free house, dispensing real ale and traditional pub food *L and E*. Dog- and child-

friendly, garden. Real fires and sports TV. B&B. *Open Mon-Thu 15.00-00.00 & Fri-Sun 12.00-01.00 (Sun 00.00)*.

🍺 **4 The Cheshire Cheese** Lewin Street, Middlewich CW10 9AX (01606 832097). Friendly, traditional establishment serving real ale. Dog-friendly, large garden. Sports TV. *Open Mon-Fri 15.00-23.00 (Thu-Fri 01.00) & Sat-Sun 12.00-01.00 (Sun 23.00)*.

🍺 **5 The Newton Brewery Inn** 68 Webb Lane, Middlewich CW10 9DN (01606 832335). 1/4 mile south of the Big Lock pub. Small friendly pub with attractive garden running down to the towpath. Real ale served. Dog-friendly. *Open Mon-Thu 16.00-22.00 (Thu 23.30) Fri 16.00-00.00 & Sat-Sun 12.00-00.00 (Sun 22.30)*.

🍺✕ **6 The Big Lock** Webbs Lane, Middlewich CW10 9DN (01606 833489; www.facebook.com/biglockmiddlewich). Canalside. Variously a bottle-making factory and canal-horse stables, this pub now serves real ale and a large menu of popular pub food. Freshly prepared meals available *Mon-Sat 12.00-21.00 (Fri-Sat 21.30) & Sun 12.00-20.30*. Family- and dog-friendly, garden. Wi-Fi. *Open daily 12.00-23.00*.

● **Middlewich**
Cheshire. *PO, stores, chemist, butcher, baker, off-licence, fish & chips, takeaways, DIY, library, garage.* A town that since Roman times has been dedicated to salt extraction. Most of the salt produced here goes to various chemical industries. Subsidence from salt extraction has prevented redevelopment for many years, but a big renewal scheme is now in progress. The canalside area is a haven of peace below the busy streets. There is an interesting town trail depicting Roman Middlewich as a Romano-British saltworks settlement in the period 150-250 AD. Interpretation boards can be found on the towpath north of Bridge 172 and beside the Newton Brewery Inn. *Stores in Wheelock Street open daily 06.00-23.00.*
St Michael's Church High Town, Middlewich CW10 9AN (01606 738005). A handsome medieval church which was a place of refuge for the Royalists during the Civil War. It has a fine interior with richly carved woodwork.

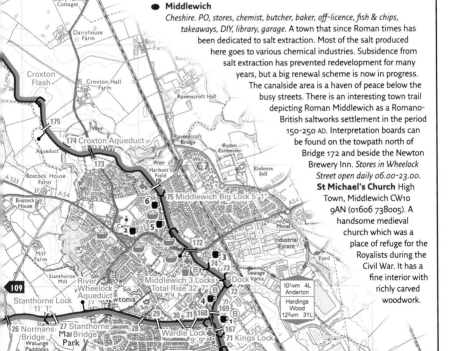

The outlying canal settlement of Broken Cross acts as a buffer between the beauty and solitude of the Dane Valley and the industrial ravages around Northwich. Beyond is another length in which salt mining has determined the nature of the scenery.

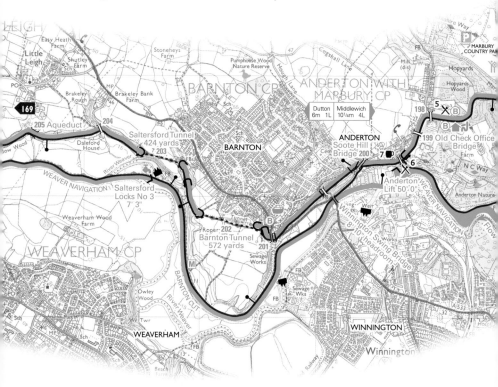

Part of it is heavily industrial, with enormous Tata Chemical works dominating the scene; much of it is devastated but rural (just), some of it is nondescript, and some of it is superb countryside. In a recent upgrade of the pipe bridges an effort was made to install decorative features devised by local consultants, Parker Design. Donkey engines can still be seen in surrounding fields pumping brine. Leaving the vicinity of Lostock Gralam and the outskirts of Northwich, one passes Marston and Wincham where there is *gas and solid fuel* available ¼ mile north east of Bridge 193. Just west of the village, one travels along a ½-mile stretch of canal that was only cut in 1958, as the old route was about to collapse into – needless to say – underground salt workings. Beyond the woods of Marbury Country Park (attractive short-stay *moorings*) and before Bridge 198, there are a full range of facilities including *toilets and showers*, followed by Anderton – the short entrance canal to the famous boat lift down into the Weaver Navigation is on the left. Gas is available 100yds south of Bridge 200. The main line continues westwards, winding along what is now a steep hill and into Barnton Tunnel. There is a useful *range of shops*, up the hill from the east end of the tunnel, including a *PO, tel, stores, butcher, takeaways and an off-licence*. You then emerge onto a hillside overlooking the River Weaver, with a marvellous view straight down the huge Saltersford Locks. Now Saltersford Tunnel is entered: beyond it you are in completely open country again. There are good moorings in the basins to the east of both tunnels.

NAVIGATIONAL NOTES

1 Saltersford Tunnel is crooked, affording only a brief glimpse of the other end. It is subject to timed passage. Northbound, on the hour to 20 min past; southbound half past the hour to 10 mins to the hour. Two boats cannot pass in this or Barnton Tunnel, so make sure they are clear before proceeding. Both tunnels are available to paddlers.

2 *See* notes on page 177 covering use of the Anderton Boat Lift.

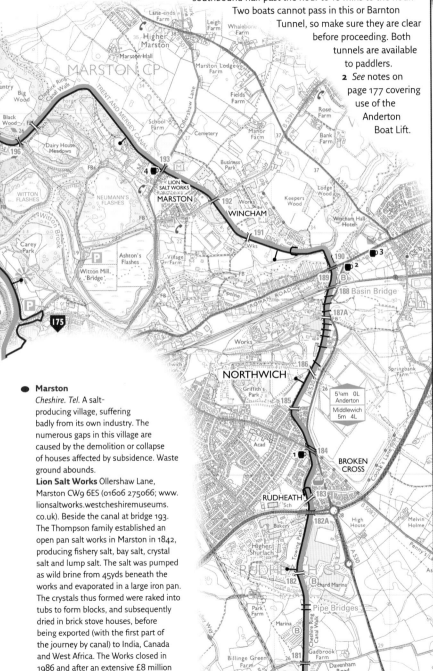

Marston

Cheshire. Tel. A salt-producing village, suffering badly from its own industry. The numerous gaps in this village are caused by the demolition or collapse of houses affected by subsidence. Waste ground abounds.

Lion Salt Works Ollershaw Lane, Marston CW9 6ES (01606 275066; www.lionsaltworks.westcheshiremuseums.co.uk). Beside the canal at bridge 193. The Thompson family established an open pan salt works in Marston in 1842, producing fishery salt, bay salt, crystal salt and lump salt. The salt was pumped as wild brine from 45yds beneath the works and evaporated in a large iron pan. The crystals thus formed were raked into tubs to form blocks, and subsequently dried in brick stove houses, before being exported (with the first part of the journey by canal) to India, Canada and West Africa. The Works closed in 1986 and after an extensive £8 million restoration project, finally re-opened to the public in 2015. Café, shop, butterfly garden and play area. *Open Tue-Sun 10.30-17.00.* Charge (for museum only).

Marbury Country Park Comberbach CW9 6AT (01606 77741; www.visitcheshire.com/things-to-do/marbury-country-park-p32091). Two-hundred-acre park occupying the landscaped gardens of the former Marbury Hall and estate, once the home of the Barry and Smith-Barry families. Overlooking Budworth Mere, the house was demolished in 1968 and the much-neglected gardens restored to their former glory by Cheshire County Heritage and Recreation service. The Information Centre (½ mile north of bridge 196) houses a display of Marbury's wildlife and history, including its use as a POW camp during World War II. Visitor's moorings and picnic area.

● **Anderton Lift**

Lift Lane, Anderton CW9 6FW (01606 786777; www.canalrivertrust.org.uk/places-to-visit/anderton-boat-lift-visitor-centre). An amazing and enormous piece of machinery built in 1875 by Leader Williams (later engineer of the Manchester Ship Canal) to connect the Trent & Mersey to the flourishing Weaver Navigation, 50ft below. As built, the lift consisted of two water-filled tanks counterbalancing each other in a vertical slide, resting on massive hydraulic rams. It worked on the very straightforward principle that making the ascending tank slightly lighter – by pumping a little water out – would assist the hydraulic rams (which were operated by a steam engine and pump) in moving both tanks, with boats in them, up or down their respective slide. In 1908 the lift had to have major repairs, so it was modernised at the same time. The troublesome hydraulic rams were done away with; from then on each tank – which contained 250 tons of water – had its own counterweights and was independent of the other tank. Electricity replaced steam as the motive power. One of the most fascinating individual features of the canal system, it draws thousands of sightseers every year. Restoration to full working order is now complete, following the original 1875 hydraulic design, using oil as the motive force rather than the chemically contaminated water that was the cause of the 1908 failure. The more recent counter balance weights, together with their ungainly supporting structure, have been retained to demonstrate the engineering development of the lift.

● **Northwich**

Cheshire. All services. Regular buses from Barnton. A rather attractive town at the junction of the Rivers Weaver and Dane. (The latter brings large quantities of sand down into the Weaver Navigation, necessitating a heavy expenditure on dredging.) As in every other town in this area, salt has for centuries been responsible for the continued prosperity of Northwich. The Weaver Navigation has of course been another very prominent factor in the town's history, and the building and repairing of barges, narrowboats, and small seagoing ships has been carried on here for over 200 years. Nowadays this industry has been almost forced out of business by foreign competition, and the last private shipyard on the river closed down in 1971. (This yard – Isaac Pimblott's – used to be between Hunt's Locks and Hartford Bridge. Their last contract was a tug for Aden.) However, the big CRT yard in the town continues to thrive; some very large maintenance craft are built and repaired here. The wharves by Town Bridge are empty, and are an excellent temporary mooring site for anyone wishing to visit the place. The town centre is very close; much of it has been completely rebuilt however, signs of decay are already beginning to creep in. There is now an extensive shopping precinct. Although the large number of pubs has been whittled down in the rebuilding process, there are still some pleasant old streets. The Weaver and the big swing bridges across it remain a dominant part of the background.

Tourist Information Centre 1 The Arcade, Northwich CW9 5AS (0300 123 8123; www.visitcheshire.com/visitor-information/visitor-information-centres). *Open Mon-Fri 08.30-17.00.*

Weaver Hall Museum and Workhouse 162 London Road, Northwich CW9 8AB (01606 271640; www.weaverhall.westcheshiremuseums.co.uk). The history of the salt industry from Roman times to the present day, housed in the town's former workhouse. Look out for the remarkable model ship, made from salt of course. Shop. *Open Tue-Fri 10.00-13.30 & 14.00-17.00 & Sat-Sun 14.00-17.00. Last admission 16.30.* Charge.

NAVIGATIONAL NOTES

1 The Anderton Boat Lift is available for use 7 days a week and pre-booked passage is essential by telephoning 01606 786777. Visit the website (www.canalrivertrust.org.uk/anderton) for more information.

2 Boaters should be careful to differentiate between the the holding moorings at the top and bottom of the lift, which are solely for lift use, and the visitor moorings.

Boatyards

Ⓑ**Park Farm Marina** Davenham Road, Rudheath, Northwich CW9 7RY (01606 44672; www.parkfarm-marina.co.uk). Short- and long-term mooring.

Ⓑ**Orchard Marina & Boat Builders Ltd** School Road, Gadbrook Park, Rudheath, Northwich CW9 7RG (01606 42082; www.orchardmarina.com). Beside bridge 182. 🛏️🏠♿D Gas, boat building, short- and long-term moorings, dry dock, boat and engine repairs, boat fitting out, boat and engine sales, DIY facilities, books, maps, solid fuel, toilets, showers, laundrette. *Emergency call out.*

Ⓑ**Colliery Narrowboat Co** Wincham Wharf, 220 Manchester Road, Lostock Gralam, Northwich CW9 7NT (01606 44672). Overnight and long-term mooring, crane, winter storage, boat building, boat sales, boat and engine repairs, wet dock, DIY facilities, toilets.

Ⓑ**Olympus Narrow Boats** Wincham Wharf, 220 Manchester Road, Lostock Gralam, Northwich CW9 7NT (01606 43048; www.narrowboats.org/canal-service/809/olympus+narrowboats). ♿D Gas, narrowboat fitting out, boat repairs, dry dock, wet dock. *Open Mon-Fri 08.0-17.00.*

Ⓑ✗♀️ 5 **ABC Leisure Group** Anderton Marina, Uplands Road, Anderton CW9 6AJ (01606 79642; www.abcboathire.com/our-locations/anderton-marina). 🛏️🏠♿D Pump out, gas, narrowboat hire, overnight mooring, long-term mooring, slipway, boat sales, engine sales and repairs, boat painting, covered wet docks for hire, chandlery, gifts, restaurant, telephone, toilets. *Open daily 09.00-17.00.*

Ⓑ**Uplands Marina** Uplands Road, Anderton CW9 6AQ (01606 782986/07931 323747). ♿ D Overnight and long-term mooring, boat sales and repairs, boat fitting out, winter storage, slipway, wet dock, gas, coal, chandlery. *Open Mon-Sat 09.00-12.00 (Tue and Thu-Fri 15.00).*

CANOEING AND PADDLEBOARDING
The Anderton Lift provides a connection between the Trent & Mersey Canal and the River Weaver for powered craft, but paddlers wishing to access the river at this point are faced with a steep portage requiring some care. The Weaver is usually a benign navigation that once carried copious salt and chemical traffic but the only commercial vessels that the paddler will encounter today are the occasional CRT work boats. However, fed by the head waters above Winsford Flash and the River Dane (a good paddle in its own right) which joins at Northwich, in times of flood the normally insignificant current becomes very apparent. Visit www.kanoroutes.nl/e-weaver.htm and *see* coverage on page 175 for further details of paddling on the river.

Pubs and Restaurants (pages 164–165)

🍺✗ 1 **The Old Broken Cross** Broken Cross Place, Middlewich Road, Rudheath CW9 7EB (01606 333111; www.facebook.com/TheBrokenCrossCW9). Once a row of canalside cottages, this establishment now serves real ale and food *daily Mon-Sat 12.00-20.00 (Fri-Sat 21.00) & Sun 12.00-19.00.* Dog- and child-friendly, garden. Traditional pub games, real fires, sports TV and Wi-Fi. *Open Mon-Thu 12.00-23.00 & Fri-Sun 09.00-00.00 (Sun 23.00).*

🍺✗ 2 **Lamb's Wharf** Wincham Wharf, 216 Manchester Road, Lostock Gralam CW9 7NT (01606 514053; www.facebook.com/lambs.wharf.7). A converted mill, still with its original water wheel, serving real ale. Live music *Sat and other nights outside during summer.* Canalside terrace. Real fires and Wi-Fi. *Open Tue-Fri 17.00-21.00 (Fri 21.30) & Sat-Sun 12.00-09.30 (Sun 20.00).*

🍺✗ 3 **The Slow & Easy** 411 Manchester Road, Lostock Gralam CW9 7PJ (07427 777858; www.facebook.com/SlowandEasy2020). Large open-plan, community pub, dispensing real ale. Karaoke *Fri* and live music *Sat.* Garden, small dog- and child-friendly *(until 20.00).* Traditional pub games, newspapers, real fires, sports TV and Wi-Fi. B&B. Camping. *Open Mon-Thu 16.00-23.00 & Fri-Sun 12.00-00.00 (Sun 22.30).*

🍺 4 **The Salt Barge** Ollershaw Lane, Marston CW9 6ES (01606 212525). Deceptively large pub with a friendly atmosphere, neatly divided into cosy areas, and with an inviting family room. Real ales, real cider *(in summer)* and food available *Sat-Sun 12.00-20.00 (Sun 18.00).* Garden, dog- and family-friendly. Traditional pub games, newspapers, real fires, sports TV and Wi-Fi. B&B. *Open 12.00-2.00 (Fri-Sun 00.00).*

✗♀️ 5 **The Moorings** Anderton Marina, Uplands Road, Anderton CW9 6AJ (01606 79789; www.themooringsrestaurant.co.uk). Canalside seating. Boaters please moor outside the basin. Small, independent restaurant and bar overlooking Anderton Marina and the Trent & Mersey Canal. Children and dogs welcome. Patio and terrace. *Open Wed-Mon 11.00-16.00 (Sun 16.30) & Thu-Sat 18.00-21.00.*

✗ 6 **Anderton Boat Lift Coffee Shop** Lift Lane, Anderton, Northwich CW9 6FW (01606 786777). Café inside the lift Visitor Centre with gift shop, serving tea, coffee, hot and cold snacks, ice creams, etc. Children welcome. *Open daily 09.30-16.30.*

🍺✗ 7 **The Stanley Arms** Old Road, Anderton CW9 6AG (01606 77661; www.stanleyarmsanderton.co.uk). Friendly real ale pub where children and dogs are welcome. Food available *daily 12.00-20.00 (Sun 18.00).* Quiz *Wed* and *occasional* live music. Traditional pub games, garden and Wi-Fi. *Open 12.00-22.00 (Fri-Sat 23.00).*

167

Dutton

This, the northernmost stretch of the Trent & Mersey, is a very pleasant one and delightfully rural. Most of the way the navigation follows the south side of the hills that overlook the River Weaver. From about 6oft up, one is often rewarded with excellent views of this splendid valley and the very occasional large vessels that ply up and down it. At one point one can see the elegant Dutton railway viaduct in the distance; then the two waterways diverge as the Trent & Mersey enters the woods preceding Preston Brook Tunnel. There is a stop lock south of the tunnel just beyond a pretty covered *dry dock*; there are often fine examples of restored working boats moored here. At the north end of the tunnel a notice announces that from here onwards one is on the Bridgewater Canal (*see Nicholson Guide 5 – North West & the Pennines*). There are good moorings north of bridge 213, and to the south of Dutton stop lock.

NAVIGATIONAL NOTES

1 Access to Preston Brook Tunnel is restricted to *northbound on the hour to 10 minutes past the hour; southbound on the 1/2 hour to 20 mins to the hour.* This tunnel **is not available** to paddlers.

2 North of Preston Brook Tunnel you are on the Bridgewater Canal, which is owned by the Manchester Ship Canal Company (Peel Ports) and is described in detail in *Nicholson Guide 5 – North West & the Pennines*.

3 Craft licensed by Canal & River Trust (CRT) are permitted up to 7 consecutive days free navigation on the Bridgewater Canal, with no return within any 28-day period (without a permit). Any return within 28 days from the date of leaving, whether leaving after 3 days, 5 days or up to 7 days, will required a permit. A 7-day permit is available which applies to Bridgewater craft on CRT waters and CRT craft on the Bridgewater Canal or there is a return permit (valid for 3 days) to transit for a reduced fee of £20. Permits can be purchased on the Bridgewater Canal website (www.bridgewatercanal.co.uk) by telephoning 0161 629 8266/8432 or from an enforcement officer.

Pubs and Restaurants

1 The Leigh Arms Willow Green Lane, Little Leigh, Northwich CW8 4QT (01606 853327; www.leighatms.co.uk). ¼ mile south of bridge 208, overlooking the Weaver and Acton Swing Bridge. Attractive old coaching inn with large restaurant area serving real ales and an extensive menu of home-made food *Mon–Thu L and E & Fri–Sun 12.00–20.45 (Sun 17.00). Kitchen may close earlier in winter).* Garden and play area, dog- and family-friendly. Traditional pub games, live music *Thu*, newspapers and Wi-Fi. *Open 12.00–23.00 (Sun 22.30).*

2 The Hollybush Warrington Road, Little Leigh, Northwich CW8 4QY (01606 853196; www.thehollybush.net). ¼ mile north of bridge 209. Listed, timber-framed building, one of the oldest farmhouse pubs in the country, with unique charm and character. Wide range of interesting, home-cooked food served in bar and restaurant *Mon–Sat L and E & Sun 12.00–19.00.* Children welcome. Garden with children's play area, including bouncy castle. Traditional pub games. Quiz night *Sun.* Real fires and Wi-Fi. B&B. *Open Mon–Fri L and E & Sat–Sun 12.00–23.00.*

3 The Riverside Warrington Road, Acton Bridge, Northwich CW8 3QD (01606 852310; www.riversideinnpub.co.uk). Large open-plan, riverside pub, serving real ale and food *daily 12.00–21.00.* Breakfast *Sat–Sun 09.30–11.00. Wed* carvery. Garden, family-friendly. Wi-Fi. *Open 11.00–22.30 (Sat–Sun 09.30).*

Boatyards

Ⓑ**Black Prince Holidays** Bartington Wharf, Acton Bridge, Northwich CW8 4QU (01606 852945; www.black-prince.com/hire-bases/acton-bridge-hire-base). 🛢🛒D E Pump out, gas, narrowboat hire, day-hire craft, long-term mooring, engine repairs, books, maps and gifts, coal, ice cream. *Open Mon–Sat 09.00–16.30.*

Ⓑ**Dutton Dry Dock** 3 Tunnel End, Dutton, Warrington WA4 4LA (01928 717273; www.claymoore.co.uk). Dry dock, historic boat repairs, boat blacking, boat repairs, engineering and machine shop, vintage engine repairs.

CANOEING AND PADDLEBOARDING
There is an excellent paddlesports shop alongside the Norton Arm which is technically on the Bridgewater Canal (just west of where it meets the Trent & Mersey) – Go Kayaking North West Marina Village, Murdishaw, Preston Brook WA7 3DW (01928 710770; www.go-kayaking.com). *Open Mon–Sat 09.30–17.00 (Sat 09.00).*

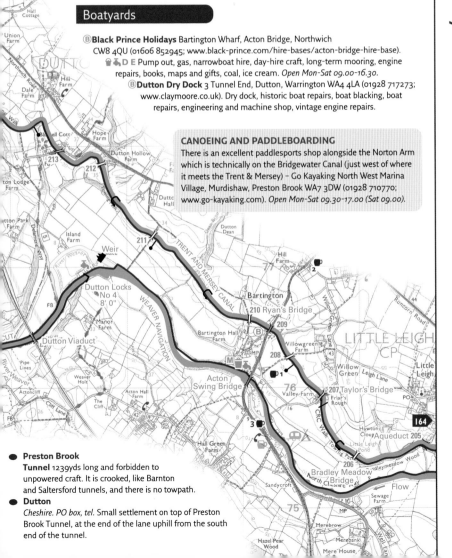

● **Preston Brook**
Tunnel 1239yds long and forbidden to unpowered craft. It is crooked, like Barnton and Saltersford tunnels, and there is no towpath.

● **Dutton**
Cheshire. PO box, tel. Small settlement on top of Preston Brook Tunnel, at the end of the lane uphill from the south end of the tunnel.

CANOEING AND PADDLEBOARDING

General Guidance for Paddlers Using the Inland Waterways

As with all navigations, whether inland, coastal or deep sea, a variety of rules, regulations and customs have, over the centuries, been established to ensure safe and efficient operation. The canals and rivers of Britain are no exception and described below are those most likely to affect canoeists and paddleboarders.

1 Boats travel on the right and you would therefore overtake a slower vessel on its left (or port) side. Meeting a craft coming towards you, you should expect to pass left side to left side (or port to port). On rare occasions boats may need to pass right side to right side (or starboard to starboard) when, for instance, their size and/or weather conditions make manoeuvring difficult. This would also be the case where a loaded commercial vessel needs to stay in the deep water channel.

2 Infrastructure – whether locks, bridges, tunnels or aqueducts – can potentially pose hazards for unpowered craft. i) In most cases, locks will have to be portaged for which a small folding trolley is often a great help. When approaching the top of a lock, beware of the draw of a swollen by-wash stream pulling you sideways, possibly away from your intended landing point. This will be more pronounced on river navigations where the same draw will be caused by an adjacent weir, especially when the current is strong following rain and snow melt. River locks are always accompanied by their attendant weirs which will be protected by large orange buoys strung across the top of the structure by a stout cable stretching from bank to bank. Note that these have been designed to catch larger powered vessels rather that unpowered craft. ii) On most canals, bridges are pinch points through which there is usually only space for one craft to pass. Judge your timing carefully, bearing in mind that your relatively small profile may not always be visible to the helmsman of a long narrowboat until he or she has committed to the bridge hole, as the structure can curtail their forward vision until the last moment (especially on bends). iii) Tunnels are clearly marked as being either accessible to unpowered craft or to be portaged. Follow instructions clearly displayed on the large boards at the mouth of the tunnel, taking account of the timings in each direction that you will often find controlling craft access on narrow-beam canals. A bright, forward-facing light must be carried on each unpowered vessel. iv) Paddleboarders, in particular, may not want to paddle across high aqueducts, therefore an assessment from the towpath should first be made!

3 In order to maintain steerage and keep on course, powered boats have to achieve a certain minimum speed so are often unable to come safely to standstill to allow a paddler to pass in a constricted space. Note also that two vessels passing under way generate an area of low pressure along their adjacent hull sides which, in turn, can create a noticeable 'suck'.

4 A waterway describing itself as a 'Navigation' will generally be a mix of river and canal, with the canal length protected from a river section by a flood gate designed to be closed to prevent the canal flooding when the river flows are swollen and levels increased. During the normal river state the gates are left open and all vessels can navigate straight through. Once closed they operate as normal locks and, with care, powered craft can still proceed. A flood lock will be accompanied by red, yellow and green bands (supported by an adjacent interpretation board) painted at the tail of the lock giving essential information about water levels, which you will also find detailed as appropriate in the Navigational Notes for that waterway. As a general rule meeting a closed flood lock after launching tells you that the river is either rising or falling but that paddling will be difficult as flow rates are increased, so don't portage around a closed flood lock unless you are used to paddling swollen rivers.

5 In the introduction to each navigation in this guide, waterways have been loosely categorised – according to their suitability for paddlers – from Category 1 through to Category 4. Paddlers encountering most of the navigations constructed as commercial waterways to accommodate vessels in access of 100ft will find that embarking and disembarking from their craft will be difficult or impossible and as such they are listed Category 4. 'Keel-sized' locks on some of the north east waterways were built for commercial craft measuring 56 x 14ft and their scale is therefore a deal good more paddler-friendly and warrants a Category 3 rating. Category 2 is reserved for waterways that would normally be rated at Category 1 (narrow- and wide-beam canals, placid rivers, etc) but can include hazards such as sharing the bed of a river for a short section, weed growth or, in the case of a stand-alone river, become hazardous in times of flood.

RIVER WEAVER

MAXIMUM DIMENSIONS
Anderton to Winsford
Length: 196' 6"
Beam: 35' 0"
Draught: 9' 6"
Headroom: 29' 6"

Western Marsh Lock to Anderton
Length: 213' 0"
Beam: 3' 6"
Draught: 10' 6"
Headroom: 59' 0"

Anderton Lift Branch
Length: 72' 0"
Beam: 14' 4"
Draught: 4' 7"
Headroom: 8' 2"

MANAGER
0303 040 4040
enquiries.westmidlands@canalrivertrust.org.uk

MILEAGE
WINSFORD BRIDGE to:
Northwich: 5½ miles
Anderton Lift (Trent & Mersey Canal): 7 miles
Acton Bridge: 11 miles
Sutton Bridge: 17 miles

WESTON POINT DOCKS (Manchester
Ship Canal): 20 miles
Weston Marsh Lock: 19 miles

Locks: 5

Canoeing and Paddleboarding: Category 2–4
depending on river conditions. Winsford Flash
Category 1.

The river itself, which rises in the Peckforton Hills and proceeds via Wrenbury, Audlem, Nantwich, Church Minshull and Winsford to Northwich and Frodsham, is just over 50 miles long. Originally a shallow and tidal stream, it was long used for carrying salt away from the Cheshire salt area. The mineral was carried down by men and horses to meet the incoming tide. The sailing barges would load at high water, then depart with the ebbing tide.

In the 17th C the expansion of the salt industry around Northwich, Middlewich and Winsford gave rise to an increasing demand for a navigation right up to Winsford. In 1721, three gentlemen of Cheshire obtained an Act of Parliament to make and maintain the river as a navigation from Frodsham to Winsford, 20 miles upstream. By 1732 the Weaver was fully navigable for 40-ton barges up to Winsford.

When in 1765 the Trent & Mersey was planned to pass along the River Weaver the trustees of the Weaver were understandably alarmed; but in the event the new canal provided much traffic for the river, for although the two waterways did not join, they were so close at Anderton that in 1793 chutes were constructed on the Trent & Mersey directly above a specially built dock on the River Weaver, 50ft below. Thereafter salt was transhipped in ever-increasing quantities by dropping it down the chutes from canal boats into Weaver flats (barges) on the river. This system continued until 1871, when it was decided to construct the great iron boat lift beside the chutes at Anderton. This remarkable structure, now completely restored and in full operation, thus effected a proper junction between the two waterways.

The Weaver Navigation did well throughout the 19th C, mainly because continual and vigorous programmes of modernisation kept it thoroughly attractive to carriers, especially when compared to the rapidly dating narrow canals. Eventually coasters were able to navigate the river right up to Winsford.

In spite of this constant improvement of the navigation, the Weaver's traditional salt trade was affected by 19th-C competition from railways and the new pipelines. However, the chemical industry began to sprout around the Northwich area at the same time and, until recently, Tata Chemical (originally Brunner Mond) works at Winnington supplied virtually all the remaining traffic on the river.

Winsford

Although Winsford Bridge (fixed at 10ft 8in) is the upper limit of navigation for shipping and the limit of Canal & River Trust jurisdiction, canal boats can easily slip under the bridge and round the bend into the vast, wonderful and deceptively shallow Winsford Bottom Flash where there are *moorings* for about eight boats, a *water point* accessible with a Watermate key and *canoe launching facilities* at Warburton Wharf. Navigation upstream of the Bottom Flash is unreliable, for the channel is shallow and winding, but can apparently be done by adventurous persons with small craft. The Top Flash is situated just beside and below the Middlewich Branch of the Shropshire Union Canal, but there is no junction between them here. Downstream of Winsford Bridge is a winding stretch that runs past the oldest and deepest rock salt mine in the country: each bank is piled high with the industrial leftovers of chemical industries and rock salt. But soon the horizon clears as one arrives at Newbridge, beyond which is the superb stretch known as Vale Royal Cut. The Vale Royal Cut typifies the Weaver at its most attractive. The river flows along a closely defined flat green valley floor, flanked by mature woods climbing the steep hillsides that enclose the valley. No buildings or roads intrude upon this very pleasant scene. Vale Royal Locks are at the far end of the cut; the remains of the old Vale Royal Abbey (believed to have been founded by Edward I and dissolved by Henry VIII) are just up the hill nearby. Beyond is a tall stone railway viaduct.

NAVIGATIONAL NOTES

1. The Weaver locks are only available *Tue, Thu and Sat for 40 mins at the following times*: Dutton *09.00 and 16.30*; Saltersford *10.00 and 15.30*; Hunts *11.00 and 14.30* & Vale Royal *12.00 and 13.30*.
2. Weston Marsh Lock, for passage onto (and off) the Manchester Ship Canal, must be booked *48hrs ahead* and is available *Mon-Fri 08.00-16.30*. Telephone 0303 040 4040 to make a booking. **On no account** should unpowered craft proceed beyond this point.
3. All relevant paperwork for passage on the Manchester Ship Canal must be in place prior to making a booking for Weston Marsh Lock.
4. Lock keepers are employed on a variety of duties and can be contacted on the following numbers: Vale Royal Lock 07748 936966, Hunts Lock 07748 936964, Saltersford Lock 07748 936965, Dutton Lock 07748 936968; by phoning 0303 040 4040 or by sounding your horn as they may simply be away from the lock station. All lock keepers can be contacted on VHF Channel 74.
5. The Weaver is a river navigation. CRT operates a number of large maintenance craft and the locks are correspondingly large and often paired. The bridges are either very high or are big swing bridges operated by CRT staff. With the exception of Town Bridge in Northwich and Newbridge below Winsford (6ft 4in) none of these bridges need to be swung for any boat with a height above water of less than 8ft. Those craft which do require the bridges to be opened should give prior notice to Canal & River Trust by telephoning 0303 040 4040. Unless there has been heavy rain, the current is quite gentle – however, as on any river navigation, an anchor and rope should be carried by powered craft, and the rules should be adhered to. There are few facilities for pleasure craft.
6. There are landing stages suitable for canoeists and paddleboarders at the locks between Winsford Flash and Dutton, although you are best to seek guidance from the lock keeper at Hunt's Lock (07748 936964). Throughout, the river banks are high. Inexperienced paddlers should confine themselves to either a return trip to Vale Royal Locks or exploring the Flash itself. (*see* page 175).

● **Winsford**

Cheshire. All services (station 1 mile east). A busy salt-mining town astride the Weaver. A huge shopping precinct has shifted the heart of the town well away from the river. Up the hill, east of the Weaver, there is a pub, takeaway, stores and a garage. To the south west of Winsford Bridge there is a cycle shop and another garage. Up the High street, west of the bridge, there are shops and the Golden Lion Pub.

● **Winsford Bottom Flash**

This very large expanse of water, in an attractive setting among wooded slopes, was created by subsidence following salt extraction in the vicinity. Three caravan sites and a sailing club are based along its banks and anglers crouch in the waterside bushes. Ideal for canoes, kayaks and stand up paddleboarders it is, however, quite shallow in places – those in canal craft *beware!*

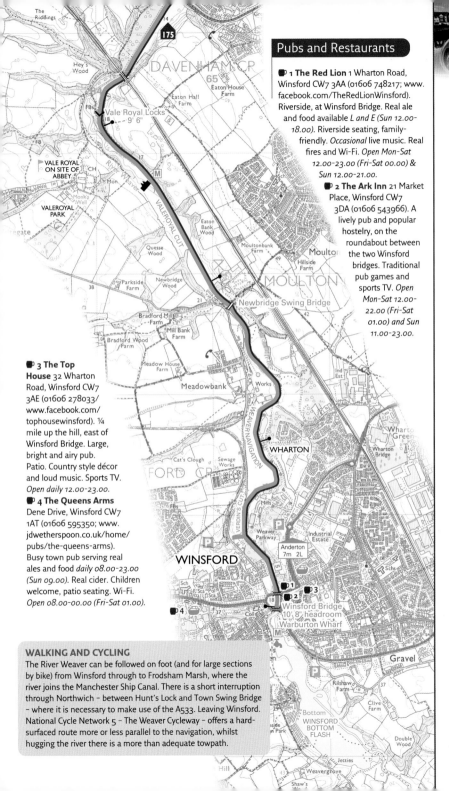

Pubs and Restaurants

1 The Red Lion 1 Wharton Road, Winsford CW7 3AA (01606 748217; www.facebook.com/TheRedLionWinsford). Riverside, at Winsford Bridge. Real ale and food available *L and E (Sun 12.00-18.00)*. Riverside seating, family-friendly. *Occasional* live music. Real fires and Wi-Fi. *Open Mon-Sat 12.00-23.00 (Fri-Sat 00.00) & Sun 12.00-21.00.*

2 The Ark Inn 21 Market Place, Winsford CW7 3DA (01606 543966). A lively pub and popular hostelry, on the roundabout between the two Winsford bridges. Traditional pub games and sports TV. *Open Mon-Sat 12.00-22.00 (Fri-Sat 01.00) and Sun 11.00-23.00.*

3 The Top House 32 Wharton Road, Winsford CW7 3AE (01606 278033/ www.facebook.com/ tophousewinsford). ¼ mile up the hill, east of Winsford Bridge. Large, bright and airy pub. Patio. Country style décor and loud music. Sports TV. *Open daily 12.00-23.00.*

4 The Queens Arms Dene Drive, Winsford CW7 1AT (01606 595350; www.jdwetherspoon.co.uk/home/ pubs/the-queens-arms). Busy town pub serving real ales and food *daily 08.00-23.00 (Sun 09.00)*. Real cider. Children welcome, patio seating. Wi-Fi. *Open 08.00-00.00 (Fri-Sat 01.00).*

WALKING AND CYCLING

The River Weaver can be followed on foot (and for large sections by bike) from Winsford through to Frodsham Marsh, where the river joins the Manchester Ship Canal. There is a short interruption through Northwich - between Hunt's Lock and Town Swing Bridge - where it is necessary to make use of the A533. Leaving Winsford. National Cycle Network 5 - The Weaver Cycleway - offers a hard-surfaced route more or less parallel to the navigation, whilst hugging the river there is a more than adequate towpath.

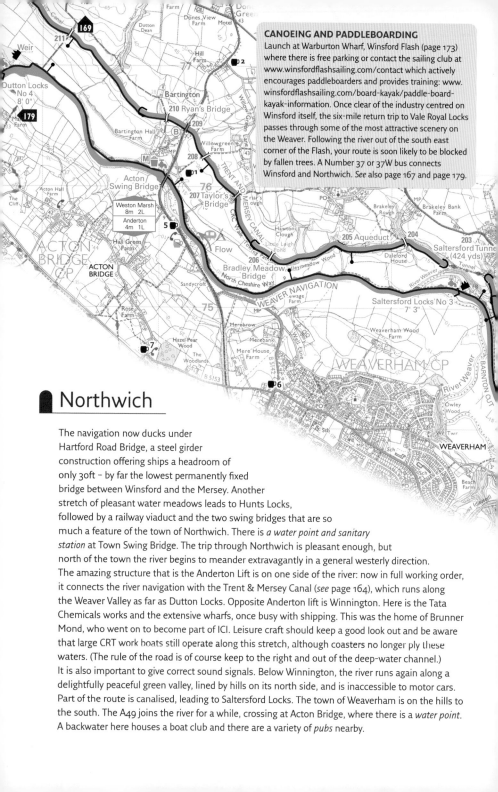

Northwich

The navigation now ducks under
Hartford Road Bridge, a steel girder
construction offering ships a headroom of
only 30ft – by far the lowest permanently fixed
bridge between Winsford and the Mersey. Another
stretch of pleasant water meadows leads to Hunts Locks,
followed by a railway viaduct and the two swing bridges that are so
much a feature of the town of Northwich. There is *a water point and sanitary
station* at Town Swing Bridge. The trip through Northwich is pleasant enough, but
north of the town the river begins to meander extravagantly in a general westerly direction.
The amazing structure that is the Anderton Lift is on one side of the river: now in full working order,
it connects the river navigation with the Trent & Mersey Canal (*see* page 164), which runs along
the Weaver Valley as far as Dutton Locks. Opposite Anderton lift is Winnington. Here is the Tata
Chemicals works and the extensive wharfs, once busy with shipping. This was the home of Brunner
Mond, who went on to become part of ICI. Leisure craft should keep a good look out and be aware
that large CRT work boats still operate along this stretch, although coasters no longer ply these
waters. (The rule of the road is of course keep to the right and out of the deep-water channel.)
It is also important to give correct sound signals. Below Winnington, the river runs again along a
delightfully peaceful green valley, lined by hills on its north side, and is inaccessible to motor cars.
Part of the route is canalised, leading to Saltersford Locks. The town of Weaverham is on the hills to
the south. The A49 joins the river for a while, crossing at Acton Bridge, where there is a *water point*.
A backwater here houses a boat club and there are a variety of *pubs* nearby.

BOAT TRIPS

Edwin Clark (01606 786777; www.canalrivertrust.org.uk/places-to-visit/anderton-boat-lift-visitor-centre/ boat-trips). The Canal & River Trust's glass-topped trip boat offering trips up and down the lift and along the connecting waterways *Apr-Oct*. Telephone or visit website for further details.

The Danny Chester Road, Sutton Weaver, Runcorn, Frodsham WA7 3EQ (www.thedanny.co.uk). The Daniel Adamson is a unique 1903 Steam Ship, listed as 15th on the Register of National Historic Ships. *The Danny*, as the vessel is affectionately known, includes stunning Art Deco saloons, restored to their original 1936 style, complete with, curved bar and wooden panelling. Static guided tours and a schedule of cruises. Visit website for further details.

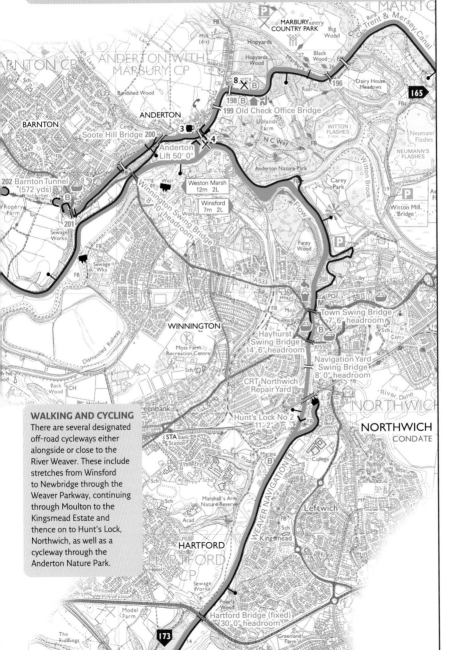

WALKING AND CYCLING

There are several designated off-road cycleways either alongside or close to the River Weaver. These include stretches from Winsford to Newbridge through the Weaver Parkway, continuing through Moulton to the Kingsmead Estate and thence on to Hunt's Lock, Northwich, as well as a cycleway through the Anderton Nature Park.

Ⓑ**Northwich Quay Marina** Northwich Quay, London Road, Northwich CW9 5HD (07967 461038; www.northwichquay.co.uk). 🚽♿D. Short- and long-term mooring, gas, pump out, slipway, coal, laundry, showers, toilets. *Open Mon-Fri 10.00-12.30 and 13.00-16.00 & Sat-Sun 09.00-14.30 (Sun 12.00).*
Ⓑ**Northwich Dry Dock Company** 30 Navigation Road, Northwich CW8 1BH (07393 978654; www.northwichdrydock.com). D Gas, short-term mooring, dry dock, wet dock, DIY facilities, solid fuel. *Open Mon-Fri 09.00-17.30.*

The following are on the Trent & Mersey Canal:
Ⓑ**ABC Leisure Group** Anderton Marina, Uplands Road, Anderton CW9 6AJ (01606 79642; www.abcboathire.com/our-locations/anderton-marina). 🚽🚽♿D Pump out, gas, narrowboat hire, overnight mooring, long-term mooring, slipway, boat sales, engine sales and repairs, boat painting, covered wet docks for hire, chandlery, gifts, restaurant, telephone, toilets. *Open daily 09.00-17.00.*
Ⓑ**Black Prince Holidays** Bartington Wharf, Acton Bridge, Northwich CW8 4QU (01606 852945; www.black-prince.com/hire-bases/acton-bridge-hire-base). 🚽♿D E Pump out, gas, narrowboat hire, day boat hire, long-term mooring, engine repairs, books, maps and gifts, coal, ice cream. *Open Mon-Sat 09.00-16.30.*

● **Northwich**
Cheshire. All services. A rather attractive town at the junction of the Rivers Weaver and Dane. (The latter brings large quantities of sand down into the Weaver Navigation, necessitating a heavy expenditure on dredging.) As in every town in this area, salt has for centuries been responsible for the continued prosperity of Northwich. The town's motto is *Sal est Vita*, Salt is Life, and there is a salt museum in London Road. The Brine Baths at Moss Farm Sports Complex are still *open throughout the year* for the benefit of salt-water enthusiasts. The Weaver Navigation has of course been another very prominent factor in the town's history, and the building and repairing of barges, narrowboats, and small seagoing ships has been carried on here for over 200 years. Nowadays this industry has been almost forced out of business by foreign competition, and the last private shipyard on the river closed down in 1971. The wharves by Town Bridge are empty, and are an excellent temporary mooring site for anyone wishing to visit the place. The town centre is very close; much of it has been completely rebuilt, with an extensive shopping precinct. Although the large number of pubs has been whittled down in the rebuilding process, there are still some pleasant old streets. The Weaver and the big swing bridges across it remain a dominant part of the background.
Anderton Lift
An amazing and enormous piece of machinery built in 1875 by Leader Williams (later engineer of the Manchester Ship Canal) to connect the Trent & Mersey to the flourishing Weaver Navigation, 50ft below. As built, the lift consisted of two water-filled tanks counterbalancing each other in a vertical slide, resting on massive hydraulic rams. It worked on the very straightforward principle that making the ascending tank slightly lighter – by pumping a little water out – would assist the hydraulic rams (which were operated by a steam engine and pump) in moving both tanks, with boats in them, up or down their respective slide.

In 1908 the lift had to have major repairs, so it was modernised at the same time. The troublesome hydraulic rams were done away with; from then on each tank – which contained 250 tons of water – had its own counterweights and was independent of the other tank. Electricity replaced steam as the motive power. One of the most fascinating individual features of the canal system, it draws thousands of sightseers every year. Restoration to full working order is now complete, following the original 1875 hydraulic design, using oil as the motive force rather than the chemically contaminated water that was the cause of the 1908 failure. The more recent counterbalance weights, together with their ungainly supporting structure, have been retained on site to demonstrate the engineering development of the lift.
Anderton Boat Lift Visitor Centre Lift Lane, Anderton, Northwich CW9 6FW (01606 786777; www.canalrivertrust.org.uk/places-to-visit/anderton-boat-lift-visitor-centre). In 1983 the Anderton Boat Lift structure was declared unsafe and in a dangerous condition and was closed pending sufficient funds becoming available for restoration. This took nearly two decades and the lift was finally reopened as a visitor attraction in March 2002 after a £7m renovation. Today there is a large Operations Centre building housing an extensive interactive exhibition with comprehensive interpretation of the whole site. Also a shop. *Open daily 09.30-16.30.* Entrance to the site and exhibition is free.
Weaver Hall Museum and Workhouse 162 London Road, Northwich CW9 8AB (01606 271640; www.weaverhall.westcheshiremuseums.co.uk). The history of the salt industry from Roman times to the present day, housed in the town's former workhouse. Look out for the remarkable model ship, made from salt of course. shop. *Open Tue-Fri 10.00-13.30 & 14.00-17.00 & Sat-Sun 14.00-17.00. Last admission 16.30. Charge.*

Tourist Information Centre 1 The Arcade, Northwich CW9 5AS (0300 123 8123; www.visitcheshire.com/visitor-information/visitor-information-centres). *Open Mon-Fri 08.30-17.00.*

● **Weaverham**
Cheshire. PO, tel, stores, chemist, hardware, off-licence, takeaways, fish & chips, butcher, baker, library, garage, station (1 mile distant). The heart of of this town contains many old timbered houses and thatched cottages – but these are now

heavily outnumbered by council housing estates. The church of St Mary is an imposing Norman building containing several items of interest. *Stores open daily 07.00-23.00.*

● **Acton Swing Bridge**
An impressive structure weighing 650 tonnes, which uses a very small amount of electricity to open it; 560 tonnes of its weight is borne by a floating pontoon. It was built in 1933, and extensively refurbished in 1999 and again in 2017.

NAVIGATIONAL NOTES

1 The Anderton Boat Lift is available for use *7 days a week* for powered craft and passage can be pre-booked by contacting (01606 786777; www.canalrivertrust.org.uk/Anderton-boat-lift). Visit the website for more information.
2 Boaters should differentiate between the holding moorings at the top and bottom of the lift, which are solely for lift use, and the visitor moorings beside Anderton Nature Park on the Weaver. Similar short-stay visitor moorings are available on the Trent & Mersey.
3 At low water levels the visitor moorings can be uncomfortably high for canoeists and paddleboarders. There is, however, a ladder at the eastern end.

Pubs and Restaurants (pages 174-175)

There are plenty of pubs to choose from in Northwich. These are a selection further out of the town:

➤✕ **1 The Leigh Arms** Willow Green Lane, Little Leigh, Northwich CW8 4QT (01606 853327; www.leigharms.co.uk). ¼ mile south of bridge 208, overlooking the Weaver and Acton Swing Bridge. Attractive old coaching inn with large restaurant area serving real ales and an extensive menu of home-made food *Mon-Thu L and E & Fri-Sun 12.00-20.45 (Sun 17.00). Kitchen may close earlier in winter).* Garden and play area, dog- and family-friendly. Traditional pub games, live music *Thu*, newspapers and Wi-Fi. Moorings nearby. *Open 12.00-23.00 (Sun 22.30).*

➤✕ **2 The Hollybush** Warrington Road, Little Leigh, Northwich CW8 4QY (01606 853196; www.thehollybush.net). ¼ mile north of bridge 209. Listed, timber-framed building, one of the oldest farmhouse pubs in the country, with unique charm and character. Wide range of interesting, home-cooked food served in bar and restaurant *Mon-Sat L and E & Sun 12.00-19.00.* Children welcome. Garden with children's play area, including bouncy castle. Traditional pub games. Quiz night *Sun.* Real fires and Wi-Fi. B&B. *Open Mon-Fri L and E & Sat-Sun 12.00-23.00.*

➤✕ **3 The Stanley Arms** Old Road, Anderton, Northwich CW9 6AG (01606 77661; www.stanleyarmsanderton.co.uk). Friendly real ale pub where children and dogs are welcome. Food available *daily 12.00-20.00 (Sun 18.00).* Quiz *Wed* and *occasional* live music. Traditional pub games, garden and Wi-Fi. *Open 12.00-22.00 (Fri-Sat 23.00).*

✕ **4 Anderton Boat Lift Coffee Shop** Lift Lane, Anderton, Northwich CW9 6FW (01606 786777). Café inside the lift Visitor Centre with gift shop, serving tea, coffee, hot and cold snacks, ice creams, etc. *Open daily 09.30-16.30*

➤✕ **5 The Riverside** Warrington Road, Acton Bridge, Northwich CW8 3QD (01606 852310; www.riversideinnpub.co.uk). Large open-plan, riverside pub, serving real ale and food *daily 12.00-21.00.* Breakfast *Sat-Sun 09.30-11.00. Wed* carvery. Garden, family-friendly. Wi-Fi. *Open 11.00-22.30 (Sat-Sun 09.30)..*

➤✕ **6 The Hanging Gate** 1 Sandy Lane, Weaverham CW8 3HG (01606 852969; www.hanginggateweaverham.co.uk). "The gate hangs well and hinders none, refresh and pay and travel on" is the inscription on the exterior this cosy pub, while inside it dispenses real ale and good food *daily 12.00-21.00 (Fri-Sat 21.30).* Garden and patio; dog- and family-friendly. *Occasional* live music and a *monthly* quiz. Newspapers and a real fire. Camping nearby. *Open 12.00-23.00 (Sun 22.30).*

➤✕ **7 The Hazel Pear** 1 Hilltop Road, Acton Bridge CW8 3RA (01606 853195 854434; www.thehazelpearactonbridge.pub). Smart pub, majoring on food *(daily 12.00-21.00)* serving real ale. Garden, child-friendly *(until 20.00).* Quiz *Wed.* Real fires and Wi-Fi. *Open Mon-Sat 12.00-23.00 (Fri-Sat 00.00) & Sun 12.00-22.30.*

Also try: ✕Ɒ **8 The Moorings** Anderton Marina, Uplands Road, Anderton CW9 6AJ (01606 79789; www.themooringsrestaurant.co.uk).

Frodsham

A mile further on, Dutton Locks lead to the Dutton railway viaduct, whose elegant stone arches carry the electrified West Coast Main Line. Beyond the viaduct one comes to Pickering's Wharf, the site of a swing bridge long gone. From here down to Frodsham, the Weaver Valley is a beautiful green, narrow cutting reminiscent of Vale Royal. Woods are ranged along the hills on either side. There are no roads, and no houses except for one farm. It is a delightfully secluded rural setting epitomised by the

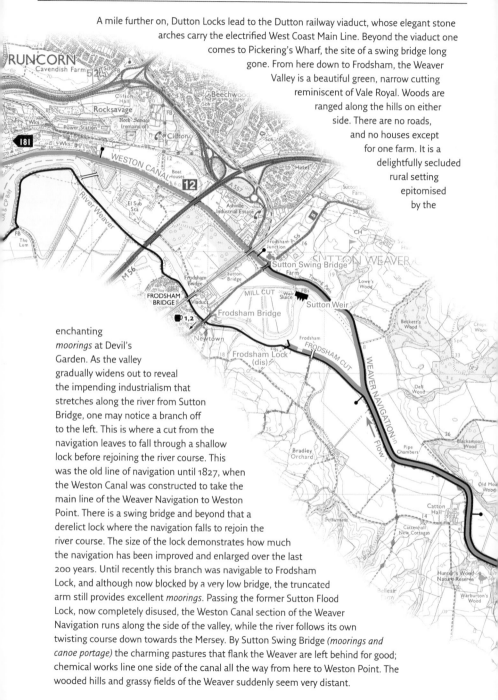

enchanting *moorings* at Devil's Garden. As the valley gradually widens out to reveal the impending industrialism that stretches along the river from Sutton Bridge, one may notice a branch off to the left. This is where a cut from the navigation leaves to fall through a shallow lock before rejoining the river course. This was the old line of navigation until 1827, when the Weston Canal was constructed to take the main line of the Weaver Navigation to Weston Point. There is a swing bridge and beyond that a derelict lock where the navigation falls to rejoin the river course. The size of the lock demonstrates how much the navigation has been improved and enlarged over the last 200 years. Until recently this branch was navigable to Frodsham Lock, and although now blocked by a very low bridge, the truncated arm still provides excellent *moorings*. Passing the former Sutton Flood Lock, now completely disused, the Weston Canal section of the Weaver Navigation runs along the side of the valley, while the river follows its own twisting course down towards the Mersey. By Sutton Swing Bridge (*moorings and canoe portage*) the charming pastures that flank the Weaver are left behind for good; chemical works line one side of the canal all the way from here to Weston Point. The wooded hills and grassy fields of the Weaver suddenly seem very distant.

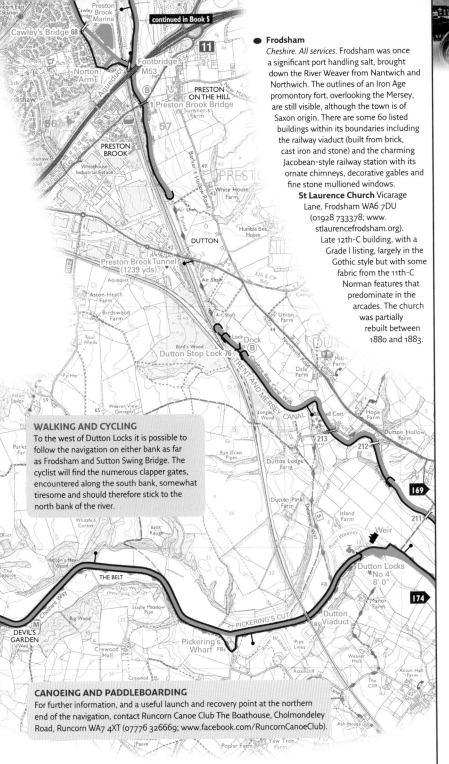

continued in Book 5

● **Frodsham**

Cheshire. All services. Frodsham was once a significant port handling salt, brought down the River Weaver from Nantwich and Northwich. The outlines of an Iron Age promontory fort, overlooking the Mersey, are still visible, although the town is of Saxon origin. There are some 60 listed buildings within its boundaries including the railway viaduct (built from brick, cast iron and stone) and the charming Jacobean-style railway station with its ornate chimneys, decorative gables and fine stone mullioned windows.

St Laurence Church Vicarage Lane, Frodsham WA6 7DU (01928 733378; www.stlaurencefrodsham.org). Late 12th-C building, with a Grade I listing, largely in the Gothic style but with some fabric from the 11th-C Norman features that predominate in the arcades. The church was partially rebuilt between 1880 and 1883.

WALKING AND CYCLING

To the west of Dutton Locks it is possible to follow the navigation on either bank as far as Frodsham and Sutton Swing Bridge. The cyclist will find the numerous clapper gates, encountered along the south bank, somewhat tiresome and should therefore stick to the north bank of the river.

CANOEING AND PADDLEBOARDING

For further information, and a useful launch and recovery point at the northern end of the navigation, contact Runcorn Canoe Club The Boathouse, Cholmondeley Road, Runcorn WA7 4XT (07776 326669; www.facebook.com/RuncornCanoeClub).

Weston Point

At Weston Marsh there is a lock down into the Manchester Ship Canal (*see* Navigational Notes opposite). Beyond here the navigation goes right alongside the Ship Canal from which it is separated by a tall bank. Eventually, after passing the entrance lock up into the abandoned Runcorn & Weston Canal, one arrives at a low (about 5ft) swing bridge. Beyond it are the Weston Point Docks and another lock into The Ship Canal. There are *shops, fish & chips and pubs* in Weston village, through the dock gates and mostly beyond A557 Weston Point Expressway.

● **Weston Point Docks**
The docks, at the junction of the Weaver Navigation's Weston Canal and the Manchester Ship Canal, are an industrial centre. The docks have been modernised and their facilities expanded to handle ships up to 2500 tonnes. However there is currently no one using this facility. *Northern Star* runs regular calcium chloride cargoes from ICI Runcorn's plant, on Weston Canal, to Ireland via Weston Marsh Lock and the Ship Canal.
Christ Church Situated between Weston Point Docks and the Manchester Ship Canal, this church was built by the Weaver Navigation Commissioners. Known as the island church, its tall spire is a distinctive landmark.

● **Runcorn**
Cheshire. All services. Runcorn's industrial growth began with the completion of the Bridgewater Canal in the latter part of the 18th C. The old town is to be found down by the docks, where the elegant curved 1092ft single span of the steel road bridge (built 1961), with the railway beside, leaps over the Ship Canal and the Mersey. West of the bridge, by the Ship Canal, is Bridgewater House, built by the Duke as a temporary home to enable him to supervise the construction of the Runcorn end of the canal. The

massive flight of ten double locks which connected the canal to the Mersey was finally abandoned in 1966, and filled in, much to the dismay of thousands of industrial archaeologists and canal enthusiasts. Since 1964 Runcorn has been a new town, its rapid growth being carefully planned. It is interesting to note that Runcorn, following local government reorganisation, is now part of Halton (which includes Widnes on the north bank of the Mersey), an echo of the time following the Norman Conquest when it was a dependent manor of the Barony of Halton.
Catalyst Science Discovery Centre Cossage Building, Mersey Road, Widnes WA8 0DF (0151 420 1121; www. catalyst.org.uk). Unique, award-winning museum of the chemical industry. Interactive exhibits and hands-on displays. 'Industry in view' is a computer and video based exhibition 100ft above the Mersey, embracing spectacular river views. Reconstructions and original film footage trace the development of the industry from ancient times to the present day. Café with riverside views. Shop selling educational toys, etc and activity guide for home-based experiments. *Open Tue-Sun (& Mon B Hol and during school holidays). Open Tue-Sun 10.00-17.00.* Charge. Any Widnes bus will drop you close to the museum.

Pubs and Restaurants (pages 178-181)

◆╳ **1 The Queens Head** 92 Main Street, Frodsham WA6 7AR (01928 730064; www.classicinns.co.uk/queensheadfrodsham). Busy town-centre pub, serving real ale together with food *daily 10.30-21.00* – including breakfast. Dog- and family-friendly *(until 21.00).* Garden. *Occasional* live music, real fires and Wi-Fi. Quiz *Tue. Open Sun-Wed 10.30-23.00 (Sun 22.30) Thu 09.00-23.00 & Fri-Sat 10.30-01.00.*

◆╳ **2 The Helter Skelter** 31 Church Street, Frodsham WA6 6PN (01928 733361; www.thehelterskelter.co.uk). A haven for real ale lovers, with eight hand pumps and comprehensive tasting notes for the range of beers that tend to favour local and national microbreweries. Also real cider and perry. Excellent food available *Wed-Fri L and E & Sat-Sun 12.00-21.00 (Sun 17.00).* Dog-friendly. Live music *Sun E.* Newspapers and Wi-Fi. *Open Mon-Tue 15.00; Wed-Sat 11.00-23.00 (Fri-Sat 23.30) & Sun 12.00-22.30.*

◆ **3 The Prospect** 70 Weston Road, Runcorn WA7 4LD (01928 561280; www.facebook.com/TheProspectInnRuncorn). Friendly, welcoming pub serving good value food *daily E* together with real ale. Garden, dog- and family-friendly. *Regular* live music. Traditional pub games and real fires. *Open Sun-Thu 16.00-23.00 (Sun 22.30) & Fri-Sat 16.00-00.00 (Sat 14.00).*

◆ **4 The Round House** 121-123 Heath Road South, Weston Village, Runcorn WA7 4RP (01928 770879).

Friendly local, dispensing well-kept real ales and food *Sun L and Wed-Fri E.* Dog- and family-friendly. Traditional pub games, newspapers and sports TV. Wi-Fi. *Open Sun-Thu 16.00-23.00 (Thu 00.00) & Fri-Sat 12.00-00.00.*

◆ **5 The Royal Oak** 187 Heath Road South, Weston, Runcorn WA7 4RP (01928 577781). This pub serves excellent real ale and real cider. Dog- and family-friendly, garden. *Occasional* live music, real fires and sports TV. *Open Mon-Fri 16.00-23.00 (Fri-23.30) & Sat-Sun 12.00-23.00 (Sat 23.30).*

◆ **6 The Ten Lock Flight** 1 Crosville Way, Runcorn WA7 5BD; 01928 352094; www.tenlockflightpub.co.uk). Newly built, family-friendly, open-plan pub majoring on food which is available *daily 12.00-22.00 (B Hols 21.00).* The name is reminder of the derelict navigation that once connected the Bridgewater Canal to the Weston Point docks. Real ale. Garden. *Open 12.00-23.00 (Sun 22.30).*

◆ **7 The Ferry Boat** 10 Church Street, Runcorn WA7 1LR (01928 583380; www.jdwetherspoon.co.uk/home/pubs/the-ferry-boat). Celebrating the ferry service, that used to cross the Mersey between Runcorn and Widnes, this one-time cinema lies in the centre of the old town and serves real ale and cider, together with food *daily 08.00-22.00.* Children welcome. Outside seating and Wi-Fi. *Open 08.00-00.00 (Fri-Sat 01.00).*

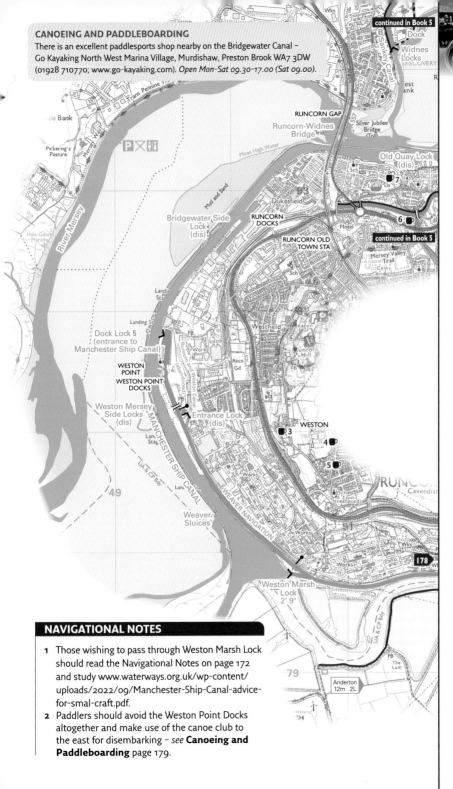

CANOEING AND PADDLEBOARDING

There is an excellent paddlesports shop nearby on the Bridgewater Canal – Go Kayaking North West Marina Village, Murdishaw, Preston Brook WA7 3DW (01928 710770; www.go-kayaking.com). *Open Mon-Sat 09.30-17.00 (Sat 09.00).*

continued in Book 5

NAVIGATIONAL NOTES

1 Those wishing to pass through Weston Marsh Lock should read the Navigational Notes on page 172 and study www.waterways.org.uk/wp-content/uploads/2022/09/Manchester-Ship-Canal-advice-for-smal-craft.pdf.

2 Paddlers should avoid the Weston Point Docks altogether and make use of the canoe club to the east for disembarking – *see* **Canoeing and Paddleboarding** page 179.

INDEX